THE PENA FILES

THE PENA FILES

**One Man's War Against Federal
Corruption and the Abuse of Power**

OCTAVIO G. PENA

with Bruce C. McKenna and Dary Matera

ReganBooks
A Division of HarperCollins*Publishers*

This book is dedicated to the special agents and supervisors of the FBI, IRS, CIA, U.S. Customs, as well as to police officers, attorneys in the Justice Department, and many honorable members of the press who have assisted me during my career. Many of them bucked their own superiors to point out government corruption to me; it is my hope that these honest agents become more of the norm in our government than the lowered standard of what constitutes "integrity" in our federal bureaucracy today.

THE PENA FILES. Copyright © 1996 by Octavio G. Pena, Bruce C. McKenna, and Dary Matera. All rights reserved. Printed in the United States of America. No part of this book may be used or reproduced in any manner whatsoever without written permission except in the case of brief quotations embodied in critical articles and reviews. For information address HarperCollins Publishers, Inc., 10 East 53rd Street, New York, NY 10022.

HarperCollins books may be purchased for educational, business, or sales promotional use. For information please write: Special Markets Department, HarperCollins Publishers, Inc., 10 East 53rd Street, New York, NY 10022.

FIRST EDITION

Designed by Laura Lindgren

Library of Congress Cataloging-in-Publication Data

Pena, Octavio.
    The Pena files : one man's war against Federal corruption and the abuse of power/by Octavio Pena.– 1st ed.
        p. cm.
    Includes index.
    ISBN 0-06-039175-8
    1. Pena, Octavio.   2. Private investigators–United States–Biography. 3. Commercial crimes–United States. 4. Organized crime–United States. 5. Political corruption–United States. I. Title.
HV8083.P45A3   1996
363.2'89'092–dc20
[B]   96-7139

96 97 98 99 00 ❖/HC 10 9 8 7 6 5 4 3 2 1

Contents

Acknowledgments

Special thanks to Mr. John T. Lynch, who gave me my start as an investigator, and to my associates in Mexico, England, and Panama who have helped me on numerous cases throughout the years. They must remain anonymous for their own safety, but without them many of the cases in this book would never have happened. Most important, I would like to thank my wife, Grace. Without her, none of this would have been possible.

— Octavio G. Pena

Thanks to my wife, Maureen, who not only tolerated the long hours and disruptions any book demands, but also provided valuable editorial comments.

Grace Pena also went far beyond the call of duty editing our numerous drafts.

I would also like to thank my coauthor Octavio Pena, who gave me much more than the most incredible raw material any writer could ask for. He taught me the meaning of loyalty, the value of honesty, and the power of perseverance.

— Bruce C. McKenna

Special thanks to Fran Matera, Ph.D., of the Walter Cronkite School of Journalism and Telecommunications, Arizona State University, for all her assistance and support.

— Dary Matera

Gracias to:
"Rick," George, Jorjeu, Ron, "Mr. Hope," Debbie, Debra, Marie, Mary, Sandy, Allan, Dan, Jeff, "Mr. George II," Thom, Rosa, Daniel, Roberto, Bob, "Don C.," "Rudy," Rudolph, "Mr. Hoffman," Abe, "Mr. Felix," "Mr. Tony," "Jean," "Mr. Brendan," Fransisco, Emmanuel, Jesus, Sally, Karen, Cherryl, "Liberty," "Mr. Bob," "Sonia H.," "Kathy C.," "El Señor," "Gallo," Daniel, Armando, Patricia, John, Marilyn, Paul M., Greg, Jesus, Kathy H., Tom R., Benedict, Erica, Victor S., Jorge D., "El Ingeniero," "Rolando S."

Authors' Note

The names of the following characters have been changed, sometimes to protect their safety. Occasionally their physical descrip-
tions and backgrounds have been disguised as well.

Rocco Scallino
Wilma Kurtz
Steve MacNair
Rich McPherson
Jason Dunston
Ricky O'Neal
Roberto Salazar
Claudia
Margarita
Paul Conte
René Dubois
Ramon Garcia
Craig Anderson
Jerome, Pete, and Jimmy—the scalping team
Mr. Chen
Wu Fong
Andreas Offerman
Jose Duran
Jack
Mr. Brown
John Maguire
Jody
Jesus, Manuel, Antonio, and Jose—the Mexican team

Introduction

IT WAS APPROACHING midnight on a crisp October evening. I was in the middle of a case, and that meant eighteen-hour days for weeks on end. That night I was tired and eager to get home to my wife, Grace, and my two young children, Elisabeth and Richard. The kids would be asleep when I arrived, but at least I'd be able to look in on them, stroke their hair, be with them in spirit for a while. During this period of my life there were far too many nights spent out of town or, like this night, at my desk, poring over investigative materials until the early hours.

I had just finished speaking with a pair of IRS agents. For the past two years they and other insiders had outlined so much fraud and dirty dealings inside the tax collection agency, including ties to organized crime, that if the public ever found out, people would start tossing their W-2 forms in the wastebasket. But the IRS wasn't going anywhere, and I was tired.

I tucked my .38-caliber revolver into a well-worn leather shoulder holster and tossed some materials into my briefcase. The remaining papers on my desk were fed into a shredder. I then encrypted all the data on my computer and turned it off. Sidestepping around the ganglia of electronic wires that snaked down from my large oak desk, I switched off the electronic bug detector. It monitored changes of electromagnetic energy in my Fort Lee, New Jersey, office, indicating the possibility of hidden listening devices. Finally, I set the infrared detectors inside my dark, wood-paneled office—an alarm system with some custom-made peculiarities that my own people had installed. When all that was done, I activated the security system that shrouded the entire building. It's not your average nightly corporate ritual, but after twenty-five years of undercover investigations, I've learned that it pays to be careful.

As I walked out into the cool autumn air to my Corvette, I checked the pistol to make sure the safety was off. This IRS business had me rattled.

I stood for several minutes under the dark trees surrounding the stone house that served as my office. My eyes adjusted to the dark. As far as I could tell, nobody lurked in the grove of trees by the car, nor were there any suspicious cars parked on the street by the driveway. Satisfied, I got into the gray sportscar and headed for my condo, perched a few miles away above the Hudson River across from Manhattan. I pulled out onto the street, phoned Grace, and told her to wait up.

I glanced into the rearview mirror. A beam of headlights flashed across my eyes. There was nothing unusual about sharing the road, even at this time of night, but I wasn't about to get lazy now. As a precaution, I began a series of driving maneuvers—in my line we call it "dry-cleaning"—to see if I had a shadow. I accelerated the Corvette down a dark, narrow suburban street, slowed to a crawl, and then sped through a couple of yellow lights and intersections. A nondescript sedan aped my every move.

I struggled to recall the pattern of streets that lay in front of me, then considered the possibilities. Was I being herded into a "choke point," a spot where additional cars would suddenly appear and cut me off? Should I stomp on the gas and lose him, or should I turn the tables on the stalker and counterattack?

The hell with running. It just delays the inevitable. If there is one overall strategy I've learned in all my years of corporate intelligence work, it is when attacked, attack back. I gunned the Corvette toward the grimy waterfront area of West New York, just below the row of apartment complexes that dominate the New Jersey skyline above the Hudson River. There was a sharp curve there off River Road where I could double back on my pursuer.

The closer I got to the point where I could spin the car 180 degrees, the more conscious I was of the heavy revolver pressed against my ribs. I was thankful for the Corvette's superb handling: Even while it hurtled at over ninety miles per hour down the twisting dark street, the low-slung sportscar hugged the asphalt. The headlights behind me flickered in and out, revealing that I had the distance I needed to maneuver.

When his lights disappeared again, I whipped the 'Vette around the curve and slammed on the brakes. The car slewed toward the curb in a squeal of burning rubber. I jumped out and crouched down behind the rear of my car. As the whine of a straining engine moved closer, I drew my revolver.

The sedan screeched to a stop about twenty-five feet away. An indistinct form jumped from the car. I looked for another person, which would have been bad news, but the stalker was alone.

"What's your problem!" I yelled, fingers gripping my weapon.

A man's voice responded out of the darkness, "Be cool." The dark form moved closer until it was caught in the wash of the car's headlights. I strained my eyes and made out some kind of uniform. A hand hovered above a holstered gun. It was a cop! Alarm bells went off inside my head. A uniformed officer in an unmarked car? I studied the badge on his shoulder. Even from a distance, I could make out the markings of the West New York Police Department. Why had a West New York policeman followed me from Fort Lee? Something wasn't kosher.

"I could have killed you!" I shouted. "Why are you following me?" The man was close enough for me to make out his features and memorize his name and badge number—Robert Gomez.

"You were speeding," he said, his breath misting in rapid bursts. I stepped back and gripped my revolver tighter.

"Are you on duty?" I challenged him. "Where's your red light? I could have shot you."

He didn't answer. He just stood in front of me, his eyes shifting back and forth as if he were confused about what to do next. For a terrifying instant, I feared this was a hit. Was this guy a button man, sent to take me out?

If so, he was at a distinct disadvantage. I had the drop on him and was shielded behind my car. He stood in the glare of both our headlights. Cop or no cop, if he made the wrong move, he was dead. We faced off in the cold night, the tension increasing with every heartbeat. It was a Mexican standoff, and I was the Mexican! Seconds passed. If he was a real policeman, a dozen patrol cars would have surrounded us by then. Nobody came.

Something unspoken passed between us. He realized that he couldn't do what he wanted to, and that I wouldn't shoot him unless he did something stupid. I carefully eased back into the Corvette, watching for any sudden movement from his hands. I gunned the engine and sped off. As I expected, Officer "Gomez" didn't follow. It was only when I pulled into the secured garage below the high-rise building where my family waited that I put away the pistol. Then I leaned against the steering wheel. For the first time during the entire ordeal, I could feel my heart thump inside my chest.

The following morning I called on a captain in the West New York Police Department named Carl Olsen to inform him that one of his cops was a rogue who might be picking up some extra dough as a hit man. It didn't surprise me, however, when Olsen informed me there was no Robert Gomez in the West New York Police Department. The guy was bogus.

That was close. If the alleged assassin had taken the time to add a bubble-gum light to his arsenal—or worse, pinched a patrol car—he could have blown me away with little trouble. I pushed that ugly thought away and considered a bigger question: Who was the asshole working for? The IRS? The U.S. Attorney's Office in New York? A cadre of powerful Beverly Hills businessmen? I was investigating a web of intrigue that linked them all, so the list of suspects was large.

The midnight rider was just the latest in a series of events aimed at scaring me off the trail. In the past month, my mail had been tampered with, including routine bank statements. My phones had been bugged, and creepy surveillance vans dotted the streets around my office. Someone even placed a tracking device on my wife's car. Someone was telephoning my kids when I wasn't home.

Where would it end? I'd faced down some bad *hombres* in my career, but it had never reached this level of retribution. Even when I had battled the Mafia or confronted cutthroat Communist rebels in Central America, it never got this personal. For the first time in my life, I considered backing off, afraid for the safety of my family.

Then again, once you back down from anything, you're never the same. And anger fueled my resolve. I'd never been intimidated off a case before, and I wasn't about to start now. I'd just have to find a way to protect my loved ones, and then go on the offensive. It's the only way.

But this one, this battle against the most powerful enemy imaginable—the United States government itself—would force me to lean on everything I'd ever learned in more than two decades of undercover work in order to survive.

Fortunately, I had a lot of experience to lean on.

1

GASOLINE ALLEY

"Octavio, you have to get over here right away!"

The voice on the phone sounded very worried. That surprised me because the caller was Harold Bernstein, the tough, no-nonsense co-owner, with his brother Raymond, of Northville Industries, a huge gasoline and petroleum products conglomerate based on Long Island.

"What's going on?" I asked. I'd solved several security problems for Northville over the years, so I knew that Bernstein's behavior was out of character. Something had rattled him in a way I'd never seen before. You don't become a billionaire without having nerves of steel.

"I can't tell you over the phone. But it's serious. Please, we're having an emergency meeting this evening. We need your help."

When I was ushered into the plush boardroom at Northville's Melville, New York, headquarters, it was like walking into a wake. The gasoline tycoon and his assistants were—to a man—unusually subdued.

Bernstein didn't waste time. "We've got problems with Rocco Scallino again."

Rocco Scallino? I shook my head.

Scallino was a tough, blustery associate of Michael Franzese, the suave and handsome *capo* in the Colombo crime family. A blue-blood Mafia prince, Franzese was the son of Sonny Franzese, a fierce, highly respected, widely feared, old-school mobster who once reigned as the underboss of the legendary New York crime family.

Scallino and Franzese were the vanguard of a band of Young Turk New York mobsters carving out a foothold in the state's multi-billion-dollar independent gasoline business in the early eighties. As always with the mob, once they got inside, they quickly took over.

How did this happen? Independent gasoline distributors, especially in New York, often operate in an Old West fashion in which anything goes. Crime, extortion, wholesale theft, shell games, hijackings, and protection rackets run rampant. On top of that, the industry is poorly policed and loosely regulated on the federal and state level.

Respectable companies, though loath to admit it, sometimes find that it initially makes economic sense to hook up with a "traditional" protector—meaning one of five entrenched Mafia families that have ruled the New York/Long Island/New Jersey area for nearly a century. This protects the firms from being bled to death by smaller, more treacherous criminal factions, like the vicious bands of Russian immigrant gangsters that began washing ashore in disquieting numbers around the same time.

There isn't a gas or oil company on the East Coast that hasn't tangled with the Mafia. Any firm that relies upon trucking, shipping, labor unions, and the docks—in other words, any distribution company—must deal with the mob at one time or another.

In Northville's case, they kept bumping into one particular mobster: the colorful Rocco Scallino. Rocco and I had crossed paths before—only he didn't know it.

A few years earlier, Northville had hired me to solve a perplexing problem. Hundreds of thousands of gallons of oil were vanishing from various Northville storage facilities. The baffled executives had been unable to determine how it was happening.

There was nothing supernatural going on. Cloaked UFOs weren't sucking up the fuel in the middle of the night. Someone powerful was simply stealing the liquid gold and carting it off. Given the cutthroat nature of the gas and oil distribution business in the New York area, Northville immediately suspected the mob. The question was, which mob?

The Long Island company had hired me to answer their many questions. I began an undercover operation in and around the affected storage tanks, setting up around-the-clock surveillance with 1000-millimeter infrared cameras. I also paid some of the truckers to let me know if they saw anything out of the ordinary.

Although it took a considerable effort to put my operation in place, once established, it wasn't difficult to flush out the mob associate who was purloining Northville's petroleum products. The first thing I discovered, as I'd expected, was that it was an inside job. The tanks were being drained by truckers working for one of Northville's own independent gas distributors—Rocco Scallino. Fleets of Scallino's silver heating-oil trucks were chugging up to Northville storage tanks and siphoning copious amounts of extra fuel for Rocco to sell through his own company.

The more Scallino stole, the bolder he became. After signing on with Franzese and tapping into La Cosa Nostra's power, the crude, rough-edged tough guy began strutting around Long Island like a mobster from central casting. But he wasn't just hot air: Scallino raked in millions of dollars a week from stolen oil and gas to augment the income from his car leasing company, gas stations, and fuel oil distributorship. The mobster was so successful that by the mid–eighties, he was regularly tailed by FBI agents assigned to pry the lid off of his illegal empire.

And if Scallino's exaggerated mob behavior wasn't obvious enough, his associates left little doubt. His direct contact to Franzese and the Colombo family was Franzese's right-hand man, a scary little dude known throughout Long Island as "Frankie Gangster." So much for subtlety.

As often happens with industrial espionage, I presented my findings to Northville, collected the fee, and let them take care of it. From past experience, that can amount to anything from calling in the FBI and prosecutors and pressing charges, slapping the way-ward partner or employee on the wrist, or doing absolutely nothing. I hadn't heard what avenue Northville took, other than forcing a plant manager to resign for looking the other way as Scallino's tankers stole Northville's oil. But given the fact that Scallino had returned to haunt the giant energy company, my guess is that their response had not been to call in the authorities.

"So what has Rocco done this time?" I asked Harold Bernstein.

"Over a period of years we gave his company a line of credit to purchase fuel oil and establish a distributorship. The line of credit ballooned to five million dollars. The loan came due today, and Scallino told us to kiss off. He offered us ten cents on the dollar, and then told us if we pressed him, he'd 'take care of us.'"

I glanced over at Harold's brother and partner, Raymond. A tough guy like his brother, Raymond clearly took Scallino's cement-shoe threat seriously. They now finally understood who they were playing with.

The Bernsteins were leery of going against the Mafia. New Yorkers seem to have it bred into them that the Mafia is invincible, and any attempt to fight back will result in pain, death, or explosive violence. But the brothers couldn't roll over and play dead, either.

Frightened as they were, they knew that once you let a rat crawl through the woodwork of a company, it grows and grows until it can eat the business alive. They needed something done, and they wanted somebody else to do it.

"He's a tough man, Octavio," a terrified executive warned, referring to Scallino. "His bodyguard carries an Uzi."

"He's got a reputation for violence. Keeps a sawed-off shotgun in his Ferrari," another piped up.

"Does he have anything on Northville?" I asked.

"Do you mean is he blackmailing us? No way," an attorney assured. "He's got nothing."

I looked at the Bernstein brothers, trying to detect the telltale twitch or downturned glance that would reveal any personal unpleasantries, scandals, or preferences that Scallino might be holding over their heads. They appeared to be in the clear.

"Okay. If he doesn't have anything, then we can attack the man. It's that simple. We go on the offensive. Right away. We hit hard and hit fast. Can you handle this?"

The men nervously glanced at each other. They desperately wanted someone to strike back at the mobster, but they feared the consequences of such an action.

"I'll arrange protection for Northville's top executives and your families," I assured them. "The guards will arrive here and then station themselves at your homes within the next couple of hours. They're experienced, well-trained New Jersey police officers and state troopers that I trust."

I could tell that this quick action impressed them. The executives let out a collective sigh of relief.

"Why from New Jersey?" Harold Bernstein asked.

"The mob has New York and Long Island cops on their payroll. That would have been our first mistake."

The meeting lasted until well past midnight. I showed unwavering confidence, depicting Scallino as a blowhard who could be defeated. It was important that I show no fear.

Mobsters are no different from any of the other big-time criminals that I've gone up against all over the world. They're by no means invincible. The key is to find their pressure points, and then exploit them. My investigations are like chess games, each with a different grandmaster. You probe your enemy, discover his weakness, and then move the pieces to lay your trap.

Scallino operated on a less refined level, through fear and violence. Knowing that, I had to come up with a strategy that would take advantage of his hot temper and macho posturing, letting him destroy himself.

The hours wore on, and the executives' backbones stiffened. The meeting transformed from a business gathering into a council of war—right in the heart of corporate America.

One of the attorneys told me that Northville's loan contract gave them access to the mobster's books if he failed to make a payment on time. I smiled when I heard that. It gave me a way to fluster the cocky gangster in an aggressive manner he'd never expect.

The strategy we developed was to stage a lightning-fast raid on Scallino's office, grab his records, and put him out of business. This would also provide Northville with the necessary ammunition it needed to prove its case in court.

While getting the records was important, I viewed the early-morning assault in a much different light, one that I wasn't sharing with my skittish clients. Rocco Scallino no longer lived by any sense of corporate etiquette. The minute he got word that we were swarming his office, he was sure to go ballistic.

Which was exactly what I wanted.

I call it my "Goon Gambit."

After the meeting, I phoned a contact I'd made during my previous investigation of Scallino and let him know that there was easy money to be made if he was willing to perform a favor. Contrary to popular belief, a degree of loyalty may exist among the close-knit fraternity of "made-men" Mafiosos and their criminal captains, but such loyalty rarely extends to the mob's beleaguered associates and employees. It came as no surprise that one of

Scallino's truck drivers stepped forward and volunteered to turn "mole."

All he had to do was keep me advised of the mob associate's movements over the next forty-eight hours, and he'd earn a cool $10,000. After I guaranteed his anonymity, he agreed.

The next day, I gathered my team of off-duty New Jersey cops and briefed them on the operation. I didn't mince words with these guys. They were front-line soldiers who needed to know who and what they would be going up against. I explained that this was a legal action to seize documents and that it would probably go smoothly, but that it also could result in bloodshed if we weren't careful. As I expected, none of them backed out.

As a precaution, I wanted a law enforcement official on board to assist in serving the seizure papers, which allowed the Bernsteins access to Scallino's documents because the gangster had signed a "Confession of Judgment" several years earlier. However, this was another touchy area. Whoever we selected, chances were that he would know Scallino, Frankie Gangster, Franzese, or someone else in the Colombo family. This last-minute addition to the team might hop on the phone and warn the mob of our plans the moment we left his office. The object here was to pay well and tell the person as little as possible about the raid.

Going right to the top, I chose a high-ranking member of the Sheriff's Department. This was going to be a quick in-and-out strike, so worrying about long-term leaks wasn't an issue.

It took me most of the afternoon to track the man down. When I found him, he was playing poker at a local country club. I hoped he was losing money.

Accompanied by a Northville attorney, I gave him the fact. "Northville Industries needs to take some records from a delinquent client. To insure that everything's legal, I'd like you to come along. I know your time is valuable, so I've been authorized to offer you five thousand dollars for your services. It should take about an hour."

The cop's eyes nearly bugged out of his head when I mentioned the money. He was familiar with Northville, so he quickly agreed to rendezvous with us at five the following morning.

I was nearly out the door when the man popped the question. "By the way, who's the target?"

"I don't know," I dodged. "Some little company I've never heard of. There probably won't be anybody there when we arrive."

The cop, visions of five grand dancing in his head, let it go at that. He'd find out when we got there.

As the sun dipped down that evening, the plan was in place. We rented a moving van to load the documents. Heavily armed bodyguards were in place at the executives' homes, equipped with walkie-talkies. My mole was diligently keeping me informed of Scallino's wanderings.

The next morning at five sharp, we picked up the officer and headed for the combined gasoline station and car dealership that served as Scallino's headquarters. As expected, the cop nearly freaked when he saw where we were heading. He grew visibly nervous and made a weak effort to bail out. It was too late. He was already in too deep. Any attempt to interfere would expose his relationship with the mobster.

"You can wait in the car," I said.

Our eyes met. For an instant, I spotted a flicker of the shame and guilt that even the most jaded law enforcement official feels when forced to confront his or her corruption. I also sensed gratitude. He knew that I knew the score. What he didn't know is how much of a scumbag I thought he was. But the time and place didn't jibe with being overly judgmental. The guy could still cause problems.

My men sprang from their vehicles, quickly neutralized Scallino's two guards, and broke into the building. I surveyed the interior, determined where the records were kept, and ordered my team to start lugging out the paperwork. There was no time to be selective. We just carried out entire file cabinets, which was sure to inflame Scallino's legendary temper.

Twenty minutes into the raid, Scallino himself roared up in a shiny red Ferrari. The tough guy sported a blue jogging suit and multiple gold chains and bracelets, a rather interesting set of fashion accessories for so early in the morning. He leapt from the sportscar, gold glistening in the morning light, and immediately began pushing and threatening everyone within earshot. His fury reached a crest when he spotted the police officer ducking sheepishly in a nearby car.

"Rocco, I didn't know it was you," he pleaded. "I swear!"

"Fuck you!" Scallino screamed. "Who you gonna call next time you need a new Cadillac?"

I marveled at the damning public exchange, glad they were both dumb enough to reveal themselves so openly. Our video man captured the whole thing in living color.

After dressing down the sheriff, Scallino tried to bully his way into his office. My men blocked him. He ranted and raved and was beside himself as we continued to strip the place of its file cabinets.

Inside the building, we discovered several shotguns and a machine gun—not exactly the typical tools of trade for a Long Island businessman. The off-duty cops unloaded the weapons and handed them to the stunned guards.

We left as quickly as we had arrived, packing up the materials and taking off for Melville, where the cabinets were stacked in an empty office at Northville's headquarters. Then we waited.

The next move was Scallino's.

THE GOON GAMBIT

A COUPLE OF HOURS after the early-morning strike on Scallino's office, a convoy of Porches, Ferraris, Cadillacs, and Mercedeses—bookended by two stretch limousines—roared up the driveway that led to Northville's suburban headquarters. It was an impressive display of mob power—in number, boldness, and, quite frankly, luxury.

"It's showtime," I announced, looking down from a second-story window.

The fleet of angry Mafia associates squealed to a stop around the circular drive that curved outside the building's entrance. An army of businessmen intermingled with broken-nosed gorillas poured out of the expensive cars. As a nice touch, they were all well-groomed and nattily dressed in suits.

I squinted, searching for any sign of Franzese or Frankie Gangster. They were nowhere to be seen. As I continued to scrutinize the enemy for familiar faces, my ears picked up a deep rumble from off in the distance. For an instant, I felt a tinge of fear, not so much from the ominous vibration, but from the unknown source. What the hell was coming next?

As if in answer to my question, two huge gasoline transport

trucks thundered up the driveway. They threaded their way through the cars and ground to a screeching halt just a few feet from the building's entrance. I could tell from the way they rolled that they were full.

Scallino had outdone himself—this was no idle threat. Franzese's men had blown up tankers all over the island when he was taking over. Now it was apparently the Bernsteins' turn.

"Stay calm, everyone," I exhorted my skittish associates. "It's just a bluff. Remember, they've come to us. This is our home turf. We've got them where we want them," I said, hoping they didn't catch my concern. I wanted Scallino out of control, but not this far out of control. The hotheaded maniac could easily kill us all if I didn't come up with a quick way to neutralize his bomb.

I turned to the off-duty cops. "Make sure your guns are visible. I want Scallino to know what he's up against."

I immediately allowed Scallino and a few select associates inside the building to negotiate. Coming along for the ride was a meek older man—the gangster's father—two aides, and his buxom bookkeeper, swathed in a low-cut dress.

After ushering them upstairs, I stood back and studied Scallino. Unlike his *GQ* associates, my opponent hadn't bothered to dress for the occasion. Decked out in gold, he looked as if he had just come from Jogger's Night at the local disco. The man was livid with uncontrolled rage, his face red, the veins in his neck bulging. He was all but foaming at the mouth. I knew instantly that instead of a game of wits, I needed to make a show of force to show the mobster who was in control.

I snapped my fingers, signaling for my men to brutishly frisk, disarm, and manhandle Scallino and his crew.

"Where's Bernstein?" Scallino screamed. "I want my goddamn documents back. Get your fuckin' hands off of me!"

It was time for me to come out of the shadows and inform the gangster who was running the show. Such an action might have long-term, life-threatening consequences, but the mob usually leaves civilians alone. Or so I hoped.

"You can't come in here with weapons. This is private property," I calmly informed him.

"The hell it is! I want my documents back!" Scallino faced me. "Who the fuck are you?" he snarled.

I didn't answer him right away. The less he knew, the more his imagination would overheat.

"Don't do anything rash," I said. "All these men are armed, and most of them are state troopers. We're going to handle this calmly and legally. Northville's attorneys are waiting for you in the conference room. You can discuss your loan payment with them."

Scallino stomped around the corner and burst into the rectangular office. To his dismay, the Bernstein brothers were nowhere in sight. I'd advised Northville's owners to get out of town to keep them out of harm's way, and to force Scallino to deal directly with the barristers. That would take some of the steam out of his threats. I then emphasized to the attending lawyers and executives that they had to do everything in their power to remain calm. They were to make their demands, hold their ground, and most of all, show no fear. No matter what the hot-headed mobster did, they weren't to be intimidated.

The lawyers and executives held together. Scallino continued to rave, curse, and threaten everyone's lives, but it was to no avail. The attorneys kept their cool and repeated their demands that Scallino repay the $5 million he owed Northville.

Suddenly the Colombo family associate stopped talking and backed toward the door. He stared hard at the Northville execs.

"Fuck you all! I ain't payin' a fuckin' cent! If I don't get my documents back in five minutes, I'm going to blow this whole fuckin' building. I got two tankers loaded with gas down there, and I'm going to blow this joint sky-high. Do you assholes hear me!"

No one said a word.

"You guys are history!" he screamed. "I've had it."

Scallino pointed a knobby finger at each attorney as if it were the barrel of a gun. I heard someone gulp.

Don't crack now, I thought. *Hang tight, guys.*

Almost to a man, the trembling attorneys and executives glanced toward me. Smiling, I slipped behind Scallino and blocked his exit.

"Rocco. Rocco. You can't blow up the building," I said, barely above a whisper. I looked him square in his cold, bloodshot eyes.

"The hell I can't," he spat. "Get out of my fuckin' way!"

"Rocco, I think you're making a big mistake . . ."

"No, it's you guys making the mistake," he hissed.

"Maybe. Maybe not. But allow me to let you in on something. You, your old man, and your lovely bookkeeper are standing right here in the building with us. I'm not letting you out. If you want to blow us up, be my guest. Only you're going down with us."

I grinned at the portly gangster and moved my jacket aside to show him the butt of my gun. Two cops moved into position beside me.

"Go call the police," Scallino ordered his buxom assistant. That was a novel move, a mob associate screaming for the cops. Unfortunately, I knew that such a request meant that Scallino might have the police department in his pocket. If Scallino could get the local cops to do his bidding, things could get ugly.

I nodded for my men to allow the bookkeeper to make the call. I felt that we were in the stronger position. Corrupt or not, it was doubtful that a force of suburban blues would choose to shoot it out with a group of off-duty New Jersey state troopers inside a private business, all to protect a brutish mobster. Even bad police have to keep up appearances.

As we waited, Scallino took the opportunity to vent his spleen at me.

"So you're the motherfucker in charge of this! You'll be the first to die! You know that, don't you? The first bullet goes to you!" he said, puffing out his chest. "I'll kill you! I'll kill your whole friggin' family!"

"Rocco," I said. "Why do you fight so much? I don't have a beef with you. Why would you kill me? This isn't personal. It's just business. You made a mistake with Northville. Why don't you just settle it like a man? Pay the loan, then everyone will be happy and you won't have to blow up your old man and your beautiful bookkeeper."

"Fuck you," he screamed. "You're a dead man!"

Scallino's redundant oratory was interrupted by a commotion downstairs. After a tense confrontation with Northville's security, a team of local police officers appeared at the top of the building's broad circular staircase. They had their guns drawn. The lead officer tried to frisk one of my men.

I rushed over. "Excuse me. What are you doing?"

"Why are these men armed? We're going to have to . . ."

"You're not going to do anything but save your jobs," I insisted, cutting him off. "This building is private property. Northville is the largest private company on Long Island."

I stopped to let that sink in, then pointed to Rocco. "And that man has threatened to blow up the building."

I could tell that the police were thoroughly confused. I softened my tone to let them know who the good guys and bad guys were.

"My name is Octavio Pena. I'm with Northville security. These are my men. They are off-duty police officers and state troopers. We're all licensed to carry weapons. Now I suggest that you perform the civic duty that you are supposed to perform and uphold the law in this city. If you are going to arrest anyone, arrest these clowns making the threats. And get those gas trucks out of here before a lot of innocent people get killed!"

The officer politely asked to see our gun permits. After we obliged him, the tension eased. The police then turned their attention to Scallino and his crew, escorting them from the building. After huddling with the goons downstairs, the cops ordered the tankers to hit the road. I heard their massive gears shift as they backed away. The fleet of luxury cars packed with Colombo family associates followed in tow. So did the local press, which had caught wind of the "tanker drama" unfolding in their sleepy little corner of Long Island.

The first stage of the crisis had passed. The Northville attorneys and executives, thinking it was over, shook hands and were in a celebratory mood. I didn't have the heart to tell them that the worst was yet to come.

It wasn't hard to figure out what was going on in the enemy camp. Scallino, if he was smart, would be calling upon the far-reaching power of the Colombo crime family to repair the damage to his so-called honor and dignity. A meet would be held in the age-old Mafia enclave of Brooklyn where the old-timers lived. If Scallino were persuasive enough, a hit would be put on the Bernstein brothers.

The mob now had time on their side. There is something about officially putting a hit on someone that can cool the most hot-headed mobster's temper. Once a hit is decreed, the aggrieved party can rest assured that his enemy is as good as dead, so there's no need to keep stewing about it. The actual hit may come that evening, the following week, the next year, or five years down the road, whenever the opportunity arises. The mob plays their cards at their discretion.

I couldn't let that happen to my clients. I couldn't walk away, collect my check, and leave them alone to live in fear, waiting for the dime to drop. This had to be settled—one way or another—in the next few days. Scallino had to have his wings permanently clipped. The threat against the Bernsteins had to be removed.

I reached out to my mole in the mobster's camp.

"Hang on," he said. "Something big's going down. I'll call you later when it shakes out."

An hour later, at dusk, I received the call.

"The guys are planning a hit," the mole whispered from a pay phone.

"When?"

"Tonight."

"Tonight?"

I was truly surprised. I didn't think the Colombo family would be stupid enough to react this quickly. I figured the more level-headed thugs in Brooklyn—the old, war-scarred mobsters who had survived their violent youths—would calm the impetuous Rocco and advise him to bide his time. The mole's report indicated that Rocco was probably acting alone, handling it within his own army. It was doubtful that even Franzese—who controlled most of Long Island and should have been informed—knew what he was planning.

If Scallino was truly acting alone, that was a break. His titanic temper would override any reasoned response. He'd make a mistake.

"What's the operation?" I asked.

"They're gonna machine-gun a couple of houses, then set them on fire with Molotov cocktails."

The driver paused, overwhelmed by the ridiculousness of it.

"At least, that's what they're talking about now. Scallino is really breathing fire."

This lamebrained scheme proved beyond a doubt that Scallino was acting alone. The mob generally likes to lay low and do their dirty work in the shadows. A dramatic, explosive hit against two of Long Island's leading business tycoons would do nothing but bring the full brunt of the law not only against the Colombos, but all five New York Mafia families. Scallino would become a pariah among his own wiseguy people.

I asked the mole where the meeting was and who had attended. This would further confirm that Scallino was acting alone.

"At his office, the gas station."

"Any sign of Franzese or Frankie G?"

"No."

"So who was there?"

The mole rattled off some names. I scribbled them down. The identity of the players was critical. During my previous investigation of Scallino, I'd developed a file on his army. I knew the names of his lieutenants, their families, where they lived, home phone numbers, nicknames, where they ate, and who their girlfriends were. Usually, this information is overkill. Occasionally, however, it comes in handy.

I doubled the guards around the Bernsteins and the other nervous Northville execs, then phoned the Nassau County police. They said that as far as the law was concerned, until Scallino actually broke the law, they had to stay on the sidelines.

My client was vulnerable. Time to take the initiative.

I called Donald Calogero, one of my assistants. The two of us came up with a plan.

Don cross-checked the names of the various Scallino associates with my computer database and quickly put together a file. I rounded up some of my trusted associates and prepared to launch our counterattack.

The heart of my strategy was to literally and figuratively hit the goons where they lived. I wanted them to know that violence can go both ways, that they and their families were just as vulnerable as the Northville executives.

Early that evening, Don and a couple other associates lined themselves in front of a bank of phones and began playing a game of psychological warfare. They called the assassins' families, professed to be "concerned friends," and mentioned their wives by name, "just to make sure they're safe."

"Hi, is Maria home yet?" Don would ask the wife of a particularly nasty henchman. "I'm just a friend, and I want to make sure she's back." Click.

This page was taken right out of the Mafia handbook. We mirrored the special, insidious language the mob uses to sow fear in the hearts of its enemies.

My crew called every five minutes, each time revealing more vulnerable pressure points to the mobsters. Within the hour, Scallino's goons had disbanded and retreated to their homes, concerned that some kind of a hit was going down against their families.

I knew our scheme was working when the first male voice answered the phone. "Who the fuck are you!" he frothed. "I'm going to kill you, you sonofabitch!"

In house after house, the roped-in gangsters railed against us, cursing and making ominous threats. That was exactly what I wanted. We taped the responses, edited the tapes, labeled them, then worked the phones again.

This time, Don played the enraged gangsters' threats to each other. Through the magic of Memorex—taped phone calls, when replayed over phone lines, seem like the real thing—I had Scallino's most trusted soldiers cursing each other and threatening to slit each other's throats—including Scallino's.

The mobsters went nuts. They braced themselves for an assault from within their own ranks. All thoughts of attacking the Bernsteins went out the window as the assassins' resolve disintegrated into fear and paranoia. Before they figured out the ruse, I was told later, they began calling each other and making actual threats.

The ploy had a devastating, long-term effect upon Scallino's soldiers. The distrust they felt for each other that night could never be forgotten nor forgiven. They were reminded, rather vividly, that the man standing next to them during any operation was a potential killer, just as they were, and was not to be trusted.

Most of all, they realized that Northville was playing hardball. Northville seemed to know them inside out, where their soft underbellies lay. Scallino and his men understood that they would forever be at the company's mercy.

The following day, Scallino called off the hit and agreed to settle the issue in court. Checkmate.

With Scallino finally calmed down, the drama moved to court. At a hearing a couple of days later, Scallino cornered me in a hallway and went into his foaming, "I'm going to kill you" rant. I was surprised. I knew he wasn't happy that I'd gotten the best of him, but I was under the impression that he wasn't holding any grudges.

"What's the matter with you, Rocco? I thought we agreed to let everything slide. There was nothing personal between us."

"You still got my wife under surveillance!"

"Hey, that's not me," I protested. "Our case is over."

"Bullshit!"

"I'll prove it to you. Do you have the license plates of the cars tailing your wife?"

Scallino made a call, came back, and handed me a slip of paper. I called Don. By the next recess, I had some names to show Rocco. I didn't recognize them, but Scallino sure did.

"Sonofabitch!" he exclaimed. "These assholes are trying to muscle me out!"

They were Franzese's men. It seemed that the so-called "Yuppie Don" had heard about my pressure tactics on Scallino and was using them as a cover to engage in a little intimidation of his own to muscle in on his associate's operations.

"Okay, Pena, I owe you one," Scallino said.

"How about paying up right now?" I answered, jumping at the opportunity.

"Shoot."

"Who do you have on the inside at Northville?"

Scallino gave me a sly smile. "A guy in finance. And someone in the credit department."

"The credit department?" I was shocked.

"Sure," he smirked. "How do you think I got so much credit?"

We both laughed at that.

"I paid them cash, usually," he added. "If you don't believe me, check out their cars. They were all gifts from my dealership."

Sure enough, the executives had nice shiny cars courtesy of Rocco Scallino.

I passed the information to the Bernsteins, who settled the matter to their satisfaction.

Meanwhile, Scallino didn't appear to be too upset about the whole affair. I soon discovered why.

As I stood outside the courtroom, I watched him pour his large frame into a big white limo. Then I stared with utter amazement as an officer of the court jumped in beside him! The pair cruised off to parts unknown.

I turned to an FBI agent standing beside me. "Did you see that?"

"Yup," he said laconically. "There goes another one." He sighed.

The last I heard of Rocco Scallino, some thugs tried to blow up his gas and heating oil terminal, then beat him so badly he was in a full body cast. It's rough out there in corporate America.

3

MIKE AND THE FAT MAN

NORTHVILLE MAY HAVE been free of Scallino, but my dealings with the feared Colombo family were far from over. I received a telephone call a few months later that again immersed me in the rough-and-tumble world of the New York mob.

The call was from Robert McPherson, an FBI agent on the New York Organized Crime Strike Force. "Octavio, can you give us a hand? We'd like you to help us find out what happened to a Colombo family associate named Larry Iorizzo."

Given the amount of evidence I'd amassed on the mob's gasoline empire, it wasn't surprising that the Feds wanted my help from time to time. I was proud to help the government break a few of the tentacles the Mafia had wrapped around New York's businesses.

We arranged a meeting at a Fort Lee, New Jersey, diner a stone's throw away from the George Washington Bridge. The FBI agent outlined what he needed. It seemed that I was about to collide head-on with Scallino's boss and Larry Iorizzo's Cosa Nostra protector on Long Island—the "Yuppie Don," Michael Franzese.

Michael Franzese's story reads like that of Michael Corleone of *The Godfather* fame. (In fact, some actual dialogue between Franzese and Gambino family mob boss John Gotti was used in *The Godfather, Part III*.) The brightest of the Franzese sons, Michael was the one who was supposed to go straight and become a doctor or lawyer, or perhaps even Senator Franzese.

Michael Franzese may have been well on his way to doing just that when a family upheaval shattered his life. His father was arrested and convicted in the late sixties on bank robbery charges that many believe had been manufactured to nail the elusive gangster. Sonny Franzese's subsequent long-term imprisonment was followed by the assassination of Colombo family boss Joe Colombo, a hit ordered by famed mobster Joey "Crazy Joe" Gallo.

Like any family business going through tough times, the weakening and disarray of the Colombo organization forced numerous sons to the rescue—including the very ones their fathers had wanted to shield from the dangerous life of crime. Michael was forced to abandon his premed studies at Hofstra University in order to shoulder the burden of supporting his mother and siblings.

Once he crossed over into the dark side of the force, the younger Franzese used his breeding and business smarts to introduce the mob into avenues of income that had previously been beyond their grasp. With a suit and briefcase replacing a fedora and machine gun, Michael Franzese was able to lift the family out of the traditional lowbrow areas of gambling, prostitution, loan sharking, smuggling, and protection, and usher it into the once-pristine automotive, banking, insurance, and gasoline industries.

Franzese quickly discovered what white-collar criminals have known for centuries—if you can avoid paying taxes, profits can skyrocket. With gasoline, a commodity burdened by heavy taxation, this strategy produced an unprecedented gold mine. Back then, the federal, state, and city governments demanded a combined twenty-seven-cent-per-gallon bite out of each gallon of gas sold in New York State. (It's even higher today.) By raking the tax money off the top through a series of ingenious schemes, Franzese and his cohorts, including Larry Iorizzo, were able to put hundreds of millions of dollars into their pockets—and into the coffers of the suddenly replenished Colombo family.

During his reign, Franzese became one of the richest and most powerful mobsters in Cosa Nostra history. His companies grew to the point where they were shipping 500 million gallons of gasoline a month in five different states. Do the arithmetic. At twenty-seven cents a gallon, that was more than $4 million dollars a *day* to kick around—before factoring in regular profits! The Colombo family's gasoline capers were costing the U.S. taxpayers billions of dollars.

Naturally, with such wealth pouring in, Franzese began to attract the attention of various law enforcement agencies. The cops and prosecutors were dying to turn someone inside Franzese's organization. They ached to arrest and convict the infamous "Yuppie Don" and shut down his obscenely lucrative operation. But it wasn't easy.

Franzese, learning at the knee of his legendary father, had become a master at the age-old Mafia practice of insulating oneself from prosecutable criminal activities. Hiding behind a maze of associates, lieutenants, and underlings, the young gangster so distanced himself from the actual crimes that finding an unbroken link proved maddeningly elusive.

The Organized Crime Strike Force responded to the seemingly impregnable wall of silence around Franzese by gathering an unprecedented amount of police muscle. The special task force included top agents from the U.S. Department of Justice, the FBI, the IRS, the U.S. Attorney's Office, the U.S. Department of Labor, and various other state and federal agencies—all primed to stop the massive hemorrhaging of U.S. tax dollars.

By the mid-eighties the Strike Force appeared to be making some headway. Franzese felt the heat and fled to Florida to play Hollywood mogul and make some movies. It was a fatal move. With the big cat away, the mice began to play. (Scallino was one of them.) Plus, the handsome Franzese became mesmerized by a voluptuous teenage Mexican dancer from Norwalk, California, named Camille Garcia. The lovestruck billionaire gas thief was spending most of his waking hours—and a good chunk of the taxpayers' money— wining and dining his new girlfriend all over South Florida.

Franzese didn't exactly abandon his Long Island operations, which were being managed by Iorizzo, but distracted by the glitz of the movie business and his voracious new girlfriend (he hadn't divorced his wife yet—but that would come), the Don soon lost his focus. He made public appearances, granted interviews with newsmen, and hobnobbed with politicians. (The mayor of Miami Beach actually gave him the keys to the city for making a film there!) In short, he did all the high-profile things the secretive brotherhood of La Cosa Nostra are supposed to shun. In so doing, he dropped the ball—a 500-pound ball named Larry Iorizzo.

■   ■   ■

Damon Runyon couldn't have invented a character as colorful as
Lawrence Iorizzo. The son of a jazz musician who played in various New York burlesque houses, Iorizzo had an appetite for crime
that was only matched by his hunger for food. He grew into an
enormous, six-foot-four-inch quarter-ton hulk who could down
pizzas like Ritz crackers.

Iorizzo apparently felt that since he was the size of two men, he
needed two wives. He regularly spent the night with *both* of them—
dinner with one, and then he'd leave in the middle of the night "to
check on his gas stations" and have breakfast with the other. All
that juggling had resulted in seven children between the pair.

Iorizzo hooked up with Franzese after some mobsters from
San Diego tried to muscle in on his operations, which were pretty
impressive by the mid-eighties. He owned or supplied over 300 gas
stations around the New York metropolitan area. With his gasoline
tax-skimming operations, he grossed tens of millions of dollars a
month.

The scam part of Iorizzo's empire was deceptively simple.
Using a confusing paper trail, he delayed paying the twenty-seven-
cent-per-gallon city, state, and federal tax the law demanded. By
the time the government tried to collect the millions of dollars in
delinquent taxes, Iorizzo would have folded up the station and
moved on. Usually he just reestablished it under another fake
ownership.

Iorizzo further insulated himself by registering all of his companies in Panama, a country with lax corporate laws receptive to
hidden ownerships. Very often the supposed owners turned out to
be the two wizened *paisanos* with machetes hacking away in some
sugarcane field. Or, as I discovered, the gardener of the attorney
who set up one of Iorizzo's companies.

Franzese agreed to protect Iorizzo at a meeting brokered by an
intermediary named Sebastian "Buddy" Lombardo, a long-time
Colombo legbreaker who was a close associate of Franzese's noto-
rious father. The deal? The Colombo family would skim 20 percent
off the top, and then Franzese and Iorizzo would split the rest fifty-
fifty.

The money poured in. At the height of their joint operation,
Franzese and Iorizzo were personally pocketing the incredible
sum of *$8 million per week!* Not even Franzese's new girlfriend

could burn through a wad of cash that thick. The tough young Don was in a position to rocket toward becoming the most powerful mobster in New York, all fueled by Iorizzo's gasoline scam. But as blissful as the Franzese-Iorizzo union was, the seeds of Franzese's destruction—and the weakening of the vaunted Colombo family— were sown the day the Mafia prince sealed the deal by shaking Lawrence Iorizzo's massive paw.

McPherson, my FBI friend from the Strike Force, told me what had happened. "We nailed Iorizzo. Bankruptcy fraud, mail fraud, tax evasion, you name it. He was looking at hard time."

"And you were hoping he'd cooperate against Franzese, right?" McPherson nodded.

"That was the plan. Would you want to go to jail if you looked like him?" We laughed.

"So what happened?"

"The guy disappeared. In June, before his sentencing."

"Big surprise," I said, wondering where a 500-pound mountain of flesh could possibly hide.

Most of the federal agents on the Strike Force dealing with Franzese felt that the "Yuppie Don" had reverted to his father's ways and fed his enormous associate to the alligators in the Florida Everglades. That would ensure that Iorizzo could never rat out the Colombo family.

"Some of my guys think he's chopped up in an oil barrel at the bottom of Long Island Sound. Actually, it would take two oil barrels," my friend joked.

"But you don't think so?"

"I don't know. But if there's a chance that he's alive, I want to find him. The guy was the key to nailing Franzese. We were close to turning him."

"Hey, I'd love to help you guys. There's only one problem."

"What?"

"The expense. If he's alive, it's going to cost a lot of money to track him down. I'm not asking you guys to pay my usual fee," I said. "But if you pay my expenses, I'll find out what happened to him."

"I don't think my boss will go for that, but let me see what I can come up with," McPherson promised.

The agent called a couple of days later with a novel way of retaining me. "Look, Iorizzo's company, Vantage Petroleum, was forced into bankruptcy. The creditors include a bunch of big companies—Hess Oil, Ashland Petroleum, Merrill Lynch, some others. The bankruptcy court appointed a liquidator, and the creditors are looking for Iorizzo's money. They could probably finance your operation. If you find Iorizzo's money, they might pay you."

After some quick negotiations, that's exactly what happened. I was retained by the bankruptcy court on behalf of Iorizzo's creditors to find Iorizzo and his money. They didn't believe I could do it, but were willing to pay me 15 percent of any cash I found, plus expenses. The hunt was on for probably the fattest fugitive to ever tip the scales of justice.

The Iorizzo case began, as most cases do, with tedious paperwork. I spent weeks poring over file boxes full of data collected by the Organized Crime Strike Force and the bankruptcy court's creditors' committee. It was no small job. At one point, I was convinced that Franzese and Iorizzo's biggest crime was the thousands of trees and other natural resources that were consumed compiling the vast amount of surveillance data collected on them. There were reams of transcripts, hundreds of reports, stacks of videos of illicit meetings, boxes of candid photos, you name it.

As is my custom, I entered every name, address, and phone number I came across into a computer database so they could be cross-referenced. I also entered whatever pertinent information I uncovered, ranging from a gangster's restaurant preferences and what he ordered to the hair color of the types of women he fancied. (Franzese liked black hair, bronze skin. Iorizzo, the bigamist, was partial to brunettes.)

I was in the Strike Force offices on Long Island one afternoon, knee-deep in Franzese and Iorizzo's convoluted paper trail, when one of McPherson's cohorts sauntered over. "Give it up, Pena. The guy's chopped up. And you'll never find his money—Franzese's got it locked up somewhere," the cynical Fed said with a challenging air.

"Oh yeah?" I answered. "If that's so, then where are all the big man's bodyguards? His associates . . ."

"Franzese took them out, too. Or they're lying low in Sicily hoping they don't get whacked."

"Even his second wife? I don't think so."

My instincts told me that Franzese hadn't killed Iorizzo. The big man was the proverbial goose that had laid a golden egg for the Colombo family. I figured Iorizzo had disappeared somewhere that Franzese or his people knew about, and that by now they'd all be planning a way for the cunning mobster to start over.

In addition, my intelligence on Franzese indicated that he'd resort to violence as a last recourse. He wasn't nearly as tough or hardened as his father. Plus, he and Iorizzo were close friends, almost brothers. They partied together, both in Florida and Long Island, closing down popular discos for the night so they and a few hundred of their friends could drink and dance the night away on Uncle Sam's tab. (During one of these parties, Iorizzo guzzled down a gallon of booze and then put a flowerpot on his massive head, doing his best Carmen Miranda imitation.)

My gut told me that Iorizzo was alive, and that Franzese probably knew where he was and was hoping to keep him hidden for a while. And if Iorizzo was alive, his money was hidden somewhere.

A guy as big as Larry needs a lot of cash to sate his appetites.

I put surveillance on Franzese all over South Florida. We tailed the Don from Miami to Boca Raton, and almost immediately discovered that the Florida Department of Law Enforcement and the Fort Lauderdale cops had him under surveillance too. There was no sign of Larry.

When my surveillance around Franzese didn't bring any results, I spent the next three months grinding through the nitty-gritty of the investigation. In addition to data provided by the Feds, we collected raw intelligence on Iorizzo's associates and on the relatives of his bodyguards. "Dry" garbage (papers and letters), credit card receipts, phone records, you name it and we perused it. It's tiring work, but usually yields a gold mine of information.

A few times I actually went on surveillance details with the Organized Crime Strike Force as they watched anyone and everyone left on Long Island who had any connection with Iorizzo. Each night, my associates and I hunkered down at my Fort Lee, New Jersey, compound and analyzed the latest intelligence.

Some of the information we examined came from the surveillance the Feds had on an office building frequently used for mob meetings. Whenever they met, the gangsters paid a private eye a whopping $5,000 to sweep the room for bugs. The guy was either a hack or a con man because his costly sweep never discovered any of the government's state-of-the-art audio or video equipment. The mobsters would waltz into the room thinking everything was kosher, not realizing that they were broadcasting their every conspiratorial statement into the recorders of the Feds. When the mob found out that they'd been duped, they busted up that PI pretty bad.

Curiously, whenever Franzese was in town, he never went into the bugged office. He'd remain in a cafeteria downstairs reading the stock quotations in the *Wall Street Journal* while his minions discussed their plans. Franzese later wrote that he had a sixth sense for bugs.

Combing through the boxes of intelligence, I noticed a couple of calls to Panama from a relative of a close Iorizzo associate named Peter Raneri. Raneri's Smithtown, Long Island, steak house was a popular meeting place for mobsters. Like so many others who play up to gangsters as if they were celebrities, Raneri found himself getting sucked into a life of crime. I was told that the Colombo gang once even used his walk-in freezer to store the bodies of their victims.

Raneri, a loud, Sicilian gangster wannabe, had become especially close to Iorizzo. It seems that the pair had a lot in common. Raneri owned a restaurant, and Iorizzo, of course, liked to eat. Iorizzo and Franzese had even sealed their partnership at Raneri's eatery.

The FBI thought Raneri might have assisted Iorizzo in washing his money. That meant the restaurateur probably knew where the fat man kept his stash.

Curiously, Raneri had also disappeared at the same time as his favorite customer. Since Franzese had absolutely no reason to kill Raneri, it furthered my suspicions that Iorizzo was alive—and Raneri was probably with him.

Could they be in Panama? We all knew that Iorizzo ran his corporations through the Central American country and had solid connections there. But was he dense enough to try and hide out in the most obvious place? Iorizzo wasn't a dumb man. It didn't seem logical.

The phone number Raneri's relative dialed was at the Marriott Hotel in Panama City. That told me nothing, and everything. My gut said that Iorizzo, Raneri, and the rest of the cutthroat gang were hiding out in Panama.

Because of international laws and jurisdiction restrictions, the powerful Organized Crime Strike Force was virtually impotent in dealing with a fugitive overseas. I wasn't. If Iorizzo was in Panama, then he was playing in my neck of the woods.

The chase for Michael Franzese's weak link was on.

THE LADY AND
THE FAT MAN SING

M Y HUNCH THAT the larger-than-life Iorizzo had fled to Panama was so strong that I phoned some contacts I'd made during a previous case there and began assembling a team. When working in a foreign country, it's imperative to have knowledgeable natives on your side. With that squared away, I hopped on the first jet south and flew to the Central American country to do some old-fashioned legwork.

My first goal was to get the phone records from the Marriott. Since we didn't know who had been in what room, we had to get all the records from all the guests over a three-month period-thousands of pages of mind-numbing numbers. A handsome Panamanian associate used his considerable charms to sweet-talk the data out of a cute Marriott secretary.

I stuffed the stack into a suitcase and headed back to New York. There was no sense staying in Panama because the information I needed to cross-reference was either in my computer or in the files of the Organized Crime Strike Force.

At home, it was back to the unglamorous job of number-crunching—scouring the phone records for a match. Thanks to area codes, I was able to focus on numbers beginning with Manhattan's 212, Brooklyn's 718, South Florida's 305, and especially Long Island's 516.

Unfortunately, New York's a heavily populated state. You wouldn't believe how many calls are routed to the Big Apple from hotels all over the world. It wasn't like looking for calls to Montana.

Halfway through the skyscraping stack, I hit 516 pay dirt. Someone at the Marriott in Panama City was placing calls to a supermarket pay phone in Long Island that the Franzese-Iorizzo gang regularly used.

Coincidence? Hardly. Especially when that same pay phone number kept showing up repeatedly after the first instance.

Now I had the proof I needed. I'd been on the job three months, and I'd found the elusive Larry Iorizzo.

"Iorizzo's in Panama," I announced, presenting the matching numbers to McPherson and two other FBI agents on the Strike Force.

They were pretty shocked, but even the most cynical FBI agent couldn't argue with the phone numbers.

I explained my plan. "Now that we know the city and country, I'll fly down there and find his exact location. He's probably not at the Marriott anymore, but he's somewhere nearby. I'll keep in touch."

In Panama, the closer I came to the fat man's trail, the more absurd things became. After a week of pounding the streets and paying for information, a real estate agent provided an address.

"No, this can't be," I said to myself, double-checking the information. "No one would be this stupid."

We drove to the location, surveyed the area, then set up surveillance from an apartment on a hill overlooking the compound. I still had my doubts about the real estate agent's tip.

The doubts vanished the next day. All of a sudden, a massive human being lumbered out of the house and strolled around the back yard. It was Lawrence Iorizzo!

Chills ran down my spine. To finally spot one's prey after a long, exacting hunt is a rush that fills your body with excitement. In this case, it was the same sensation Captain Ahab must have felt when he first spotted Moby Dick.

After the initial exhilaration, I scratched my head and rolled my eyes. New York's most wanted fugitive was living in a swank Panama neighborhood populated by rich foreigners. His mansion was just a few houses away from that of the United States Ambassador!

What could the big guy be thinking? It wasn't like he could dye his hair, slap on a false mustache, and go unnoticed. It would take a bigger country than Panama to hide that stomach!

At least Iorizzo was using a different name, but even that was bizarre. He was now Salvatore Carlino. That begs the question: Why did he select an alias that sounded even more like what he was, a mob-connected Italian gangster on the run? Salvatore Carlino sounded more like a Mafia moniker than Larry Iorizzo!

Also present and accounted for in the compound was wife number two (wife numero uno stayed home in her Long Island mansion); various children; the long-lost restaurateur, Mr. Raneri; and assorted other former Long Island residents. They might as well have put up a New York state flag on the lawn, along with the green, white, and red colors of Italy.

Finding the fat man, however, was only half the battle. Although the Organized Crime Strike Force would be dancing in their offices at the news, my clients and I had our sights set on a bigger score—the cash Iorizzo had stolen from Ashland, Merrill Lynch, and the other creditors. It would have been stupid to rush in and grab him at that point. I had a better idea.

My Panamanian associates, with the help of General Noriega's best wire man, quickly placed the Long Island fugitive inside what I call an "electronic box." They tapped Iorizzo's telephones and placed bugs in his kitchen and bedroom, then rented a house in the neighborhood to use as our surveillance headquarters. Whenever the big man left the compound, we tailed him.

On two occasions, I strolled up into the exclusive neighborhood around his complex with a Panamanian team member acting as my girlfriend. Twice, as we passed in front of the walls surrounding the fat man's estate, Iorizzo's little girl and nanny ran out into the street. I actually scolded the nanny for being so lax with the child's security.

Two weeks into the "box" treatment, we intercepted a call from New York informing Iorizzo that a pair of private detectives were on his tail. Raneri immediately phoned New York and informed Sebastian "Buddy" Lombardo, the Sonny Franzese associate who had first introduced Iorizzo and Michael Franzese. (Lombardo was Franzese's way of keeping tabs on Iorizzo, making sure the fat man didn't do anything untoward—like bolt to the Feds and start singing.) Raneri and Lombardo wanted to identify the PIs and determine how close to Iorizzo they were getting.

I didn't think much about it at the time. Iorizzo had burned a lot of different companies when he left the country, and it was conceivable that one of these other firms had hired some detectives to track him down. As long as they stayed out of my way, everything would be cool.

They stayed out of my way, but everything wasn't cool. Two weeks later, I received a panicked call from my wife.

"Octavio, the FBI says the mob sent two hit men to Panama to kill you! You've got to get out of there, now!"

Despite the FBI's warning, I knew that it was the other guys the Mafia "mechanics" were after. Apparently Lombardo got a bead on the nosy detectives and decided to take care of them on behalf of Franzese or someone else in the Colombo family. At that point, Iorizzo didn't know I existed. I was just a friendly guy in the neighborhood. Still, with a team of hit men running around Panama itching to plug someone, it was possible they could stumble upon our operation.

To keep from being exposed, I had to warn the PIs that their lives were in danger and persuade them to leave Panama pronto, before they got themselves turned into fertilizer for a sugarcane field.

First, however, I wanted to determine who they were and who had hired them. I had the strange feeling that there was a leak somewhere in my chain of command, and that these guys had materialized because someone blabbed that I'd found Iorizzo.

After a day of calls and inquiries, my suspicions were verified. When I notified the bankruptcy court that I'd found Iorizzo, a lawyer for one of the creditors took it upon himself to tell his client. They selected a pair of loud and aggressive ex-New York cops who flashed Iorizzo's picture around various downtown Panama City hotels, clumsily alerting everyone in Central America that they were there.

That's no way to conduct an investigation against the mob, to say the least. The buffoons were setting themselves up to be killed. They were in a foreign country, a country where burying a couple of troublemakers under a banana tree was as easy as hiring a two-dollar hooker.

Complicating things, the FBI got wind of the hit and figured the killers were after me. They called my office. Thinking they were talking to my secretary, they presented the frightening news to my wife!

After calming everyone, I tracked down the flatfoots at their hotel and had a fatherly chat with them.

"You two have been made. I suggest you return to New York with haste. Tell your client that everything is being taken care of, and they'll get their money when it's found."

"What the fuck you talking about?" one of them growled.

"You're here looking for Lawrence Iorizzo. A team of seasoned Mafia killers are on their way right now to make you disappear, permanently. Is that blunt enough for you?"

The detectives, eyes bugging out of their heads, checked out of their rooms on the spot. That was the last I heard of them.

With that problem solved, it was back to the tapes and earphones. The bugs the Panama team planted paid off the minute they were switched on. Thinking he was safe in Panama, Iorizzo made free use of Madre Bell. The fat man's carelessness immediately bore fruit. We were able to identify a bank account in Panama City where Iorizzo had stashed more than $5 million.

Finding it was easy. Getting the stolen money back was another matter. In order to grease the wheels of justice, my Panamanian associates arranged for a late-night rendezvous with the Attorney General of Panama. We wanted the country's top legal officer to freeze Iorizzo's accounts so the American bankruptcy court could then seize the cash. After the meeting was set up, an attorney for the court and I were whisked through the dark, trash-strewn streets of Panama City into the swankier section of town where the Attorney General had one of his villas.

The Attorney General greeted us in his bathrobe. It may have been 3:00 A.M. and he may have been in his pajamas, but Panama's top barrister quickly proved he was wide awake.

"I want half of the money. Fifty percent. Then I freeze everything for you," he said without a twinge of shame.

After some consultations the next morning, the attorney and I decided that $2.5 million was too much grease. Plus, it didn't strike us as the smart move for agents of a federal court in New York to bribe the Attorney General of a foreign country. If I had been working for a private client, I might have figured out a way to get around the corrupt Attorney General, but the attorney and I decided the pittance we'd end up with didn't warrant the risk of an international incident involving the so-called Justice Department of General Noriega. We had no choice but to leave Iorizzo's Panama mad money alone.

After we hit that wall, it was time to return to Iorizzo's telephone calls to see if anything else turned up. I found several of his routine conversations particularly intriguing. For instance, Iorizzo was regularly calling and meeting with international drug dealers.

Second, one of Iorizzo's smuggler buddies, a suave Argentinean drug lord, used the Fat Man's phone to contact a mole he had developed inside the U.S. Embassy. This source fed the drug kingpin information about various U.S. intelligence agency activities, along with, presumably, information about the efforts to find Iorizzo. (I subsequently learned that this same Argentinean drug dealer may have later used the embassy mole to warn General Noriega that the U.S. Army was coming to bust him. The tip enabled Noriega to go into hiding, and resulted in the dangerous standoff that was shown on television around the world.)

It was the third series of conversations that interested me the most. Iorizzo kept in frequent contact with a sultry-voiced woman in Vienna, Austria, who had a most interesting job. She handled many of the gasoline mob's bank accounts in Europe.

Bingo! That's what I was looking for. I now knew where the bulk of Iorizzo's money was, and who could lead me to it.

I contacted the Organized Crime Strike Force. "I've got what I need down here. He's yours now," I said.

It didn't take long for Iorizzo's fate to be sealed. I was still in Panama and had the big man under surveillance when the dime was dropped. Raneri, Iorizzo, and a beefy bodyguard left the compound one morning and drove their big American Chevy to a local gas station. Raneri, acting as Iorizzo's Uzi-carrying main bodyguard, went inside to get some cigarettes, leaving the deadly machine gun in the trunk. That was his first mistake.

While the restaurateur was inside, an unmarked sedan pulled in front of the Chevy. Two grim-faced military officers got out and approached Iorizzo.

"Señor Carlino. Please come with us. The General [Noriega] wants to see you."

Raneri rushed out as Larry reluctantly lumbered out of the Chevy, but there was nothing he or the bodyguard could do as the officers pushed the defenseless Iorizzo into a sedan and whisked him away.

Raneri and the bodyguard recovered from their momentary paralysis. They jumped into the car and followed the now-sagging sedan. A second military vehicle skidded to a stop and blocked them. Raneri watched in horror as the Colombo family's prized money machine disappeared around the corner.

What happened from there reads like a Tom Clancy novel complete with the long arm of the American government, double-dealing politicians, international criminals, and frantic American gangsters. Big Larry was taken to a Panamanian safe house owned by the military and put on ice. Meanwhile, Raneri and the now-contrite bodyguard ran to the home of a shady Austrian duke named Henri Alba-Teran d'Antin, a con man buddy, and begged for help. The duke put on a suitable frown, and promptly began scheming to extort Iorizzo's family!

You can imagine Iorizzo's surprise at all this. It was widely believed (and confirmed later in Michael Franzese's book, *Quitting the Mob*) that Iorizzo had paid General Noriega upwards of a million dollars for asylum and protection in Panama. Apparently a million bucks doesn't go as far as it used to: Noriega coughed up Iorizzo like a cat spitting up a furball.

The following day, Panamanian military escorted him onto a regularly scheduled flight to Miami to be turned over to the Feds. The soldiers tucked him into a seat and handed him a seat-belt extender so the fat man could weather the bumpy ride ahead.

In Miami, Iorizzo was met by three FBI agents from the Organized Crime Strike Force. As expected, Iorizzo immediately offered to cut a deal. Point out a crime and a suspect, and Iorizzo was willing to link the pair. The FBI was happy to accommodate him.

When he was brought into the Metro Detention Center in Miami, the FBI—afraid that the Colombo family would put a hit on the fat man—made sure nobody knew that he was even in the country. The Feds weren't the only ones thinking along those lines.

When I debriefed the Panamanian military officers who squeezed into the seats next to Iorizzo on the flight into Miami, they told me that Iorizzo was sweating heavily, terrified that his former buddy, his "almost brother," the Yuppie Don, was going to rub him out.

Iorizzo was so scared he decided not to call anyone until he had cut his deal with the Feds. That momentary delay gave me the time I needed.

As soon as Buddy Lombardo put two and two together, the phones began buzzing in Panama, Miami, and New York—and all over the country. One of the first calls came from the duke. He dialed Iorizzo's wife in Panama and asked her for a quick $50,000 to help spring her husband. That turned out to be nothing more than an extortion scheme. The duke, figuring the fat man was down for the count, was trying to take advantage of the situation and make a quick score. There is indeed no honor among thieves.

The rest of the calls were of the mass panic nature. Raneri and gang burned up the lines calling Colombo family associates around the country in order to warn Franzese that his money man had vanished. Raneri called their drug dealer associate, who claimed that his pal Noriega didn't know where "Salvatore" was.

The panicked calls lasted three days, while Iorizzo relaxed in a Miami jail cell. (He even faked a heart attack on the second day to better his accommodations.)

I couldn't believe how lax these mobsters' security had become. After months of sneaking around to phone booths, calling collect, and so on, they were now openly discussing the Iorizzo disaster on their home phones!

One of the more interesting conversations was between Raneri and Lombardo, the Colombo strong-arm man who was supposed to keep tabs on Iorizzo. The two had an animated chat establishing the fat man's value on the ransom market.

"We're not gonna pay more than two million for Larry," Lombardo groused, still unaware that their golden goose was in custody in the United States.

The pair then began naming associates who might have to be killed in order to obliterate the trail that connected Iorizzo, Franzese, and the stashed millions.

"Is Wilma reliable?" Raneri asked.

I perked up at that. "Wilma" was Wilma Kurtz, a British woman who handled Iorizzo's money in Vienna. She was also one of Lombardo's girlfriends.

"We might have to kill her," Lombardo answered without a trace of humanity or compassion for the woman he supposedly loved. I was stunned. I knew the mob could be vicious, but that was sinking to a new level.

For me, however, it was a wonderful new level. The threat was my key to Iorizzo's overflowing bank accounts.

I grabbed the tape and jumped on the first jet to Vienna. It was time to meet Ms. Kurtz.

Before landing, I contacted a friend in German counterintelligence. Klaus and I had crossed paths on a previous case, and kept in touch. I asked him to help me with the critical Wilma Kurtz phase of the hunt.

After settling in at a hotel, I met Klaus and we drove to Kurtz's apartment complex. I told my German associate to take the elevator up to her apartment and tell her that I was working for the U.S. bankruptcy courts and had important news from the States.

"Explain that we've uncovered some information that is vital to her safety."

I wanted Klaus to talk to her in German and put her at ease. The intelligence officer went upstairs. After a brief conversation, he invited me to join them inside Wilma's nicely furnished apartment. The tall, distinguished-looking woman tried to act cool, but I could tell she was nervous.

"Ms. Kurtz, I'm a consultant working for the courts investigating Larry Iorizzo." Her face went blank, but her eyes narrowed a bit. "I know that you know he's disappeared."

"What does this have to do with me?"

"We've received a tape recording from some Panamanian agents who monitored the communications of Iorizzo's men, and your name came up. Let me play what these two gentlemen said."

I plunked the cassette recorder on the table and started playing the tape.

Lombardo's voice boomed out. I switched it off.

"Do you recognize that voice?"

"That's Buddy," Wilma shrugged.

I played some more. Raneri's voice echoed through her apartment.

"How about this gentleman?"

"That's Peter," she said.

She was unraveling. Her eyes were unnaturally bright. I pushed the button again, letting the tape roll to its damning conclusion.

"Is Wilma reliable? Can we trust her?" Raneri asked.

"We might have to kill her."

I saw the blood drain from Wilma's face as she listened to her lover elaborate on how he was going to have her silenced.

I switched off the recorder. After a long pause, Wilma composed herself and spoke. "What can I do?"

I leaned forward. "I have been authorized by the court to protect you if you so choose."

"Who are you? How do I know you're not one of them?"

Klaus tried to reassure her—again in German—that I wasn't a mobster.

Wilma was shaken, but she wasn't stupid. She wasn't about to accept me on face value. Fair enough, but proving my claim turned out to be more difficult than I imagined. The U.S. Embassy refused to vouch for me. The government did its usual dance, ignoring my efforts on its behalf in case something went wrong. (Of course, they'd take all the credit if I succeeded.) I was pretty upset that the State Department withheld comment. Here I was, closing in on nearly $15 million in stolen tax money. The official arm of the government could have been a tad more helpful.

The embassy snub forced me to call Ron Noel, a highly placed friend in Washington.

"Listen, you have to get someone in Europe with a diplomatic passport to vouch for me. Tonight."

A few hours later Ron called back and promised that an American diplomat would arrive from Switzerland to convince Wilma that I was legit.

That night, Alan Ringgold, the FBI's assistant legal attaché in Bern, Switzerland, flew to Vienna and met me and Wilma at a local wiener schnitzel emporium. He flashed the proper credentials, and told Wilma that I was on the level. Once assured, Wilma asked me for help. I told her that my client would pay her 2 percent of any money she helped them recover from Iorizzo. She readily agreed to turn.

Phase two began. I called in some British operatives who wired Iorizzo's Vienna office, Wilma's apartment, and any other place the mob frequented in Vienna. I then waited to see what happened.

It was a good thing we worked as fast as we did, because events quickly took another turn. Lombardo calmed down and decided not to bury his girlfriend in some Austrian glacier. Instead, he simply telexed the Austrian bank and made sure he was the only person authorized to withdraw the money. He then flew to Vienna to cuddle with his sweetheart, assure her that everything was all right despite Iorizzo's problems, and explain that things would proceed as normal.

Although Wilma was furious that Lombardo had considered killing her, she remained his lover. She wasn't exactly ecstatic about sleeping with someone who had contemplated rubbing her out, but she realized that it was the only way to protect herself and earn her fee. Nevertheless, the fact that she was still shacking up with Lombardo muddied the waters. She was my mole, her place was wired to the hilt, and she was still entertaining the tough Italian in her bed! I didn't know how long the flustered accountant could handle the stressful double-agent drama, or which side really held her loyalty.

I had to spend a great deal of time with Wilma, reassuring her that I could protect her. Like most people, she considered the mob almost omnipotent, its long tentacles powerful enough to snuff her out anywhere at any time. It was my job to show Wilma that Buddy and his cohorts weren't quite up to Don Corleone standards.

I put Lombardo under such tight surveillance in New York that the tough guy panicked and flew to Vienna. One night, while the British team's tape recorders whirred in the hotel room next door, Lombardo and Iorrizo's son, Larry Jr., talked openly about how unnerved they were about the surveillance in New York. The legendary legbreaker was so terrified that he was being targeted for a hit that he stayed in his hotel room for two days, refusing to order food from room service because he couldn't stomach the local cuisine. The Colombo tough guy made Larry Jr. go to the local McDonald's to get some hamburgers.

When Wilma heard those tapes and realized that her boyfriend was as scared as she was, she calmed down. The more she realized how well we were protecting her—I had a team of covert bodyguards around her whenever anyone from the Colombo family came to Vienna—the more relaxed she became.

I couldn't relax, however. I needed to know if the mob actually suspected her, and if they did, whether or not they planned to kill her and how they might go about it. So I eventually came up with another plan to protect her.

From all the intelligence I had gathered on the family, I was able to find a weak link fairly high up, someone who was vulnerable and easy to turn. I'd been waiting to play this card, and now, in order to figure out if the mob really planned to kill Wilma, it was time.

This Colombo high-ranking soldier flew to Vienna and arranged a meeting with the lawyer who handled the family's legal and financial interests. (Wilma just handled the money.) The attorney's name was Dr. Erhard Weber, and he had a nasty reputation—sort of the Germanic version of Bruce Cutler, John Gotti's brawling barrister.

The mole told Weber that "an enforcer" was coming to Vienna to "roll up the carpet" on the whole Iorizzo mess, and that Weber should help the killer sort out who should get whacked to protect the mob's money in the future.

Armed with this ironclad introduction, I marched into Weber's office one bitter Vienna morning using my best hit man swagger.

Weber was a walking poster boy for Hitler's SS: he had cold light blue eyes, and an arrogance as refined as his custom-made suits. But this morning he decided to leave his Teutonic attitude at home. Meeting a "Mafia hit man" has a way of doing that to even the coolest of customers.

"Please, can I get you some coffee? Strudel?" he groveled in perfect English.

"No," I said with nary a smile. "We have to solve this problem as quickly as possible."

"Yes, yes. A disaster," he said, eager to please. "What can I do for you?"

"I want to know who handled what, so we can avoid this in the future. You got anything to help me figure this out?" I asked.

"Of course, of course."

Weber jumped out of his chair and gathered up copies of the mob's most intimate business records faster than the Wermacht rolled through Poland. I popped the papers into a briefcase for perusal later.

"We have to take care of some of these people," I said ominously. I stared at him like he was my first choice, trying hard not to blink. I could see him swallow. By now his hands were shaking.

"I agree. We could have a disaster over here."

"Who's at the top of your list?" I asked.

"Wilma Kurtz."

My stomach dropped. I kept a straight face, but inside I felt a chill.

"You think she's ratted out on us, like Larry?"

"I don't know. I suspect. She's been acting strange lately. Buddy still trusts her, but I'm not sure. She should be the first to go."

"You got any evidence? I don't want to terminate someone who doesn't deserve it."

I let the word *terminate* sit there in the room.

"No. It's just suspicions," he responded, wringing his hands.

I left after extracting a promise that he wouldn't talk to anyone about our little discussion.

Forewarned that the family suspected Wilma, or at least that Weber did, I finished the gambit by having my contact Klaus make a call on Weber about a week later, pretending to be an "informant" with some pertinent information. Klaus told the mob lawyer that, based on "German counterintelligence intercepting phone calls" and some other cockamamie stories, the mob suspected *him* of ratting out and that Wilma was in the clear.

I still laugh when I think about Weber buying into my act. He probably didn't sleep for a week. Neither did I. I was up all night deciphering Weber's papers on the mob's financial empire in Austria.

More importantly, though, the mob left Wilma alone. Wilma, for her part, stayed true. She didn't alert her lover about the bugs. Maybe it was her revenge for the death threat. Whatever her reasons, when I invited her to the United States to meet with the FBI, she accepted as long as I accompanied her. Once there, she was extremely cooperative, telling them about Iorizzo's and other mobsters' numbered accounts at the Creditanstalt Bankverein and Bankhaus Feichtner & Company banks in Vienna. She went on to take the agents through the intricate trail of transfers from bank to bank around the world that the mob used to launder its money.

Despite Wilma's help and information, we still couldn't grab the money. Austrian banking laws are tough. To access the accounts, we needed Lombardo's passbooks. Separating the volatile Italian from his prized possessions wasn't going to be easy. But I had a plan.

Lombardo and his crowd had no idea that their money was at risk. What we needed to do was figure out a way to freeze the accounts. The only way to do that was to use the Austrian courts. The only problem was that it had never been done in Austrian history. After we hired and fired about half a dozen Austrian attorneys who flat-out refused to help us pry open their country's arcane banking laws, we finally found one who thought he could help.

While our attorney looked into innovative ways to freeze the Colombo family accounts, my associates in Panama and New York kept Buddy Lombardo under tight surveillance. The plan was, when he came to Vienna again, we'd hit him with legal papers and take the money.

Lombardo flew to Vienna all right. But as soon as he got there, he withdrew the $15 million and stuffed the bills into a half dozen suitcases. Somebody at the bank had apparently tipped him off that there was a move to freeze his money.

Fortunately for us, Lombardo told Wilma where he was stashing the money. He converted the money back into about twenty passbooks to special numbered accounts, which were as good as cash, and shoved the surrogate money into two rented safety deposit boxes at another bank. Once again, we knew where the money was, but it remained just out of reach.

Still, Lombardo's activities brought us that much closer to the money. To get his passbooks, all we needed was a couple of deposit box keys.

After bidding another fond goodbye to Wilma, Lombardo and his bodyguard went to the airport, tailed as always by my British team. When they reported that Lombardo and his bodyguard were headed for New York, I called the FBI and the bankruptcy court and requested that they greet Franzese's legbreaker/banker with a court order to confiscate his safety deposit keys.

The Colombo enforcer was nabbed at Customs at Kennedy Airport. He was ushered into a side room and strip-searched while I watched with a team of FBI agents through a two-way mirror. The gruff gangster took it in stride. He didn't appear panicked, miffed, or remotely concerned, even when the customs agents made him bend over in order to check his most intimate hiding places.

His mood changed when one of the agents rummaged through his pants and then dangled a pair of keys in Lombardo's face.

"What's this, tough guy?"

Lombardo went white. The agent left the room, walked next door into ours, and handed the keys to the lead FBI agent. The G-man promptly gave them to me.

"Happy hunting," he said, smiling.

I knew enough not to waste time. The race was on. The next flight to Vienna was that night. I had to hustle to get ready. I was ten minutes into the drive back to my apartment to pack, when the first of a series of baffling hurdles was thrown into my path.

My car phone rang. Laura Brevetti, the head of the Brooklyn Organized Crime Strike Force, wanted to talk. At that time, the ambitious young prosecutor was one of the most powerful law enforcement officials in America. She could marshal police detectives and federal agents at a moment's notice. She even had some nasty IRS officials at her disposal. She was definitely someone you didn't want to cross.

"I can't tell you how proud we are of you," she opened. "What you've done is incredible. You're the best."

It was a wonderful compliment, and I thanked her, but I kept waiting for the other high-heeled shoe to drop. It didn't take long.

"I have to meet with you tomorrow. It's urgent. You can't go to Vienna right now," she ordered.

"I have to go before the money disappears," I argued. "If I don't get the money, then all the praise you just gave me will be meaningless. My job is to get the money."

"I've arranged for the money to be frozen," she insisted. "There's no rush. I really need to see you first."

I protested some more, but she insisted. Something was up.

"Okay," I said, turning back in despair. Although Brevetti promised the money would be there, I had my doubts. Powerful as she was, I didn't think her reach extended across the ocean. If she really had the ability to freeze foreign safety deposit box accounts on a moment's notice, the mob would have been out of business.

Despite my misgivings, there was little I could do. Brevetti wanted to have a sitdown, so the trip had to wait twenty-four hours.

The next day, I drove to Brooklyn, eager to hear the important news that had yanked me from the flight and stalled me in my tracks. After some polite chitchat, Brevetti, a stern, stocky woman with brown hair, proceeded to praise me again. That was followed by . . . nothing!

I stood there in shock. I couldn't believe that I'd been derailed from my objective for no other reason than to hear some warmed-over compliments.

Something was fishy. Even so, I couldn't fathom that the head of Brooklyn's famous Organized Crime Strike Force could be compromised, and could be capable of so obvious and blatant a ruse. There had to be an explanation.

The next day, I got it via Austria. It wasn't what I wanted to hear.

"Octavio. You won't believe who's here."

Wilma Kurtz's voice was low and etched in fear.

"Who?"

"Buddy."

"Lombardo! How the hell—"

"He somehow lost his safety deposit box keys. So he had the bank drill open the boxes. He took the money and passbooks."

"Okay, hang tight and keep your ears open. Call me if anything else happens."

My body went numb as I hung up the phone. Was I intentionally delayed so the mob could get their money back? I could understand having to run a gauntlet of gangsters all the way to Vienna, but to be stopped dead by an influential U.S. Attorney? Unbelievable.

I phoned Brevetti.

"Laura. Lombardo's in Vienna! He's got the money back."

"Are you sure?"

"Positive. How did that happen? I thought you had it frozen?"

"I did. I can't believe it."

"You can't believe it? That's exactly what I warned you was going to happen!"

I slammed down the receiver. What was going on here? Could someone have touched Brevetti—the head of the Brooklyn Organized Crime Strike Force?

I made some calls and put Brevetti under tight surveillance. I wanted to know where she ate, drank, and slept, and who she ate, drank, and slept with. I put my men on particular lookout for any sign of "Buddy" Lombardo. This move appeared to have his fingerprints all over it. I didn't think Lombardo, Iorizzo, and their underlings had the class, smarts, or moxie to get to a U.S. Attorney.

I watched Brevetti for weeks, but came up with nothing. No contacts with anyone shady. No sight of Lombardo anywhere. She was apparently spic-and-span clean.

The only fireworks came when Brevetti got wind of the tails and reported that she was being watched by the mob. The FBI knew it was me, but they didn't say anything. They were as curious as I was to see what I'd uncover.

"The prosecutors just want all the credit," a high-placed source told me. "They want to get the money themselves, then hold a big press conference to announce it. Remember, they've been hunting Franzese a lot longer than you. There are what, fifteen government agencies involved? You gotta understand, the Feds have never recovered money from the mob. This is a big coup for them. So it might not have been Brevetti's call. You can't just point the finger at her."[*]

---

[*] Brevetti's boss, famed Organized Crime Strike Force head Edward McDonald, supports this explanation: "I'm sure she just wanted to officially retrieve the money herself. That was a big score for the task force. There's no question as to her integrity. Laura Brevetti put too many mobsters in jail even to hint that."

Brevetti's integrity notwithstanding, she recently made the news when her husband, Marty Bergman, whom the press described as someone who "swoons at the mention of gangsters like John Gotti and Carmine Persico," became the target of a criminal probe—for allegedly trying to compromise a government witness—that also raised some troubling questions about Brevetti.

It made sense. The government disavows you when things go wrong, then steals the headlines when they go right. But it's a fine line, in my opinion, between a publicity hound and the dark side of the law. What Laura Brevetti did was flat-out wrong, whatever her reasons.

With the Brevetti shadow failing to bear fruit of a mob/U.S. Attorney conspiracy, I turned my attention back to the cash. Although Lombardo had it again, he hadn't moved it out of Austria. He'd simply deposited it into some new secret accounts.

That meant the race was on again, not just with the mobsters, but with the U.S. Attorney's office as well. And that introduced another wrinkle into the fabric. I'm extremely protective of my informants. The less people involved, the better. However, in this case, Wilma Kurtz's identity was widely known among the Organized Crime Strike Force members because she had come to America and was cooperating with them. If the task force had been compromised, she would no longer be able to function, literally and figuratively.

That, thankfully, wasn't the case. And it pounded home what my source had been trying to tell me about the subtle difference between corrupt prosecutors and overly ambitious prosecutors. If they were corrupt, they would have sold out the informant.

They didn't, because Lombardo promptly gave his still-breathing lover copies of the new passbooks. She then relayed them to me. Working the Austrian legal system, I eventually found a team of attorneys with the guts to freeze the accounts. A week later, the bankruptcy court in New York was wired $11.8 million.

The story unfortunately had one more disturbing twist before we actually got our hands on the money. After freezing Iorizzo's huge stash, we were all set to wire it to the United States. All we needed was the okay of a Vienna district prosecutor. Incredibly, the guy asked our lawyers for a $100,000 bribe for his signature! I immediately put the British team onto him, and within twenty-four hours, we'd discovered that the guy was squeezing a French food company in a similar matter, and that the payoff would come in twenty-four hours. Klaus notified the local press and the police. The next day, they nabbed the prosecutor with a suitcase full of cash in a Vienna park. Needless to say, we got another (honest) prosecutor assigned to the matter, and Iorizzo's money went on its way.

As far as I know, it was the first and only time mob money hidden in secret European bank accounts was returned to the

United States. The case was a big success, but the price was high. My faith in the integrity of the American legal system took a punch to the gut. And if I was paranoid about sharing information with government officials to begin with, I was even more so now.

With Iorizzo securely tucked into the Witness Protection Program, the federal task force gunning for Michael Franzese was finally able to meet with success. Using the testimony of Iorizzo, they hit the Yuppie Don with a twenty-eight-count racketeering indictment. They also ended the careers of most of his associates, including such well-known mobsters as Frank "Frankie Gangster" Castagnaro, Frank Cestaro, and union boss Anthony Tomasso. The specific charges against Franzese included conspiracy, mail fraud, obstruction of justice, extortion, issuing a counterfeit security, violating federal anti-kickback laws, embezzlement, and wire fraud. There was also a nifty charge known as a "Kline conspiracy." This is a blanket accusation that every business Franzese was ever involved in, including his Hollywood movies, was created for the sole purpose of stealing taxes.

Florida, borrowing Iorizzo from the task force, took back their key to the city in a huff and threw an even bigger book at Franzese and his southern gang. The tropical state slapped the Yuppie Don and company with a whopping 177-count indictment, 66 of which were against Franzese personally.

Among the twenty-six codefendants were some of Iorizzo's and Franzese's closest pals, including Duke Henri Alba-Teran d'Antin, Sebastian Lombardo, Peter Raneri, and a trio of Russian mobsters named Michael Markowitz, David Bogatin, and Leo Persits.

A battalion of Feds swarmed Franzese's mansion in Brookville, Long Island. A second team surrounded the love nest condominium in Brentwood, California, where he had stashed his Mexican lover turned fiancée. In Brookville, his wife, Maria, truthfully told them her husband no longer lived there. In Brentwood, the only people the cops found at the condo were the beguiling Camille and her comely sister Sabrina. The Mexican sisters, despite being gorgeous and refined, were also pretty street-smart. They played dumb and told the agents nothing. One of the law enforcement officers ended up asking Sabrina for a date!

Meanwhile, Franzese was at the Bel Air Sands Hotel, figuring out what to do. Camille hopped down the balcony of her condo, leaped to the ground, jumped into her expensive sports car, shook a police tail, and met Franzese there for one last night of tears and passion. The next morning, Franzese flew to Fort Lauderdale and gave himself up.

With Franzese and his men behind bars, the unprecedented and obscenely lucrative empire of Long Island and Florida's "Yuppie Don" had come to a crashing end.

For me, the implications were staggering. From the simple task of locating the fattest fugitive in U.S. history, I ended up providing the government with the key ingredient that destroyed one of the biggest Mafia operations in organized crime history.

Not bad for a year and a half worth of work.

A few months later, I settled down on my sofa one evening, turned on NBC news, and watched Franzese cruise down Wilshire Boulevard in Los Angeles in a white convertible. The Don was out! Half the law enforcement officials in the country were probably going into shock, but not me. I was expecting it.

A few weeks earlier, an FBI source called with the incredible news that Franzese had cut a deal to get out of prison. There was nothing the FBI could do except fight back with the press. The bureau called a reporter at NBC, Brian Ross, who turned a magnifying glass on Franzese's miraculous rehabilitation.

I turned up the sound. Brian Ross explained that the silver-tongued Mafia devil had negotiated a whale of a plea deal for himself. He confessed to just two of the twenty-eight Organized Crime Strike Force counts—federal racketeering and tax conspiracy. He also pleaded guilty to the sixty-six Florida counts, but they were just window dressing. The nine-year Florida prison sentence ran concurrent with the ten-year federal sentence. The ten-year term, in real time, meant he had to serve just three and a half years before he could be paroled!

Franzese also promised to pay $15 million in restitution—a promise few believed he'd ever make good on.

So what was the Yuppie Don doing cruising free as a bird down Wilshire Boulevard? It turned out he had further negotiated a deal that allowed him to serve his time in a comfy L.A. halfway house. All he had to do was sleep there! His days were his own. This was arranged, according to Franzese, so he could make some more movies and earn the government the $15 million he owed. In essence, Franzese made Uncle Sam his new partner!

How did he do it? There were whispers that Franzese paid off a lot of prosecutors, but nothing was ever confirmed.

Whatever the truth, Franzese had a tougher time when it came to the media and the public. After NBC aired its report, the judge who let him go was so embarrassed by the sight of Franzese living the good life that he threw him back in prison.

The smooth criminal did his three years, was paroled, stubbed his toe on some shady real estate deals, had his probation revoked, served two more years, and is now trying to make movies again in Hollywood—one of which is supposed to be based on his life. He also waged some publicity of his own with his autobiography, *Quitting the Mob.* If the title of his interesting tome is indeed accurate, he is the highest-ranking Mafioso in history to turn his back on La Cosa Nostra.

The mob, of course, has a half-dozen contracts out to kill their fallen king, but so far he's remained unscathed, developing scripts for his production company in Hollywood.

Some prosecutors feel that the ever-resourceful Franzese may have bought his contracts back from the mob, using his vast wealth—all generated by the rotund Larry Iorizzo—to ensure himself a peaceful existence.

If true, there remains one dark cloud on the horizon. In 1994, Sonny Franzese, Michael's no-nonsense mob enforcer father, was finally released from prison after nearly a quarter-century behind bars. Rumor has it that Sonny has been given the order to "take care of" his wayward son. Sonny, who served his term with iron-jawed silence, is the kind of man who can't be bought.

A few months after Larry Iorizzo disappeared into the maw of the Witness Protection Program, he asked his keepers if he could speak to me. At our first face-to-face, the big man had a rather unique request.

"Man, you're good," he buttered me up.

"Thank you, Larry." I wondered where the conversation was going.

"I think Franzese's going to have me killed."

"I can understand that."

"I want you to protect my wife and children," he continued. "Please."

That was a novel request: a mobster asking a civilian for protection.

"I can't do that, Larry. But I'll tell you what I can do. I'll meet with her and give her some tips. Is that okay?"

Iorizzo nodded.

The following week I met with his wife and gave her some advice on security. A strange end to a long case.

Nobody's gunned down Larry or his family thus far. They've managed to destroy themselves on their own.

In 1995 the Feds kicked the fat man out of the Witness Protection Program and put him in a Texas jail. It turned out that for years, while under the protective umbrella of the government, Iorizzo went right back to what he knew best—stealing U.S. gasoline tax dollars. He's now cooling his heels in the slammer with his son, his two daughters, his son-in-law, and his good buddy Peter Raneri.

THERE GOES THE JUDGE

I T'S NO SECRET that the judicial system in America appears to be approaching meltdown. *Time* magazine said as much in a recent cover story. If you hold your nose and study the O. J. Simpson murder trial, it's obvious that *Time* wasn't exaggerating. Critics charge that O.J.'s "Dream Team" of defense attorneys made a mockery of the law in their zeal to free the famous ex-football star.

The goal was not to seek the truth, but to do anything possible, jump upon any misconception (racial or otherwise), use any thread of unrelated information, to divert attention and sow seeds of doubt into at least one juror. That's justice?

In the opinion of many observers, Judge Ito went overboard in granting the famous defense team the leeway it needed to obfuscate the mountain of damning evidence the prosecutors had amassed. Particularly galling was the parade of hired-gun experts that marched to the stand and earned their fees by attacking the police and prosecutors and saying exactly what the defense wanted them to.

Everybody knows that attorneys have the morals of alley cats. That's almost a job description. The whole process of defending clients they know are guilty forces even the best of them to do things that the rest of us would consider repugnant.

But judges are a whole different story. They're the last defense against the barbarians coming over the walls. When the judges start cracking, we're done for.

I'd been in America less than a decade when a client asked me to investigate one of the bulwarks against the barbarians—a sitting federal judge. It wasn't a task I relished. As a former law student, I wanted to cling to my illusion of an untainted legal system in the great "land of the free."

I operated under that grand notion until the day a powerful Chicago businessman named Steve MacNair walked into my office with a story so incredible that I initially refused to take the case.

I didn't believe this guy's story, and besides, I didn't like him. MacNair had barreled into the room, plopped himself into a chair, put his feet on my desk, and begun ordering me around. Whatever his problem was, and regardless of how much he was offering to solve it, I wanted him out of there.

"I'm sorry," I said. "I'm too busy right now."

He was as persistent as he was rude, bugging me every week to see if I'd change my mind. He even pestered my partner, John Lynch.

"What's the problem?" Lynch asked me. "Why don't you take this guy's case?"

"I don't like the man. We'll never get along. He's too arrogant," I responded. I was doing well enough now that I could pick and choose my cases. Why put up with the aggravation?

"You should give him a chance," Lynch said.

"I did. It's not going to work out."

The following week, I received a call from the president of a large chain of radio stations in Illinois. The president said they had a pressing problem and wanted to fly into New York to discuss it with me.

When the radio executive arrived, he said that we had to wait for the chairman of the chain. A few minutes later, in walks Steve MacNair—the same guy who'd been harassing me for weeks!

"This is one of my companies," he growled. "You have time to help him. Why can't you help me?" He had me there. It was also the first thing he had done that impressed me. It was a cute stunt.

"Okay. Okay," I said, smiling and putting out my hand. "I'll take your case."

MacNair quickly briefed me on his operations. He was the owner of, among other things, one of the largest grain storage operations in the country. MacNair built and leased huge grain distribution centers for the largest food companies in the Midwest.

As is so often the case with dynamic entrepreneurs like MacNair, he constructed his rapidly expanding empire on a razor-edged profit margin. That left him vulnerable to dramatic shakeups in the economy.

For MacNair, the shakeup came in the form of the real or contrived worldwide gasoline shortages that plagued the early seventies, and the subsequent out-of-control rise in interest rates. Hit by this double whammy, his only option was to seek protection under the Chapter 11 bankruptcy code. That would enable him to shield his grain storage firm from creditors long enough to ride out the economic storm and save his multimillion-dollar business.

At least, that's what he thought Chapter 11 would do. The truth, as he put it, was that he exposed his weakened company to an even bigger threat than rocketing inflation and coldhearted bankers. He was at the mercy of a federal bankruptcy judge.

"The judge has appointed some of his cronies to oversee my firm, and they're robbing me blind!" he exclaimed. "The court-appointed trustee has started liquidating my assets!"

"I thought that's what Chapter 11 is supposed to protect against?"

"Exactly! But they're doing it anyway. Right under the judge's nose. And they're stuffing the money into their pockets."

"Have you notified the judge?"

"I've done everything but picket his courtroom! But he ignores me. He has to be in on it."

"That's hard to believe. A federal judge? In the United States?"

"Believe it! Just look into it. Snoop around for a week or so. If you think I'm crazy, then we'll shake hands and part company, no harm done."

I agreed to peruse the records, firmly convinced that MacNair was merely suffering from the stress and paranoia of watching his hard work and once-bustling empire suddenly crumble.

The records, however, revealed some alarming curiosities. The Midwest accounting firm hired by the trustee was partly owned by the judge's brother. The man selected to manage the grain storage facilities was one of the judge's best friends.

That wasn't illegal, but it did raise eyebrows. I dug deeper.

With every plunge of the shovel, more curiosities surfaced. It didn't take long to strike a vein where all pretense of propriety vanished.

The court authorized an expensive roof repair for one of Mac-Nair's warehouses. When I checked the bill, the invoice was sent to an address that was an empty lot.

"You're right, Steve," I apologized to my client. "They're ripping you off. And this is only the beginning."

"See! What did I tell you? I knew it. What can we do?"

"We go by the book. We gather the evidence and build a case. There has to be somebody above the judge who won't tolerate this kind of abuse. Somebody honest."

"Yeah, let's break out the kerosene lamps," he said cynically.

"Don't worry. We'll find someone."

Fueled by anger, I cleared my schedule and began battling the court-ordered cancer before it overwhelmed my client's entire half-billion-dollar operation.

To obtain a clearer picture, I developed a mole inside the construction company that supposedly repaired the roof.

From there, it was off to the races. Both the informant and the court records detailed how the judge was handing out fat fees like so many polished apples. When the dealing was done, His Honor had showered $700,000 of MacNair's supposedly court-protected money on the new managers, including $137,000 to his brother's accounting firm and $80,000 to a lawyer pal.

At least those people were real. Another foray into the paperwork unearthed a series of canceled checks made out to companies that didn't exist. Empty Lot, Inc. was doing great business that year.

That was only the half of it. His Honor had a bigger score waiting on the horizon, one that would make all the looting up until then look like so many nickels and dimes. The judge was preparing to return MacNair's lapsed mortgages, some as high as $50 million, to the financiers who had issued them. In return, the banks and mortgage companies would kick back millions to the helpful attorney friends of the black-robed adjudicator.

Digging deeper, I was told that a few of those lender bailouts had already gone through. And the payoff was so bold that the money was brought into the courtroom in a suitcase!

That was the last straw. I don't know about anyone else, but Samsonites stuffed with cash is where I draw the line when it comes to magistrates. I gathered my evidence and paid a visit to the local U.S. Attorney, fully expecting the United States Justice Department to crush this bench-sitting bad seed. The U.S. Attorney studied the materials, whistled long and loud, then called in the FBI. The G-men promptly initiated a top-secret investigation of the federal bankruptcy court. I took special pride in the fact that the bulk of the investigation was carried out from my office, and the agents relied heavily upon me.

I quickly learned why. In order for the G-men to legally obtain certain records or information, they had to first get court orders from other judges. At worst, these justices could be doing similar things and tip off our target. At best, they might feel compelled to protect a member of their exclusive fraternity.

It was easier to send me out to continue doing things my way —with no approval or interference from anyone.

Weeks passed. I kept gathering the goods while the FBI investigated, and investigated, and investigated. They were investigative machines. Yet nothing changed.

"What's going on?" MacNair kept asking as his hemorrhaging firm crept closer to the abyss. "Why haven't they arrested this clown? What are they waiting for? You have enough evidence to convict ten judges!"

"Be patient," I advised. "It's not easy taking down a federal judge. The FBI needs time to get up to speed, and they have to build an exacting, slam-dunk case for the prosecutors."

I cautioned MacNair to remain cool, but he couldn't take it anymore. He brought one of my reports to a famous muckraking investigative journalist. The journalist passed the materials to a young reporter at a local paper. Not long afterward, a front-page story appeared in the paper under the blaring headline U.S. JUDGE UNDER INVESTIGATION.

The FBI and the prosecutors were furious, but I was quietly pleased. The whole world was now aware of His Dishonor. The paddy wagon was sure to be on the way to the judge's chambers, with a quick stop at the offices of his relatives and pals.

I was naive. Instead of rounding up the scoundrels, everything ground to a screeching halt. The FBI packed up their things and bolted from my office like ticks from a dying rat.

The judge quickly resigned, but was never indicted or prosecuted. He merely put out a shingle and became a top bankruptcy attorney, practicing before the same courts he had shamed. His friends and relatives also skated away scot-free, pockets bursting with my client's cash. Baffled, I relayed a more colorful version of MacNair's lament to the U.S. Attorney.

"What the fuck's going on?"

He looked a bit chagrined, and then came clean. "The other justices flew into a rage because we investigated a sitting judge without first notifying them," the prosecutor shrugged.

"So why didn't you?"

The U.S. Attorney gave me a look that told me he didn't trust them either.

In the end, everybody walked away rich and happy—everybody, that is, but the taxpayers who financed a long, aborted investigation, and my client, the poor schmuck who placed his faith and his multimillion-dollar company in the protective arms of the American judicial system.

And when the protectors became predators, my client wasn't even given the satisfaction of seeing the bad guys get their just desserts. A few months later, another paper reported that a "special committee of federal judges" had looked into the matter and decided that there was "no basis for criticism" of the judge who shafted MacNair. He just showed "poor judgment" in approving his brother's accounting firm to pick apart MacNair's company.

The whole case hammered home something everybody should realize when they step into a courtroom. Judges are lawyers, too.

THE FRITO
BANDITOS

ONE HAZY SUMMER afternoon in the late 1970s, I received an SOS from Cartha DeLoach, a man whose considerable reach extended into both business and politics. At the time of the call, DeLoach was an executive vice-president of PepsiCo, the soft drink giant. Before his jump into the private sector, DeLoach had served as an assistant director of the FBI, as well as J. Edgar Hoover's liaison officer to the White House during the Kennedy and Johnson administrations.

During his government stint, DeLoach had an office inside the White House, making him the first and only FBI liaison so privileged. DeLoach was especially close to Lyndon Johnson, and was on the short list of those being considered as Hoover's replacement when the legendary lawman died.

With Richard Nixon disgraced and the Democrats, in the form of Jimmy Carter, now back in control, DeLoach once again had access to the top echelons of power in Washington, an advantage he no doubt used for his new employer.

I was familiar with PepsiCo's operation, having worked several successful cases for the $4-billion-a-year conglomerate in the past. I solved a bottling scam at their Queens, New York, plant (the employees were skimming thousands of cases a month), which resulted in the largest number of indictments for one case in Queens County history. In another case I had determined that the president of PepsiCo Puerto Rico was embezzling millions of dollars from the company through an intricate scheme. He borrowed money on behalf of PepsiCo, but then pilfered the cash, laundering it by buying expensive art.

(This one's worth a brief digression: I discovered the identity of the artist washing the executive's money and visited him, pretending to be a rich Mexican businessman who wanted to launder money through high-priced art. The minute I said that, the famous Cuban artist smiled, turned to his mother, who was in the next room, and said, «¡Cómo Carlos! ¡Cómo Carlos!» He then explained how he was doing precisely that for his buddy Carlos. That, suffice it to say, was the end for Carlos, PepsiCo's man in Puerto Rico.)

The trouble this time wasn't at PepsiCo per se, but with Frito-Lay, the snack company PepsiCo swallowed in one of those typical corporate takeovers. PepsiCo had heard rumors that the Frito-Lay engineers and plant managers at the various food-processing facilities were taking sizable kickbacks.

I told DeLoach that if it were true, the problem was a relatively common species of corporate theft, the kind that's generally not too difficult to ferret out. I marked it down as a routine assignment, signed on with DeLoach, and headed for Dallas, the place where the fun and games were going on. It proved to be a most interesting and illuminating trip.

In cases of this nature, the weak link is generally the subcontractors. Frito-Lay had tremendous influence in Dallas and thus had enormous economic leverage over the local economy. The chip company's engineers and buyers could tap into this power and browbeat the subcontractors into virtually any scheme they could dream of.

Combing through the records that covered capital improvements, I identified a contracting firm that appeared to have the most—and most obvious—irregularities. This firm was ripe for squeezing.

Along with my associate Karen Kronman, who had a Ph.D. in psychology, I paid the company's president a visit. We intercepted him with a team of grim-faced security officers in the lobby of his office as he arrived early one morning. That strategy was designed to knock him off guard right from the get-go.

The contractor was a tall, balding man with a weak hand-shake. I sensed from the opening introductions that he would crack at the first sign of pressure.

"We work for PepsiCo security," I explained, affecting a prop-erly serious expression. "We're investigating allegations of extor-tion carried out by the Frito-Lay engineers."

"Extortion?" he gulped.

"That's what they call it in the criminal codes. Here's what I think is happening. The Frito-Lay engineers are forcing companies like yours to pay kickbacks."

I was throwing the man a life preserver, but he was so flus-tered he couldn't see it. I had to spell it out when we reached the privacy of his office. "Now, I could be wrong about this. I think it's extortion on our end. But then again, it could be bribery. Maybe our guys are the ones being hustled?"

I let that sink in for a few seconds, then tossed the raft again.

"My instincts tell me it's extortion. So if you help us out, we can put this bribery angle to bed right now."

The man sighed, sat down, and nodded his acquiescence. Within minutes, a runner appeared and handed me a canceled check for $25,000 made out to a Frito-Lay engineer named Claude Smith.

The check all but had the word "kickback" written on the memo line. I got a complete explanation from the contracting firm president as to who, when, where, and how often.

I thanked the contractor, assured him that I would pass a good word about his cooperation to PepsiCo, and left with the damning evidence. At this point, a less experienced investigator might have marched into DeLoach's office and proudly announced that he or she had snared the rat. That would have been a mistake. If the con-tractors were bold enough to pay kickbacks by check, then we were on the way to catching an even bigger rat—or uncovering a building overrun with rodents.

Plus, the contractor revealed that there was more involved here than just kickbacks. Frito-Lay was a sleeping giant that wasn't being policed very well. Its executives were picking it clean, bit by bit, like ants swarming a child's discarded lollipop.

If my suspicions were correct, then Claude Smith was merely one of the greedy ants. The object was to confront him, turn some psychological screws, and see if he would lead us back to the nest.

To achieve that end, I relied heavily upon Karen Kronman,

whose psychological acumen gave her a special talent for velvet-hammer interrogations. The tall, attractive, black-haired shrink helped me analyze the Frito-Lay executive as we made our move.

Smith was a big, Texas-sized man with reddish-blond hair and bulging muscles. Physically, he made for a formidable opponent. Fortunately, I wasn't there to arm-wrestle. For several hours we peppered Smith with questions about his activities. He stayed calm. Karen watched him like a hawk, looking for signs of nervousness or guilt.

"We're investigating corporate fraud here in Dallas for Frito-Lay," I explained. "We know that some engineers are taking kickbacks from local contractors, looting the treasury, the usual things. You wouldn't happen to know anything about this?"

"Shit, no! Folks, look, I'm real busy. If'n you got nothing else to talk about, I'd like to get back to work," he said in a hard Texas drawl. His anger lay just below the surface.

I stared at Smith. Collecting himself, he stared right back. I began to push him. "We have evidence to the contrary, Claude. We know that you've been taking kickbacks for several years from various contractors."

"Bullshit!" His cool was starting to melt.

I chose my next words carefully. There's nothing more dangerous than a man using anger to cover up a lie.

"I'm afraid it's not bullshit."

With a slow and deliberate motion, I pulled the canceled kickback check from a thick folder and handed it to the tough Texan. The starch went out of his backbone the moment he saw it.

"Claude, do I have to show you all the other ones in here?"

It was a bluff. We only had the one check, but he looked down at the bulging folder, and then he stared at me. There was no more bluster, just fear and resignation. He folded his cards.

"There's nothing you can do. The jig's up," I said, softening my tone. "You did something wrong and got caught. But there's a bright side to this. There's a way you might be able to get out of it."

Smith perked up. This was one wheeler-dealer who didn't need to be beaten over the head with a life raft.

"How?"

"If you help us, and your help results in other people getting indicted, I'll tell the FBI and the IRS that you cooperated. If they want your help, you might cut an immunity deal with them."

I made sure to drop all the government initials because I

wanted Smith to know exactly what kind of hell was about to crash down on him if he didn't play ball.

He played.

"All right," he conceded, the fight drained from his powerful body. "What do you want me to do?"

"Obviously, you're not the only person here involved in this. You're just lucky, extremely lucky, to be the first one caught. Right now we need you, and that's your edge. Pretty soon, we won't need anything but a paddy wagon to transport all the crooks out of here.

"My job is to break this kickback ring, then get out the soap and brushes and clean this company up," I explained. "And you're going to help me."

Smith nodded.

As things turned out, I was right. Smith was the right person to squeeze. He was almost the official "Vice-President in Charge of Corruption" at Frito-Lay. He not only knew what he'd done to line his pockets, he pretty much knew what everybody else was doing. And what they were doing was mind-boggling. Virtually every deal the company was involved in—from New York to Los Angeles— was larded with kickbacks and skimoffs. Anything the company purchased, from salt to cooking oil, was rife with side deals.

My associates and I got to work, huddling with Frito-Lay's general counsel and internal auditor. Perusing their records, we began to spot patterns that helped us flush out the players. There were dozens of them, all over the country.

I detailed the crimes and continued my investigation, uncovering layer after layer of theft. The corruption was so pervasive, I sometimes doubted whether such a company could ever be cleaned. Each time I thought we had mopped the floors for the final time, Smith would lead me into another, even dirtier room.

After I got a handle on what was going on in and around Dallas, Smith expanded my horizons. He directed me to a contact in Illinois who was ready to talk about Frito-Lay's special arrangement with some shady commodity traders in Chicago.

In order to bone up on the commodities market, PepsiCo flew me and Karen out to the headquarters of the Archer Daniels Midland company in Decatur, Illinois. For two days we soaked up as much as we could about the mysterious, rough-and-tumble world of commodities.

(Archer Daniels Midland were the right people to teach us the "game." Just last year a senior ADM executive pleaded guilty to price-fixing and embezzlement in return for his testimony against practically the entire upper echelon of the huge agricultural products company. I'm still convinced that nobody from the outside should ever play this market, because it is totally manipulated by a few players. Just ask Hillary Clinton about her huge $100,000 windfall from the Chicago commodities market. I have a hard time believing it was simply luck.)

As with the building contracts in Texas, the scam here was based upon Frito-Lay's power as a consumer. In this case, what was being consumed were potatoes. Tons and tons of them. The subterranean vegetable is the heart of the chip company's product line, so you can imagine the quantity it needed to be fed.

I checked the figures. Frito-Lay bought about 25 percent of all the potatoes grown in North America. That placed them second only to McDonald's, the french fry and hash brown king, in potato purchasing power.

When a buyer has that much influence, it can affect the entire market by altering the free-enterprise price structures. The key here was knowing exactly when the Frito-Lay orders would be sent through. If outside brokers were given advance knowledge of precisely when, and how much, the next Frito-Lay order was going to be, they could use the knowledge to speculate on potato futures.

Say Frito-Lay was having a bumper year and upped their regular order by 10 percent. That leap would send shock waves through the commodity and farming industry and bump up the price of potatoes. With such a massive purchase, even a small jump, a few cents a bushel, could make a commodity trader—and his friends on the inside at Frito-Lay—a bundle.

I reported my findings to DeLoach and his right-hand man, Hobson Adcock. Like DeLoach, Adcock had come from government and the FBI. To my pleasant surprise, instead of dealing with the problem internally (namely, covering it up), the two former law enforcement officials wanted to prosecute. That, I speculated, was partly due to their backgrounds, but mostly to the fact that they were working for PepsiCo and needed to clean up the mess they inherited when they purchased the chip company.

I was directed to a pair of Dallas FBI agents named George Clow and Ed Kresewski. After briefing them, I went to the IRS and laid out the scams to George De Los Santos, an eager young IRS Criminal Investigations Division (CID) investigator.

Running with Claude Smith's info, and backed by the weight of the FBI and the IRS, we were able to trace the cancer inside Frito-Lay back to one of its major sources: a commodity purchasing manager named James Stafford who had been at the company for as long as anyone could remember. Stafford was responsible for buying more than $150 million in raw agricultural products per year, making him a huge player on the commodities market. He had learned very early on how the game could be played for his benefit, and had been engaged in personally profitable behavior for more than twenty years.

Stafford's scheme was as ambitious as it was ingenious. He funneled a healthy chunk of Frito-Lay's annual purchase through a West Texas commodities corporation. Nothing wrong there. Then I checked the corporation's stock holdings: a substantial amount was owned by James Stafford.

When he wasn't enriching his own secret company, he was forcing the other commodity traders to pitchfork over hundreds of thousands of dollars in kickbacks for everything from corn, salt, vegetable oil, and peanut oil to spices.

Combing the records, I discovered that Stafford had routinely used another neat trick when going to market—the ol' split-bill scam. Bill-splitting is a common way to steal tax money. For instance, instead of paying one bill for a million gallons of vegetable oil at 50 cents a gallon, the supplier sends two bills for 500,000 gallons each. The first overstates the value of the oil, say as 75 cents a gallon. The second understates it at 25 cents per gallon. The average comes out to the same price, but the billing makes a world of difference when dealing with complicated IRS corporate tax codes designed to protect firms from extreme fluctuations in the price of raw materials.

Frito-Lay's accountants were able to use this split-billing technique to report that they were forced, for whatever market reasons—a bad crop, a drought, a fire, overseas supply cut off by war, and so forth—to pay too much for half of its oil purchases. That enabled them to write off the expense as overstatements of capital expenditures.

Through these various schemes, Stafford had become a very wealthy man. We estimated he siphoned $10 to $20 million from Frito-Lay and Uncle Sam during his two decades on the job.

When the digging was done, Frito-Lay fired Stafford and sued him for $13 million, which he paid. (The payment, of course, leads me to believe he had a lot more to spare.)

As big a fish as Stafford was, he turned out to be just another link in the Frito-Lay chain, but what he was linked to was far bigger than the routine kickback schemes we unearthed. Ever the trader, he agreed, for "plea considerations," to direct the IRS to a wider scam, this one reaching into the highest levels of the U.S. government itself.

Stafford sat down with government prosecutors and investigators and laid it out. In the middle and late seventies, the U.S. government stockpiled millions of gallons of peanut oil in order to subsidize the farmers. Occasionally, to stabilize prices or correct crop problems, they auctioned the oil to the highest bidder, a process designed to achieve fair market value. Stafford and some other conspirators arranged for the government to forgo the scheduled 1977 auction and sell the entire stock—some eighty million gallons—to a small Georgia company, Camilla Inc. Stafford, of course, had an interest in Camilla Inc.

"We bought it dirt cheap," Stafford explained. "Twenty cents a gallon."

The Frito-Lay executive then turned around and sold the oil to his bosses at the big chip firm for twenty-one cents a gallon. It was the kind of classic deal where everybody came out smiling—almost everybody. The government unloaded their oil. Stafford and Camilla were happy to take it off their hands, and Frito-Lay was happy to get it at twenty-one cents a gallon, still far below market price, which was around sixty to seventy cents per gallon. (Camilla and Stafford pocketed more than $700,000 for about ten minutes' work in that transaction. This didn't include the $300,000 in "walking-around money" to close the deal.) The U.S. taxpayers, who bought the oil at its highest level, were left holding the bag.

It gets better. According to Stafford, Frito-Lay foisted the oil off on overseas firms (which pay far more than market price for a commodity that is relatively rare in certain countries) in an elaborate paperwork scheme that netted Frito-Lay millions of dollars in illegal profits. The sale violated U.S. law, which mandated that the oil could only be sold in the United States, and only 90 days after the purchase.

The overseas monkey business wasn't really necessary. Within weeks of the Camilla purchase, the price of peanut oil shot up. So Frito-Lay stood to double its investment anyway.

Based on Stafford's testimony, the U.S. Attorney for the Dallas Texas District convened a grand jury to start handing out indictments. I continued to work for PepsiCo in conjunction with the FBI and the IRS, in order to bring evidence to the grand jury.

We interviewed all the major peanut commodity brokers, including the Gold Kist corporation, which leased the Georgia peanut operations owned by the Carter family—as in President Jimmy Carter. The President's farming operations were managed in a blind trust by a family trustee named Charles Kirbo—"blind" in order to create a Chinese wall between the President and his investments so he couldn't be accused of any conflicts of interest.

Nothing wrong there, right? Except Gold Kist managed to get a piece of the discounted oil action, purchasing a percentage at 25 percent of the market price.

I didn't know whether Gold Kist and the Carters were involved in this peanut oil scam, but when the Gold Kist executives refused to talk to us, I began to smell a big rat.

Could the peanut oil's apparent whirlwind tour and disquieting final destination be written off as merely a coincidence? A check of Stafford's records dispelled that notion. Before the Frito-Lay executive snatched the much-traveled oil from the government, his phone logs indicated that he'd been in contact with Kirbo, various Department of Agriculture executives, and one other fellow—a simple country-bumpkin gas station owner named Billy Carter.

Yep, that Billy Carter, the President's highly opportunistic, beer-swilling, side-of-the-street-peeing, redneck brother.

The implications were clear. Stafford had used his connections to stop the auction and buy the oil at a cut-rate price. The shell game across the Atlantic and back was performed so everybody could get their piece of the action.

Never one to miss an opportunity, Stafford also falsified the purchase invoices so that Frito-Lay was able to buy the oil from Camilla tax-free. And he revealed that the original $16 million used to purchase the oil was fronted to Frito-Lay by PepsiCo.

I had now reached what I like to call the get-out-of-town-fast point in my investigation. That's when the trail of corruption suddenly leads to a place where the people who hired you don't want it to go. This is the point where I'm usually called in, handed my fee on the spot, thanked profusely, and told, in so many words, to hit the road, Jack.

Remember, I was hired by Cartha DeLoach, a man with heavy connections in politics, specifically Democratic politics. A Democrat, Jimmy Carter, was back in office after years of Republican rule. And now DeLoach was sitting on a peanut oil scandal which, at the very least, could embarrass the President and give fuel to his political enemies in the coming election.

The stakes got higher.

Not surprisingly, after the Frito-Lay–Jimmy Carter connection was made, things started getting weird.

Backtracking, and acutely aware that a big fat dime was about to drop on my head, I flew back to Dallas with DeLoach's blessing to tie up the loose ends of my investigation. I called a top-secret briefing with Frito-Lay's management and unloaded everything I'd discovered on corruption in their company. This in itself was a high-wire act because I guessed that half the people in the room were either aware of the scams and had looked the other way, or were part of it! No company could have that much systematic looting going on for so long without the bigwigs catching on. They all looked extremely attentive when I finished briefing them on the run-of-the-mill corruption and started in on Jimmy Stafford.

I returned to my hotel immediately after the informative meeting. I'd barely taken my jacket off when the phone rang.

"Pena?"

"Yes."

"Stop the fuckin' investigation, now!" an angry male voice drawled. "Stop it and get outta Texas today. If you don't, both you and the lady are dead."

That didn't take long. I called Karen to see if she'd received the same warning.

"No. But how did they know where we were?" she asked

It was a damn good question. I'd only let a few people at Frito-Lay know which hotel I was staying in.

Karen and I checked out of our rooms and hit the streets. I called and met with George Clow of the FBI, who was outraged over an obvious obstruction of justice, but powerless to do anything about it.

Things moved rapidly from there. As the grand jury in Texas prepared to call Herman Talmadge, the Democratic Senator from Georgia, Richard Stone, the Democratic Senator from Florida, Dawson Mathis, a Georgia Representative, and last, but not least, Charles Kirbo, the President's close advisor and trustee of his peanut empire, the shit hit the fan.

The general counsel of Frito-Lay sent along two tough New York attorneys to my office who demanded that I turn over all my investigative files. I sensed that some manner of corporate battle was brewing, and I was caught dead in the middle. My primary responsibility was to PepsiCo and DeLoach, because they originally hired me. However, through some typical corporate channeling, my fee was coming from Frito-Lay.

You can see where this is heading. I refused to turn over my confidential files, and Frito-Lay refused to pay my fee and expenses. What Frito-Lay really wanted was to dump me and Karen into a boiling vat of cheap peanut oil.

I retreated back to New York and waited for the possible grand jury indictments to solve my problem. (I also knew that the IRS Criminal Investigations Division had started an investigation into President Carter's peanut empire, and that the FBI had opened a file on his brother Billy, as well as on some people in the Department of Agriculture.)

Almost immediately after Frito-Lay slammed the door on me, the fires I'd started down in Texas were furiously put out. The grand jury investigation was hamstrung when the U.S. Attorney in charge, Dan Guthrie, resigned to take a position in the private sector. Guthrie publicly stated that his resignation was due to "the pressure which you [U.S. Attorney Kenneth Mighell] and other high Justice Department officials have attempted to exert upon me." A less experienced assistant U.S. Attorney was plugged into his slot. Not long afterward, the grand jury quietly disbanded without issuing a single indictment!

Then came a rash of promotions and reassignments that scattered the investigators. FBI agent George Clow was dispatched to Fort Worth to become the Special Agent in Charge of that office. The IRS's De Los Santos was shifted to management.

Before his miraculous upgrade, De Los Santos received a visit from two White House officials and a senior IRS honcho from the tax agency headquarters in Washington. The suits ordered him to turn over all his investigative files on the peanut oil purchase to the White House. (The White House has no power to investigate anything.)

It was the same with Ed Kresewski and Clow. While the Dallas agents were at the FBI office in Atlanta, they were instructed to turn their records over to a team of special agents from the Washington, D.C. office of the FBI. They were told to forget about the case. "Washington" was taking over.

That was the end of the peanut oil caper. I never heard another peep about it. Frito-Lay, on the other hand, did some housecleaning. Six managers entered guilty pleas to income tax evasion and were given some jail time. Included among the group was Claude Smith, the guy who helped us start it all. I was under the impression he'd been granted immunity, but the deal got bungled.

Adcock, DeLoach's hatchet man at PepsiCo, called me and told me to stop paying Smith. My deal with Smith was that in return for his cooperation, I'd pay his salary until the government verified his allegations, and then I'd bill PepsiCo for what I paid him.

"Why?" I asked.

"He's going to be indicted. The Feds need some bodies to throw to the press."

I couldn't believe it. That was dirty pool, but there was nothing I could do. De Los Santos told me that his attorneys were handling it, and that only they could grant immunity. Smith had been promised immunity, but the deal was never formally finalized by the U.S. Attorney. Bad break for Smith. Even though they never read him his rights, or let him consult an attorney, he pleaded guilty. They needed sacrificial lambs to close their case, and Smith ended up *baaaaaing* all the way to the big house.

I was enraged that the government would use his cooperation to break open the case, then toss him in jail like a used piece of tissue paper. They were supposed to be the good guys.

More illusions shattered. After that, I made doubly sure that all my future informants had their immunity deals in writing before they opened their mouths. And from that moment on, I vowed to tape all my conversations with any representative of the U.S. government.

Along with Smith, the six who took the fall were just small fry. The guys pulling all the strings—including, no doubt, the person who threatened my life on the phone—escaped to extort again.

None of Frito-Lay's subcontractors, the guys who paid out the bribes and kickbacks, were indicted. They escaped to bribe again.

I eventually got paid all but the final $21,000 I was owed, so I wasn't completely burned. Because of that final stiff, however, I never worked for PepsiCo again, even though they later asked me for help on numerous occasions.

It was disquieting to see how corruption can ensnare a famous U.S. company. It was sad to see that even when the fraud was exposed, it went mostly unpunished. I'd left Mexico because I became tired of what had become almost institutionalized corruption in every facet of society.

For the first time, the scales fell from my eyes and I saw that perhaps the land of the free wasn't so free. I'd seen the raw power of the U.S. government abused to cover up a crime and to protect the powerful.

It still bothers me. I would have liked to have determined, for my own peace of mind, if the dirty deal went all the way to the White House. Did they know what was going on, or was it a case of others in the government taking advantage of the situation?

What I do know is that someone reached out to someone very high up in the federal government, someone with the power to free eighty million gallons of taxpayer-owned peanut oil. Someone who knowingly allowed a cadre of profiteers to bounce the oil around the domestic and international markets, taking huge cuts at each stop, and gouging the taxpayers at every turn.

It was a sobering lesson. For the first time since I had emigrated to the United States, I witnessed how the raw power of money could subvert justice. I expected this kind of corruption south of the border. But I always thought—I suppose with the naivete of a recent immigrant—that the American legal system would protect citizens against this kind of abuse. After the White House apparently interfered with an investigation that might have involved the Carter family, after the bigwigs at Frito-Lay sacrificed Smith to save their own skins, I no longer had such illusions.

7

THE WILKINSON SWORD

BACK WHEN THE dinosaurs ruled the Earth, in the days before disposable razors, men had to pop a double-edged razor blade into a crude, heavy, metal shaver with a flip-up, winged top. This, believe it or not, was a revolutionary, Darwinian advance from an even more brutal device: the nasty, lip-amputating, throat-slicing straight razor.

To feed the public's demand for the ammunition that fed the wing-tops, the shaving industry manufactured razor blades by the zillions. One of the leaders in the field was Britain's Wilkinson Sword company. Wilkinson produced its gleaming blades under the catchy, and heavily advertised, Old English–themed moniker.

Wilkinson's brand of blades, according to the ads, was made from the same precision steel used to construct the glistening sabers once used by British knights, French musketeers and their heroic ilk.

To pound the saber connection home, the blades were marketed in packages embossed with the crossed swords that clanged so strikingly in Wilkinson's memorable television ads.

With a multimillion-dollar advertising and PR campaign designed around such positive images, you can imagine Wilkinson's horror when hordes of angry men started blistering the company with complaints. The famous swords were hacking up their faces like a band of marauding peasants armed with rusty coat hangers.

A frantic investigation pinpointed the problem—someone was counterfeiting the blades by the tens of thousands. And although the packaging was crisp, and the same kind of tempered steel was being used, the manufacturing process was different. Apparently one layer of coating was missing, resulting in an inferior product—and a subsequent bloodbath in the sinks of American males.

For a major company like Wilkinson, this was the kind of corporate disaster that has CEOs lurching out of their beds in the middle of the night. Each new sunrise, Wilkinson was losing thousands of angry, screaming customers. The company needed to find the source of the dull counterfeits, and fast.

"There's no way to tell the blades apart," an alarmed Wilkinson executive, Jason Dunston, told me during a briefing in his office at the company's New York headquarters. "And the packaging is nearly perfect."

"Nearly?"

He handed me two packs of blades, one real, the other phony. I studied them with keen interest. Looking back and forth, back and forth, I finally spotted the fatal flaw. One of the crossed swords on the counterfeit package was thicker than its legitimate counterpart. It appeared that it was being overstamped, giving it the echo effect that sometimes happens in printing (and is more commonly found on televisions equipped with rabbit-ear antennas).

"That's it, the second sword," the executive confirmed. "Without that, we'd be in deep shit."

"Thank God for small favors and sloppy counterfeiters," I cracked.

After signing on, I spent the next week combing New York for counterfeit Wilkinson Swords. To my shock, and Wilkinson's utter dismay, the dupes were everywhere. From the smallest mom-and-pop grocery to the largest chain drugstores, the faux Wilkinsons packed the shelves.

This was definitely a well-financed and professionally organized criminal outfit. To reach the buyers at the major chains, people had to be paid off big-time. Wilkinson had a hell of a problem on its hands.

After running background checks on the purchasing people of various New York area drugstore chains, we decided to zero in on a vice-president who looked promising. This fellow, Ricky O'Neal, liked to live the high life: thousand-dollar suits, a red sportscar, revolving babes, and an attitude to match his expenses. Not surprisingly, O'Neal racked up some pretty heavy debt. When I started sniffing around, I found out he was asking for kickbacks from the vendors supplying his employer. That's what I call a suspect.

Pretending to be a cash-laden Mexican importer, I paid O'Neal a visit. "These new Wilkinson Swords are the best," I gushed. "We have nothing like them in Mexico. I want to corner the market there. Introduce me to your supplier, and I'll cut you in."

This was a highly improbable offer. Why a Mexican businessman would go to a drugstore VP, and not directly to Wilkinson, should have immediately raised red flags. Unless, of course, something shady was going on.

Without either of us having to spell it out, the VP must have either figured that I knew his swords were special or that I was one pretty dumb dude. Whatever the thought process, O'Neal jumped at the offer. "You gotta buy them through me, okay? I'll introduce you to my supplier," he crooned.

From then on the pace quickened. I bought $2,000 worth of fake blades "for the Mexican market." I paid for them with a check made out to him.

With that check, I had O'Neal by the balls, but he was strictly small fry. I wanted his distributor. After the initial purchase, I contacted him again and explained that I wanted to go through his supplier.

"Don't worry, you'll get a percentage, but the cash has to come from the supplier, not me, okay?"

Ricky was learning that I wasn't dumb. He thought about it, talked with his big supplier, and then agreed. "You got a deal, on one condition. You gotta make a $5,000 purchase. When we deliver, you can meet the supplier."

"Great. We're in business. Mexico is a big country, my friend," I said. He grinned from ear to ear.

I was rarin' to go when I reported back to Wilkinson. But they weren't! Dunston promptly thanked me and said they'd take it from there.

"How?" I asked.

"Our lawyers want the cops to handle it from this point. You've done a great job. Thank you."

"Cops and lawyers? What the hell do they know about undercover operations? All the cops know how to do is arrest people."

"I'm sorry, but we have to follow the recommendation of our lawyers," Dunston said sheepishly.

"Okay. It's your company. Your funeral."

Two days later, the frantic Wilkinson executive was back on the horn. "Octavio, you've got to help us!"

"What happened?"

"The cops botched it."

I shook my head. There was no sense giving him the I-told-you-so. "How bad was the botch?"

"Bad. We need you to reestablish contact with the distributor."

"How can I do that? The cops were made. He won't go near me now."

"No, it wasn't like that. The police never met with him. They just watched from a distance, then tried to follow him back to the plant . . ." Dunston said over the phone, his voice trailing off into silence.

"Let me guess. They lost him?" There was a sigh on the other end.

"They lost him," the executive said.

"Must not have had New York's finest on the job," I answered. I wondered at that. A guy who doesn't even know he's being followed loses two crack NYPD bloodhounds. I had used several off-duty New York cops over the years for surveillance who were quite good. I guess these guys were from a different precinct.

"Look, I'm sorry. We should have listened to you. But our attorneys, the police . . . you know how it goes."

Yeah, I knew how it went. Everybody has their own agenda.

"I gather you want me back on the case."

"If that's okay with you," Dunston said.

"Okay. But the only way I go back in is with complete control. I'm the boss. The cops, the lawyers, the DA, everybody follows my orders. Got it?"

"It's your show from this point on. I promise," he said. "The only thing is—"

"Only thing?" Here we go again, I thought to myself.

"The DA wants you to wear a wire."

"You've got to be kidding!"

"Come on. We've got to stop this thing. They're killing us. There's only so much you can do. We're going to eventually need the legal muscle to shut them down. Work with the DA. Please."

I paused to think it over. Dunston had a point. I was indeed limited in my scope. Once I found the creeps, I'd need the cops and prosecutors to throw the net over them.

"Okay. I'll wire up. But I want to be shadowed the whole way by cops, good cops. I don't want to end up being patted down in the bowels of some dark warehouse surrounded by a bunch of Neanderthals armed with razor blades!"

"That seems fair."

I dropped the receiver, rolled my eyes, and prepared to do some fast talking, and no small amount of shit-eating, with my ol' pal Ricky "the flash" O'Neal, the drugstore VP.

"I had an emergency back in Mexico," I pleaded when I got him on the phone. "You have my sincerest apology."

"You could have at least called," Ricky said.

"Sorry. But things were hectic. It won't happen again. I promise."

"I don't know. The guy was pissed. Came all the way from Long Island just to get stood up. I don't think he'll go for it."

"Look, I had to go to Mexico to widen my pipeline. I need twice as many. Ten thousand dollars. I've got the cash right now."

That piqued his interest.

"I don't know, the guy's pretty pissed . . ."

"Hey, if you'd given me his number, I could have called him directly. What am I supposed to do? I don't want to compromise you."

"I'll get him on the phone," O'Neal relented.

Meet Numero II was set for the next day at 2:00 P.M. at the Barclay Hotel on Manhattan's Lexington Avenue. As soon as the meeting was scheduled, I called the Wilkinson attorneys, who notified the cops, who moved on up the food chain to tell the DA. The day of the meeting, I sat down with the cops to prepare. Right off the bat, I knew I was in for a long day.

The first problem involved the cops' idea of a wire. My eyes bulged when I saw the tape recorder they planned to strap to my torso. Instead of a modern, fly-sized transmitter, this was a complete recorder the size of two cigarette packs.

"Gentlemen, there's no way that thing will fit underneath my suit," I said, pointing to my tailor-made threads. I was going to have to go to Discount Dan's and buy some ill-fitting aberration off the rack to cover their wire. The recorder practically had vacuum tubes instead of transistors. "Don't you have anything smaller than that?"

They shook their heads. I sighed and took off my jacket to prepare for the cumbersome wrap. In a small inside pocket of my suit, I had stashed a small can of Mace—a last resort in case something went wrong.

"Hey, this guy's packing Mace!" a sergeant screamed. "That's illegal. We should arrest him."

He motioned like he was going to do just that. I could hardly believe it. Here I was getting strapped with their own nineteenth-century equipment to nab some criminals they couldn't catch a few days earlier, and this jerk was actually going to arrest me—an hour before I was supposed to meet with a big-time crook the DA wanted to bag.

It was so absurd I actually started to laugh. Wrong move. The beefy sergeant actually took his cuffs out and was moving for me when the DA arrived.

"What's going on?" the DA asked.

"This wiseass is packing Mace!" the sergeant said. Before he finished his sentence he knew what a jerk he was. The DA just looked at him.

"Just confiscate the stuff and let's get on with this."

"Hey, I need a weapon," I protested. "I'm on the front line here. I don't want to go in there naked!"

"We'll be backing you up," the DA said.

"Who? This asshole?" I said, motioning to the sarge.

"When push comes to shove, he'll do the right thing, right, Sarge?"

The sergeant growled.

"Come on. We're a team. You two kiss and make up and let's get this show on the road."

After the fireworks, I left the office, taped like a mummy, lugging a suitcase stuffed with $10,000. I headed for the rendezvous with the phony razor blade salesman.

When I arrived at the hotel, O'Neal was there with a middle-aged man in a nice suit. That surprised me. I was expecting someone rumpled or seedy. He shook my hand in a relaxed, easy manner, putting me at ease. He said his name was Bill. We quickly got down to brass tacks (which he also probably could have sold me).

"I'm interested in importing your blades to Mexico. How much can you provide?"

"Whatever you can afford. Ten thousand. A hundred thousand. A million. You name it. If it's blades you want, we got 'em," Bill said with a cocky gleam in his eye.

"Good. That's what I wanted to hear."

"We aim to please."

"And you can take care of our friend here?" I said, motioning to Ricky.

"Sure. He set up the deal, he'll get his percentage. Don't worry. I take care of everybody," he said with a broad, magnanimous smile. Ricky smiled back.

"My friend said you're ready to take delivery today? Ten grand, right? Cash, right?" Bill continued.

"That's right," I answered, opening my briefcase and flashing the wads of bills. I couldn't help thinking that this was going down more like a heroin deal than a razor blade sale.

"I see. Okay. Are you prepared to take delivery?"

"I've got a truck waiting downstairs."

"Good. Let's roll "

We hopped into Bill's four-door sedan and headed to parts unknown while I tried to ease the pain of the recorder grinding into my back. As we pulled away from the hotel, I made note of all the plainclothes cop cars jumping on our tail. I memorized each vehicle to make sure my "protective" shadows kept up as we threaded our way through traffic down into the Midtown Tunnel.

Halfway out to Long Island, I looked around and spotted ... zip. The cops were gone! The only person still with us was the guy driving the rental truck. And he was one of my associates!

Great. No cops. No Mace. No weapon. And I'm wrapped up like a mummy carrying the world's largest undercover tape recording device that practically squeaks when the tapes roll.

"Hey, I just remembered something," I said, looking at my watch. "I need to call Mexico. Let them know the supply's coming. Can you pull over up ahead?"

"Sure," the affable sales rep said, turning into a Howard Johnson's motel. "There should be a pay phone inside the restaurant."

I ducked through the door, pushed some change into the slot, and dialed the DA's office. The sergeant answered, the same asshole who tried to arrest me.

"Where the hell are you?" he snarled.

"Where am I? Where the fuck are you guys?"

"Looking for you, cowboy."

"I'm at the Howard Johnson's on the Sunrise Highway. In Valley Stream."

"How'd you get there?"

"We drove. Slowly. Just tell your guys to catch up, dammit! Shit!" I shouted, slamming down the receiver. I had to stall the deal until New York's finest could get out an atlas and try to find me. I took a deep breath to calm myself and strolled back to the car.

I gave Bill a big thumbs-up. "Mexico's very excited. But I have to call back in ten minutes to handle some things at the airport when the blades come in. Is that a problem?"

"Relax, we got time," the sales rep said. Ten thousand dollars in cash stashed into a briefcase apparently worked magic on Bill's nerves. We sat in the car and chatted—Ricky told us all about his new girlfriend. Ten minutes passed. Fifteen. Ricky's love life was getting stale, and still no cops. I sighed, got out, and pretended to make another call. I jabbered in Spanish to the dial tone for ten excruciating minutes until I saw the cops finally start pulling into the lot, kicking up gravel and making themselves as obvious as the cavalry. I then called the sergeant and told him that his crack team had apparently navigated their way out of the paper bag they'd been trapped inside.

I got back into the sedan, and we made it to the Suffolk County warehouse without losing the blue bloodhounds.

While my truck waited outside, I waltzed inside the expansive storeroom and began to inspect the merchandise. Slicing open a box, I lifted out a package, noted the fat, double-stamped crossed sword on the wrapping, peeled away the paper, took out one of the thin slabs of metal, and peered at it like I was some kind of razor blade expert.

"Nice work," I cooed.

It was crazy. I did everything but whip out the test tubes and chemical kit cocaine dealers use to check the purity of their purchases.

"Okay, I'm hooked," I announced. "Let me get my guy ready for the stuff." I walked outside and motioned to the detectives. They were supposed to crash the party and cuff everyone on my signal.

Nothing happened. I signaled again. Nobody moved. I did everything but wave the stiffs over, but they wouldn't budge. It was like their feet were rooted into the ground.

I finally threw up my hands and walked to where the four detectives were standing, big as life.

"They're here. This is it. Show time. Go get them."

The cops looked down.

"What's wrong? We've got 'em red-handed. This is where you guys come in. Do your thing!"

"We can't," one of the detectives finally said. "We're out of our jurisdiction."

"You're out of your jurisdiction? What the hell is this? Didn't you know that all along?"

The cops suddenly all looked behind me. I gripped the handle of the briefcase that still had the DA's ten grand in it. Then I turned around. There stood the crooked sales rep and Ricky O'Neal. They'd followed me outside!

"What's going on?" Ricky asked, glancing at the detectives.

It was a good question. I looked at the paralyzed cops, then back at Bill and Ricky. No one said a word.

"Okay, here's the scoop," I said, turning to the two crooks. "These men are cops. You guys are counterfeiters. I represent Wilkinson Sword. I'm out of it now. You guys work it out among yourselves."

With that, I walked away—thoroughly exasperated.

By some miracle, the DA was able to patch together the Botched Razor Blade Case II. Bill led investigators on a trail that crossed the Atlantic to England and Europe. Hopscotching continents, the police and prosecutors determined that a former high-level Wilkinson executive in England had absconded with the formulas and molds and set up his own bogus operation in Germany.

The disgruntled ex-employee took everything, it seems, but the printing mold for the crossed swords on the package. Big mistake.

Thanks to the echoing sword, Wilkinson was able to sweep the market free of the phony blades and reaffirm their billion-dollar identity as a maker of fine shaving instruments—including, as the future would hold, plastic disposable razors.

MURDERING MARXISTS

EARLY IN MY CAREER, when I was eager to make the switch from providing private security to taking a more active investigative role, a Central American businessman named Roberto Salazar strolled into my office.

The thin, cultured Latino sat in a chair across from my desk with his legs crossed. His casual posture bespoke respect and friendship. Although we both spoke fluent Spanish, he addressed me in heavily accented English, much like my own.

"I have a problem. I hear that you might be the man who can solve it for me," he opened.

I was curious as to how he'd learned of me. He explained that he knew many attorneys in New York and that one, a trusted friend, had recommended me for the "special kind of problem" he had.

"And what problem is that?" I inquired, growing excited by the prospect.

Salazar's friendly smile vanished. I surmised that his troubles were personal rather than professional.

Without being boastful, he gave me a brief bio. He was a wealthy landowner from El Salvador with business interests in

New York, Miami, San Francisco, Brazil, and Mexico. His coffee plantation in Brazil was particularly impressive. It was larger in size than the entire country of El Salvador, his native land.

"As you probably know, we are having serious problems with Communists in my country," he said, squirming a bit. It was obvious that the Communist infestation of his homeland was a personal affront. "A group of terrorists, an organized cell, kidnapped my son and asked for a million-dollar ransom. I was willing to pay, but the army bungled the exchange and shot the courier before my boy was released. The next morning they found his body in the trunk of a car in San Salvador. That was the price my family paid for the army's blunder."

Salazar relayed this tragic story in a calm, dignified manner. His body appeared relaxed, except for his hands. He gripped them together so tightly in his lap that his knuckles were white. He was trying desperately to hide his rage and grief.

"I'm sorry," I said. "Things can be tough in our part of the world."

The shattered aristocrat nodded sadly. We both shared an unpleasant bond in that area. We were both born in countries where the ancient terrors of kidnapping and murder-for-profit remain a common practice for rebel factions, political groups, or simply savage criminals. The rule of law was the rule of the jungle.

"Why did the army handle the exchange?" I wondered.

Salazar sighed. "I am a very influential man. The army handled it. They didn't want the money to fall into the Communists' hands. Their screwup made sure it didn't."

"You have my deepest sympathy for your loss. But, Señor Salazar, if you have problems like this again, call me first."

I had no idea why he was there. To me, the issue seemed closed. His son had been kidnapped. The army botched the exchange and got a man killed. End of story.

"I cannot trust anyone in El Salvador. I want you to find the Communist cell that did this to my family," he said, slamming his palm on my desk. "I want them brought to justice!"

This sudden burst of anger caught me by surprise, momentarily masking the startling nature of his request. I shook it off and focused on the proposed assignment. This wasn't a simple matter of finding a crook inside the purchasing department. This man was asking me to go after a heavily armed insurgent army!

I was eager for excitement, but this was pushing it.

Aside from the obvious danger of the case, I was troubled by a number of factors. Justice, to a man like Salazar, usually means that the culprits, once captured, will be impaled on the nearest spiked fence post. Although I hated what they did, and have long had a distaste for Communists, I couldn't see myself as a hired assassin.

"You want them killed, don't you? Justice Latin American style, right?"

"I don't operate like that," he assured me, his voice once again calm and dispassionate. "I want them to stand trial. It would be very important for democracy in my country."

That, I could handle. Capture the murderers and allow the legal system to take it from there. If the government of El Salvador subsequently found the perpetrators guilty and sentenced them to die, then that was justice defined.

Salazar was correct about the symbolic importance of such a trial. Rebel factions who kidnap and murder civilians should be treated as the common criminals they are, rather than as heroic soldiers or oppressed freedom fighters.

"This isn't a routine investigation," I said, shelving the justice issue for the moment. "It's going to cost a lot of money. And I'll need to check you out first. I don't want you to be offended, but I can't work for people who I feel don't have integrity. I'm not saying you don't, but I just need to make sure for myself. Can you under-stand my position?"

"Of course."

"I'll need my fee, plus expenses, which will be considerable. And if I find the guilty parties, I want a bonus."

"How about one hundred thousand dollars?" Salazar cut in.

I nodded and tried to remain calm. If I succeeded, it would be my largest bonus to date.

"I'll consider it," I said. "Call me in two days."

I immediately discussed the meeting with some associates, people with more experience tracking terrorists than I did. They warned me to be careful.

"Operating in a foreign country—particularly Latin America—is always rife with danger. You never know who's on your side and who isn't, and who you can trust. The police and army can be your friends one day, and your bitter enemies the next. Be careful," an old friend of mine, Paul Conte, warned me. Conte had worked on the Central American counterintelligence desk at the State Depart-ment, so he knew his stuff.

It was chilling advice, but again, no different from the way things are in Mexico. I had grown up in that kind of treacherous environment.

My investigation of Salazar found him to be one of the biggest and wealthiest landowners in all of Central America. Men like that, especially in Latin countries, are often noted for their callousness and cruelty. They live amid incredible riches while the vast majority of their countrymen wallow in abject poverty.

Yet other reports said that Salazar was not without compassion or integrity, and was a man of his word. If he'd made me a promise, he'd be expected to keep it.

I decided to take the case. It wasn't so much the money, or even the belief that Salazar could be trusted. It was the challenge that proved to be irresistible. This was the exact kind of adventure I was looking for, and such opportunities don't come along every day. Personally, I was eager to test my mettle under fire. If I could successfully infiltrate an army of hard-core Central American revolutionaries whose beliefs I despised, I could do anything.

Salazar shot me a smile of relief when I informed him that I was going to take the case. He was shouldering a tremendous psychological burden over what happened to his son. He was being eaten up with guilt, rage, and frustration. He needed to feel that he was actively taking steps to repair the damage done to his family honor. He also needed to vent his anger so he could cling to his own sanity. My signing on eased some of the stress and pressure.

The land baron spent the next two days bringing me up to speed on his family history, his relations with the military, the president of El Salvador, the clergy, and even other powerful Central American families. He told me about his experiences with the rebels, who frequently threatened him. At my request, he detailed his personal and professional security operation. He also provided sophisticated surveillance photographs of men he described as close colleagues of the slain courier. That raised my eyebrows. They were intelligence photos.

Salazar no doubt had CIA contacts. The American intelligence agency regularly reaches out to rich natives in foreign countries for assistance in combating Communist uprisings. After all, Salazar and the American government shared a common interest in quelling the growing leftist revolution in El Salvador.

I glanced at the photos again and studied the captured faces. The guerrillas appeared painfully young, all university students.

They were pawns in someone else's political game. Still, I knew I couldn't be caught off guard by their youthful appearances. At that juncture, even the youngest among them had transformed into sociopaths capable of the most gruesome savagery imaginable.

"Most of these people have disappeared," Salazar said, pointing at the pictures. "The rebels usually train, and hide, in Cuba, Chile, East Germany, or Czechoslovakia. Do you think you can find them?"

"I wouldn't have taken the case if I didn't."

Before I flew down to El Salvador, I arranged to meet with some informants and sources within the student councils at the University of Mexico. Tapping some sources from my previous CIA activities, I picked up vague rumors that the gang in question had escaped to Chile. Another source pointed me toward a woman who worked at the University of El Salvador's student library and who was known to be a guerrilla sympathizer.

Prior to pursuing these leads, my first task in El Salvador was to establish a solid cover. That was critical. Although the rebels were young, their operation was well supported. The guerrilla leaders could tap into Russian or Cuban intelligence and easily get an accurate make on a new recruit or sympathizer.

I had to select something that I truly was, or at least, used to be, so that my story would wash. If it didn't, I'd end up hanging skinned from a banana plant, or hacked to bits in a car trunk like Salazar's boy.

Before coming to America, I'd been the distributor for Esso oil in central Mexico. I knew enough about that business to pass myself off as an automobile oil filter salesman trying to set up a distributorship in San Salvador. Anyone snooping around would indeed find records of me working in that industry.

Just to be safe, I called in some favors and had my name placed on a filter company's payroll in Mexico City. With luck, whoever was charged with checking me out would stop after making the initial connections.

For the first few weeks, I only worked on my cover. During the day, I motored around San Salvador, contacting businesses and actually trying to sell oil filters, while at night I met with potential sources to develop intelligence. I made myself obvious: People would remember the brash Mexican businessman trying to get a foothold in the local market.

One afternoon, returning from a sales pitch, I fell into a situation that gave me the in I needed. Driving through downtown San Salvador, I suddenly found myself smack in the middle of a bloody skirmish that had erupted between students and the army. There was gunfire all around me, and the air smelled of blood. Bodies littered the pavement.

A soldier ran to my car, screaming. I thought he was going to shoot me.

«*¡Soy Mexicano! ¡Soy Mexicano!*» I yelled.

"Please give me a ride," the soldier pleaded. "Get me away from this shit!"

I opened the door. The terrified soldier hopped in and ducked down. I drove away, maneuvering around a half-dozen fresh corpses.

As I left the city, my mind wandered back to the 1968 Olympics in Mexico City. In order to keep the games going and not embarrass Mexico in front of the world, the army was ordered by the then minister of the interior to fire upon thousands of demonstrating students. They were cut down by the score in the Plaza Tlaltelolco in downtown Mexico City.

In those days, the international media were not as open or aggressive as they are today. They reported around fifty or sixty deaths when in fact more than one thousand students actually perished. Those who were killed were quickly burned at a nearby military camp—*Campo Militar Numero Uno*—and buried in anonymous graves. After a few stories that drastically underestimated the number killed, the whole incident was covered up and forgotten.

At the time my brother Gabriel was a law school student at the university. When the riots began, my father, knowing full well what the government could do to the naive students, locked my brother inside a closet, so he couldn't get out of the house. After the riots, my brother thanked him for saving his life.

This was the harsh reality of the streets of El Salvador in the mid-1970s, a continual carnage going mostly unnoticed in the rest of the world. And unlike Mexico, the students and rebels in El Salvador didn't even have the hope of reaching any sort of international press corps.

The next day, I drove to the university library in San Salvador and quickly spotted the young sympathizer from the photographs. She was a short, plain librarian named Claudia, with dark skin and little concern for personal style. Her hair was bobbed, she wore no makeup, and her clothing was simple and unfashionable. She completed the dowdy picture with a pair of unflattering eyeglasses. After observing her from a distance for a while, I made my move.

"I can't believe what the government is doing to the students here," I said offhandedly after a brief introduction. "I got caught in the crossfire yesterday downtown. It was scary. Bodies of young people lying around. Blood everywhere. This is terrible!"

"It *is* terrible!" Claudia spat, taking the bait. "Too many brothers in the struggle have been shot by the agents of the capitalists!"

That response was more than I expected. The woman's language and terminology clearly identified her as a Communist sympathizer, if not a full-fledged rebel herself! She proceeded to go on about the cause, ripping the rich, aristocratic government at every turn. I marveled at how she managed to survive in her position. Or survive at all, period.

Claudia wasn't too much of a firebrand to miss my Mexican accent, however. In fact, she immediately discerned that I was from the capital, as Mexicans from Mexico City have a clearly identifiable manner of speech. This endeared me to her even more.

Here I was, a fire-breathing leftist from the land of Pancho Villa and Emiliano Zapata. Mexico's revolution in the early part of the century was still a beacon to most Central Americans. She extended me a welcome that matched the respect that Mexicans often receive because of the country's history.

"My country is the same," I said. "A few rich families control everything, and they act like bandits. The poor don't have a chance. Our only hope is a revolution!"

Afraid that we would attract attention with such inflammatory talk, I invited her to share her views with me over coffee later that afternoon.

"What are you doing in El Salvador?" Claudia asked.

"I'm selling oil filters here. It's not very glamorous, just a job. I had to drop out of college because of my politics."

"And you really are from Mexico City? What part?" she pressed. My antennae rose. She appeared fixated on pinning down where I'd come from. I had to be careful.

"I know you complain, but things here are much worse. If only El Salvador could be more like Mexico," she sighed.

"We may not have a dictator, but it isn't much better," I countered. As I spoke, I noticed that the words came easily to me. I was speaking with a passion that went beyond acting. It truly was how I felt about the country of my birth. The corruption and caste system in Mexico are terrible, and should be changed. But left-wing rebels who kidnap and murder are no different from the right-wing death squads who do the same to keep the ruling class in power.

I wasn't in El Salvador to lead a democratic movement. I was there to find some murderers and bring them to justice. To that end, I began visiting and having coffee with my new library friend a few times a week, solidifying our friendship. Although Claudia was candid and outspoken in her views, she was very guarded about identifying herself or anyone in the rebel army, or saying anything that could hinder or compromise the movement. She proved to be experienced and crafty. I was patient.

During our conversations, we discussed the Salvadorian elites, including Salazar. She even mentioned the kidnappings.

"Salazar's family deserves whatever they get," Claudia hissed, hatred boiling out of her. "They should all be dead."

Throughout our lively diatribes against the filthy imperialists, I kept mentioning that I traveled all over Latin America on business, hoping that she might take the bait. I wanted her to use me as a conduit to her friends who might be hiding out, specifically the ones responsible for killing Salazar's son. They were certain to be in need of something, perhaps money, supplies, moral support, or simply a message from her.

For weeks, Claudia ignored my hints. Then finally, one cloudy afternoon, she let down her guard. "I have some friends in Mexico," she said. I tensed with excitement. Up until then, all my leads had gone nowhere. I hadn't been able to pick up the kidnappers' faintest scent.

"No kidding," I answered nonchalantly, shielding my true feelings. That afternoon the librarian said no more about her friends. I wanted to draw her out, but sensed that it wasn't the right time. She would have to come to me. The next time we met, she did.

"Octavio, could you do me a small favor?"

"Sure."

"Could you deliver a letter for me the next time you go to Mexico?"

"Absolutely. I'd be glad to. Is it something for the friends you mentioned?"

"No, no," she dodged. "I just want you to bring a letter to a bookstore in Mexico City. A place called Librería Casa Maria—you know it, I'm sure. Give it to the owner and tell him it's for Enrique. It's nothing special. I just want to avoid the censor."

"Where is it, again?" I asked. It had been a while since I'd perused the Mexico City bookstores.

"Right behind the Cathedral. Do you know that area?"

"Of course. You can't miss that."

"Can you do this for me?"

"No problem. Consider it done. For Enrique, right? Do you have it now?"

She reached into her purse, retrieved the letter, and handed it to me. I slipped it into my jacket pocket without so much as a glance.

I took the letter with me to Mexico City that Friday. Just to be safe, I didn't attempt to open it until I had touched down in my native country.

The suspense was killing me. Could this be a secret message sent to the exact men I was hunting? What were the odds of that? It might be a letter to an old boyfriend, or a missive to a relative. Claudia could even be inquiring about banned books she wanted to purchase for her library, but the fact that she didn't want it traveling by mail told me otherwise. There was only one way to find out.

My hands shook with nervous anticipation as I held the envelope over a pot of boiling water. Easing open the sticky flap, I slipped out the damp paper and unfolded it. I blinked my eyes a few times as I tried to read it. It didn't make any sense. The words were all jumbled and disconnected. It was in code!

"This is it!" I said to myself. "I'm in."

The intricately coded, three-page letter had to come from one of the major revolutionary groups in El Salvador, one that was well-financed and intellectually founded. The only faction that could construct a message of that nature was the same one responsible for the murder of Salazar's boy.

And now this top-secret rebel underground was using me as a courier to their contacts in Mexico City—or, better yet, to their brethren on the lam. Every fiber of my being told me that the murderers had to be in Mexico. There was no time to break the code as I immediately assembled a skilled team of Mexicans to help me with surveillance around the bookstore.

The core of my group consisted of three friends I'd made over the years. First there was Jesus, whom I met when we were both at law school in Mexico City. Jesus's father had been the chief of staff to the Minister of the Interior for Mexico—the most powerful intelligence-gathering entity in the entire country, and usually a stepping-stone to the presidency. Jesus was a budding lawyer who had access to the kind of intelligence information an operation like this might need. (He eventually developed a large and successful law practice.)

Next, I contacted a buddy of Jesus's named Manuel, who also worked for the Ministry of the Interior. After his stint with the powerful Mexican internal police, Manuel provided intelligence and other services to the CIA. (He later parlayed his CIA-based "engineering expertise" into a successful chain of businesses across Mexico.) Then I called in Antonio, who was a bit younger than the first two. Antonio had been born in the United States, serving on the Los Angeles Police Force before moving to Mexico. He built a lucrative real estate empire that stretched from Mexico City to Acapulco.

The trio constituted what became my "Mexican Team," which I used on many of my cases, including the infiltration of the Colombo family in New York. Occasionally we'd add another friend or two if their particular expertise was needed (including a former personal bodyguard for the president of Mexico). In this case, I brought in a young charmer named Jose who worked for Antonio. Jose had a flair for undercover work—something that can't be taught. His good looks also might come in handy.

I assembled my team, briefed them, then called Salazar.

"I think I'm inside their cell!" I announced proudly, jumping to a conclusion that I felt certain of.

"You're kidding!" He was incredulous.

"A librarian gave me a letter to deliver. It's in code. Now we just have to wait and see who picks it up. I have all the photos of the men you suspect killed your son, so let's hope I spot a match."

My colleagues and I watched to see if any of the bookstore's patrons matched the surveillance photos Salazar had provided me. People poured in and out, but none of the faces matched the snapshots. This wasn't easy. I had no way of knowing which one of the shoppers came for the letter, and the rebels could have sent anyone.

I debated whether or not I should attempt to infiltrate the bookstore. It could prove useful, but would be expensive and time-consuming. I decided not to try. I'd just have to sell some more oil filters in San Salvador and hope my new friends needed more mail drops to the mysterious "Enrique."

One of my team members kept the store under watch, and I jetted back to San Salvador. Despite my initial failure, the system must have worked well from the Communists' perspective because I was asked two more times to deliver messages.

The second trip was no different from the first. Except by this time Jose had befriended a lady working at Casa Maria, the bookstore. When a man came for the second letter, she casually introduced him to Jose, calling him Enrique. Jose nodded hello, and stayed behind as Enrique left. Then, through a prearranged signal, he let us know we had our man.

When Enrique came out, I tensed with excitement. I might be face to face with one of the murderers. One glance at the guy deflated my hopes. He may have been a revolutionary, but his image didn't match any of Salazar's intelligence photos. We tailed him back to his house.

Despite the setback, I was optimistic. After finding out where he lived, we had Enrique's apartment under tight surveillance. Some associates then befriended his sister, and we figured out his entire routine. I felt it was only a matter of time before Enrique led us to the real target. The rebels obviously were cautious about the drop and had taken pains to transport the letters to the intended parties without being spotted.

On my third letter drop for my Salvadorian librarian, we hit pay dirt. I was handling a shift across the street from the bookstore, observing the various comings and goings. A tall man with shoulder-length brown hair appeared out of nowhere and ducked inside. He didn't look like any literary buff. Less than a minute later, he darted out and walked briskly down the street.

The man's distinctive features clearly identified him as one of the rebel "soldiers" in the photographs. My instincts had been correct all along. The murderers were in Mexico!

I got on the radio, and my team swung into action. Keeping our distance and rotating positions, we followed the soldier to a bus stop, then rode with him until he got off in a section of Mexico City known as Colonia de los Doctores, near the main bull ring. From there, we continued the alternating tails until he led us right to his apartment.

Strangely enough, he didn't exercise the least bit of caution. He didn't change his route suddenly, or use any of the other standard maneuvers most trained terrorists—particularly ones wanted by Interpol, as he was—do to avoid being followed. And he had just picked up coded messages from a revolutionary sister! I filed his nonchalant behavior away for further reflection.

We watched his place, quickly determining that the tiny unit housed five occupants: the rebel, his girlfriend, their baby, and another couple also from El Salvador. The second male had blondish hair and Anglo features, meaning he was probably of post-World War II German descent, possibly the offspring, legitimate or otherwise, of an escaping Nazi. Whatever his heritage, he was no doubt a fellow revolutionary.

Before I phoned Salazar, I wanted to make absolutely certain the two couples were the ones responsible for his son's death. Salazar might jump the gun and drag the wrong people kicking and screaming back to El Salvador.

In addition, if there were other people involved, I wanted to find out. For all I knew, there was another apartment nearby with a second group of rebels watching their friends' backs.

Caution was definitely the right policy, at least for the time being. I needed to get closer, but realized it wouldn't be easy to infiltrate their tight circle. These were not verbose librarians bubbling over with revolutionary piss and vinegar. They had escaped a massive police manhunt and managed to exit the country without being caught, actions proving their cunning and skill. And if they truly were the ones who had mutilated Salazar's boy in a bloody act of vengeance and defiance, then they were dangerously ruthless. They were no doubt desperate. They'd probably stop at nothing to keep from being captured and returned to El Salvador.

I had to penetrate their clique, but it couldn't be accomplished directly. The invitation had to come through a third party. Claudia, the librarian, was not an option. She'd made it clear that she only wanted me to deliver letters. If she had wanted me to meet her friends, she'd have already suggested it. If I suggested it, it would arouse her suspicions, and the group might be spooked enough to flee to a new location. At least now I knew where they were, and I wanted them to stay put.

To move forward, I had to step back. I devised a new strategy. The only way to breach the defenses of such a well-trained terrorist cell was to have a totally innocent person approach them. It would have been very hard to train someone quickly to infiltrate the revolutionaries. Sometimes, if it's safe, it is better to have a completely clean go-between.

To initiate the infiltration phase of the operation, I told Jose to fly to Mexico City with a beautiful young Salvadorian woman named Margarita. Jose didn't tell her anything about the operation, just that they were going to have some fun in Mexico City, where he was a "food salesman." I knew that the terrorists wouldn't try anything on Mexican soil, so Margarita would be safe.

We rented an apartment for them a few blocks away from the revolutionaries. Then, early one evening, as the couple went for a stroll, Jose met up with his "brother": me.

The three of us had coffee, chatted about life, and then sauntered over to the Plaza de Toros Mexico, the site of the next phase of the operation. Jose pointed to a man sitting by the bull ring with a book in his hand.

"Let's ask him directions to a good restaurant," Jose said. The man was another "brother." This time he was a real one—Gabriel, my younger sibling.

Jose asked my brother where to eat, and from there, the chitchat took off. Gabriel effusively told Jose what sights he should show Margarita, what clubs to go to. He was a regular Michelin Guide.

"Where are you from?" my brother asked after a while.

"San Salvador," Margarita said.

"Oh, some of my neighbors are from El Salvador. You should meet them. They live down the street . . ." Gabriel said, pouring out his rehearsed lines like a pro.

"Hey, Margarita, you should meet these people. You've been lonely, I bet you could make friends," Jose chimed in. After some more small talk, Gabriel excused himself and wished Jose and Margarita a happy stay in Mexico City. He winked at me, then disappeared.

The seed had been planted. It would be up to Margarita now, and she didn't even know about it. The ruse was important because if she did meet with the terrorists and they pressed her about how she came to them, it would be from a totally innocent chance encounter on the street. At least, that's what Margarita would think.

Lonely for voices from home, Margarita did exactly what I predicted. After a few days, she sought out her countrymen, and with honest intentions, she befriended them. The terrorists were hungry for news from home, and so they quickly invited her over for dinner.

Naturally, she brought along her Mexican boyfriend. The pair dropped by the following evening. The socializing went without a hitch. The Salvadorian rebels said they were studying in Mexico and acted the part of young students. Margarita was happy to hear familiar accents and talk about shared experiences. The night went so well, the terrorists invited them back. And this time, Jose asked if he could bring along his older brother.

"He's pretty savvy about politics here in Mexico."

"Sure, bring him along," said the ringleader with the long hair, whose name was Pablo.

The three of us trooped off to the apartment the following week. Over a few beers and chips, we discussed Mexican and Salvadorian politics until the wee hours of the morning. Pablo and his petite girlfriend, Maria, said they were against oligarchies, but that was about it. No fire-breathing rhetoric, just the usual leftist slant. I told them stories from my past—like the fact that the rich bribed the teachers at my first school in order for their children to get higher grades.

They nodded politely. Obviously the four weren't going to break down and start handing out leaflets or stuffing pipe bombs right there in front of me. Keeping the evening upbeat and friendly, I made a special effort to shower attention upon Pablo and Maria's baby. This, I knew, would further endear me to the two women. Even the Germanic guy, Martin, smiled when I tickled the baby's feet.

"I don't see a crib anywhere," I said, formulating a future plan. "Where does he sleep?"

"Our apartment is so small," Maria responded apologetically. "He just sleeps here in the living room."

I filed that away.

"Next week, you all have to come again for dinner," Pablo said, extending the invitation as we were leaving.

"Yes, we'll make a special Salvadorian treat," added Maria.

"I'd like that," I beamed, promising to attend.

Jose, Margarita, and I showed up as scheduled and had another relaxing, noncontroversial evening, full of pleasant conversation and more jabs at the establishment. The critical aspect of the night came when I ceremoniously presented the baby with a large brown teddy bear.

"I bought this for him in Guadalajara," I said.

"Thank you so much," Maria beamed. "That was so kind of you."

It was kind of her to accept. My associate Jesus had sewn a sophisticated listening device that operated on batteries into the stuffed animal's stomach. I gambled that the couples, figuring they were in the clear, didn't bother to sweep the apartment with expensive detection equipment.

Later that night, I left my hotel and made my way to a Volkswagen van packed with monitoring equipment parked down the street.

Free of our presence, Pablo and Martin immediately changed their tune. The revolutionary rhetoric came out in torrents. They discussed secret projects going on in El Salvador, frequently mentioning Claudia, my librarian friend.

I listened to them for the next few days. The men, not surprisingly, were consumed with the revolution and spoke of little else. Thanks to the teddy bear's big ears—and its prime location in the living room—I was able to figure out the nicknames of the members of their revolutionary cell back in El Salvador. In Latin America, that is a key way to identify rebels: Jose "El Lobo [the wolf]," Marcos "El Mirador [the lookout]," Pablo "El Gato [the cat]," and so forth. It was a revolutionary menagerie. My librarian's moniker was Claudia "Cuatocha," which was slang for "friendly."

I even overheard detailed plans about their next terrorist attacks—bombings, kidnappings, murders, fires—which the foursome were itching to carry out upon their triumphant return to their homeland.

By the time the bear's batteries wore out four days later, I'd heard everything I needed to convince me, beyond a shadow of a doubt, that these were the men responsible for the brutal murder of Salazar's son. And the women were more than window dressing.

The diminutive Maria proved as fervent in her rhetoric and violent intentions as her zealous lover. It was strange to see such ordinary people—loving parents, even—switch to vicious revolutionaries. Who would have suspected that Pablo and his smiling wife were planning to murder up to a dozen people—all while changing their youngster's diapers?

There was only one problem with the intelligence my team gathered. The four were apparently receiving money and support from the supposedly anticommunist Mexican government! They were even given a car to use.

Either Mexico was actively harboring known terrorists, which I doubted, or they were doing the CIA a favor by herding all the bad guys into one cage, where it would be easy to monitor them. Providing sanctuary and support to foreign leftists is just the kind of thing the CIA was good at. I now saw why Salazar had hired me instead of using his CIA contacts. The spooks probably weren't cooperative.

As I lay in bed that evening after flying back to New York, a strange sensation swept over me. With a single telephone call, I could determine whether my new "friends" remained free or were returned to El Salvador, where they would probably be tried and executed.

MURDERING CAPITALISTS

A SINGLE TELEPHONE CALL did determine the fate of the four Salvadoran terrorists. But instead of making it, I was on the receiving end.

"You going to be around tomorrow?" It was the CIA contact I had spoken with about Salazar when I took the case.

"What's up?"

"Expect a package." The phone in my office went dead.

The next morning a messenger dropped off the mysterious package at my office in the Pan Am Building in New York. It contained a year-old article from one of the leading newspapers in Central America. I wondered if this had anything to do with my infiltration of the rebels. What was the CIA trying to tell me?

The lead article blared out the headline, "PLAN TO ASSASSINATE THE LEADERS OF THE PLN" over a grainy picture of a man labeled "RENÉ DUBOIS." The article went on to describe Mr. Salby's incredible story.

A middle-aged mercenary who had fought in French Algeria and worked for the OAS in France (the splinter army group that wanted to assassinate Charles de Gaulle), Dubois had been caught by the Costa Rican security forces. It seemed he was right in the middle of an operation to assassinate the entire leadership of the leftist political parties in Costa Rica. He also targeted many prominent Salvadorian exiles who had fled to the small jungle nation to avoid persecution inside El Salvador.

According to the paper, Dubois had been hired to carry out the killings on behalf of the Salvadorian and Guatemalan governing elites in order to create chaos inside Costa Rica. The Salvadorian and Guatemalan right-wing politicos could then put their own man in power in the budding Central American democracy to reduce the influence of the left in San Jose, as well as lower the chance that such political leanings could spread to the rest of Latin America. In other words, the rich families of Central America wanted to snuff out—literally—any growing signs of Marxism wherever it reared its ugly head.

Reading further, I came to the crux of the enigmatic CIA phone call and article. According to the paper, after the security forces nailed Dubois, he confessed and implicated several members of the Salvadorian security forces in the assassination plot. Nothing too upsetting there, until I read the paragraph on the alleged money man behind the *Day of the Jackal*-like operation: Roberto Salazar.

I put the paper down. My client was engaged in political assassinations inside other countries!

I had a serious dilemma. I'd found the murderers who had killed Salazar's son. But if Salazar was ruthless enough to hire assassins to kill his political enemies inside a foreign country, I doubted his idea of justice for the terrorists involved a trial.

I stared at the phone, anguishing over the consequences of my next call. On the one hand, I had a professional obligation to give Salazar the information he was paying me to uncover. On the other hand, I was pretty sure what the Central American magnate would do with it.

There was another consideration. My CIA contact hadn't sent me the article on Dubois and Salazar out of the goodness of his heart. Given the fact that the Mexican government seemed to have some sort of relationship with the rebels, I began to suspect that the CIA had turned them. Perhaps my contact was trying to tell me that the Company didn't want Salazar screwing up a top-secret operation out of his quest for vengeance.

I called Salazar in San Salvador, still not sure of what I was going to do.

"We need to discuss this matter here in New York as soon as possible," I opened.

"Have you found them?" he asked, the excitement clearly evident in his voice.

"Meet me in New York."

"Can't you tell me now?"

"No. We need to speak up here."

"Why don't you come back here, to San Salvador," he pressed.

"It's important to me for security reasons that we have this conversation in New York."

"Okay. Okay—I'll come."

We arranged a meeting at my office for two days later. That gave me time to talk to some contacts inside the Mexican government. I needed to find out the status of the terrorists and why they were being subsidized by Mexico. If they had been turned by the CIA or the Mexican DGS—Dirección General de Seguridad, the Mexican secret police—then the whole thing could blow up into a political mess.

Either way, I had to consider my options carefully. I hadn't any guilt or remorse about infiltrating the guerrillas. At first, meeting them up close and socializing with them acted to humanize the men, but after listening to the bug that broadcasted their private conversations, I was reminded anew that they were hard-core Communist revolutionaries who preached violence as a means to their ends. I suspected they would kill again, unless one of them had been turned by DGS or CIA and was informing on the others. If this wasn't the case, then they had to be stopped. The question was, how?

Salazar appeared in my office exactly on time, smiling brightly, confident that I had good news. I did and I didn't. My sources in Mexico didn't know if the rebels had been turned, but the Mexican government was definitely protecting them. I didn't want to butt heads with the DGS, or the CIA, if they were involved.

"As you've guessed, I've successfully completed this assignment," I began.

"I knew it!" he said, clapping his hands with glee.

"I have identified all six members of the cell that murdered your boy. I know where they are. At least three are still in El Salvador. The others, as you know, are in Mexico City."

"That's incredible! Octavio, you're the best. I didn't think anybody could do it. You are something!" he praised.

"I appreciate your compliments, but I was just doing my job."

"A lot of people tried to do the job you did, believe me, more people than you know. They failed. You didn't. I'll never forget that."

"Thank you," I said.

"Now I have one more job for you."

"Oh?"

Salazar's face grew angry and vengeful.

"I want you to kill them!"

I didn't think he'd be so blunt so soon. I hadn't even presented him with the details yet. If he was planning to betray our agreement, he should have gotten all the information first, then made his request. If I refused, then at that point all he had to do was hire someone else to do the dirty work.

Instead, he let his passion run wild and jumped the gun. But the brutal request unnerved me. Here was one of the most powerful men in Latin America, a magnate with deep ties inside the U.S. government and probably inside the U.S. intelligence community, asking me to commit murder for him!

"No way!" I said calmly. "I can't do that and you know it."

"How much?" he asked, an odd glint in his eye. "Name your price."

That explained why he felt no need to restrain his true intent. He was banking that he could buy me, just like he bought René Dubois. The innate arrogance of his wealth and privileged social standing finally poked through his dignified demeanor. For a brief moment, I sensed the hatred the rebels felt.

"Fuck you!" I lashed out, dropping all pretense of decorum. "I'm not a killer."

"How about a million dollars?"

The huge bounty didn't make me blink. It wasn't the first time a client had offered me a fortune to do his dirty work. I was once asked by the CEO of a Fortune 500 company under siege in a vicious takeover battle to break into his adversary's New York law firm—who used my security guards. When I turned down his million-dollar offer, he foamed at the mouth: "Who the fuck are you! I've bribed senators, judges!" It was too good a line to pass up: "Who am I? I'm the guy you couldn't bribe." No, I was going to have no trouble answering Salazar.

I leaned forward and spoke softly so that the Latin-American magnate would listen to every word.

"No. Not for ten million or a hundred million! I'm not a murderer, Salazar." I then got up out of my chair and stood over him to get my point across. "You're breaking the law. This is the United States, and I won't be an accessory to murder. This conversation ends right now."

Salazar sat back in his chair. He took a deep breath and collected himself. His tone changed from demanding to pleading.

"I want them brought to justice."

"So do I! Let's do that. Bring them to trial like you promised. You said it would be good for the whole country, remember? Have them extradited and brought to court. Let the law take care of it. You'll eventually get what you want, the proper way."

"There are too many risks. Their friends could kidnap someone and demand that they go free. We'll be putting other people in danger."

There was no reasoning with him. He was going to have his revenge, and nothing, not even his own word as a man, was going to get in his way.

I knew what I had to do. "I can't do that. I'm sorry. I can't be part of something like this."

"You can't do this to me!"

"I can and I will. They're in Mexico. You take it from there."

"That's not good enough," he said, his voice rising. "That's not what I paid you for."

"You didn't pay me to be an assassin, or act as an agent for an assassin. We made that clear before I took the assignment."

Salazar ignored my arguments and kept pressing me for a specific location. I refused to budge. Finally, exasperated, he gave up and stormed from my office. There went a cool million I could have earned—and the hundred grand bonus!

Needing someone to talk to, I phoned Roger Burman, a retired successful Fortune 100 executive who had become a trusted associate and mentor. "You did the right thing, Octavio," he said without hesitation. "You can't let clients bully you. You may have lost some money, but you can't sell out your integrity. Once you do that the first time, it'll never be the same.

"Besides, my guess is that Salazar will come to his senses and everything will work out," he finished.

That evening, I thought about the advice my father had pounded into me during my childhood. "Personal honor is its own reward," he preached countless times. "Never lose sight of that. Let it guide you throughout your life."

"You were right, *Jefe*," I whispered, then said a prayer and made my peace with God. A few days later, I received a call from Salazar. He was back in San Salvador.

"I want to apologize to you," he said, sounding sincere. "You were right. I'm sorry I lost my head. There's just been so much pain. So much anger. And don't worry, I'll pay you what I promised. You earned it and deserve it. You kept your word. I was the one who didn't. I respect that. You were able to do something even the great American intelligence agents couldn't accomplish. I appreciate it, and again, I apologize for my behavior."

I waited for Salazar to drop the other shoe, but no subsequent requests followed. He apparently wasn't using his humble-pie stance to suck me into giving him the withheld information. Because of that, I accepted his apology.

For whatever reason, Salazar stopped searching for his son's murderers. The rebels remained in Mexico, supported by the Mexican government. Despite their grandiose plans to wreak more havoc for the revolution, I don't think they ever returned to their country. Maybe they were hedged in by the CIA after all.

"See, I told you everything would turn out," Burman said. "But let this be a warning to you about getting involved in Latin-American politics. Try to avoid that if you can." It was a solid piece of advice, one that I unfortunately didn't heed.

Three months later, another wealthy Salvadorian landowner, a man named Ramon Garcia, phoned me. Normally I would have blown him off. I wanted nothing to do with powerful Salvadorian oligarchs anymore and was about to say "Thanks, but no thanks," when he floored me with his problem.

"Guerrillas attempted to kidnap my mother and during the kidnapping they killed her!" he said, his voice choking with emotion. "They've made more threats, and I'm afraid they'll carry them out."

"Calm down," I said. "Just tell me what happened." I reached for a yellow pad and started jotting down notes. Garcia, it turned out, owned coffee plantations too, although his weren't quite as large as Salazar's. But unlike Salazar, Garcia had industrial interests all over the world. He was close to being a billionaire, which obviously can have its pitfalls in Latin America, as I quickly ascertained as he continued to outline his problems.

"Another group, different than the ones who hurt Roberto [Salazar], they grabbed my mother right outside our compound. She was old and scared. Her heart gave out before they could demand a ransom. Now they're asking for a million dollars in American money," Garcia said quickly.

"Wait a minute. They want the money anyway? Even after they caused her to die?" I interrupted.

"They're demanding it as protection money so they won't kidnap and kill my father!"

"They have your father?"

"No. Not yet. But that doesn't matter! I'm going to pay. I want you to deliver the money and identify the kidnappers."

I shook my head, trying to sort out the confusion. The kidnappers, after botching the original grab, were demanding the money anyway based upon the threat of a future kidnapping? And the target was willing to pay?

If Garcia gave in to these demands, he'd never have a moment's peace. The rebels would bleed him dry.

"Don't pay them. Not a dime! Whatever you do, don't give in. I'll come right down and we'll deal with this together."

"I don't know . . ." Garcia said.

"Listen to me. Don't give the bastards a cent. You hear me?" I hoped the sharp tone of my voice would jar some fight back into him.

"Where's your father now?"

"We have a house in Key Biscayne. I sent him there. But he can't stay forever . . ."

"Just keep him under wraps for a few weeks. I'm going to assemble a crisis team and come down to San Salvador tomorrow, the day after at the latest. Don't worry, Señor Garcia, we'll take care of it."

"I appreciate that, more than you know. I didn't have any options. The police and army can't protect us anymore."

Before I left, I phoned Roger Burman again. He wasn't too happy about the instant replay in El Salvador, but tried not to be judgmental.

"Be careful. The place is a powder keg. It could blow at any time. And don't trust anybody down there."

That was true, but I couldn't let myself become distracted by the political turmoil in the Central American country. I would treat this as a criminal case, with the intention of drawing out and capturing the perpetrators. If the whole place blew while I was down there, well, that was the risk I was going to have to take.

Which didn't mean I planned on taking unnecessary chances. I made sure I was surrounded by competent assistants, both pros from America and locals, including some bodyguards, my own electronics whiz—a guy named Leon—as well as Craig Anderson, a crack lawyer who was just about the only attorney I trusted.

A brief digression about this interesting young man: Craig headed his own small but bustling firm, a pleasant departure from the staid, giant law factories with their automaton employees that I was used to working with. A handsome, charismatic go-getter with dark hair, friendly eyes, and wire-rimmed glasses, Craig was sharp as a tack, diligent, and knew the law from A to Z. More important, he was totally free of that oily, money-grubbing aura that clings to most attorneys, even the most expensive three-piece pinstripe-suited ones.

Craig wasn't along to serve subpoenas to the bad guys, however. He was a good chess player and knew a thing or two about strategy. His ability to outthink the enemy had helped me on more than a few cases.

"Blackmail cases are just like kidnappings," I briefed my associates on the plane. "Both boil down to long, drawn-out negotiations. You negotiate the bastards to death. It's like a chess game. You make small moves, probing your opponent, feeling him out. Get these people talking, believe me, and they'll make a mistake. Then you nail them."

"What if they don't want to talk?" Leon said, staring out the window, no doubt dreaming of diodes and transistors.

"Everybody wants to talk," I said with a smile. "You just have to hit upon the right subject."

"So are we going to use the Ruy-Lopez Defense?" Craig offered with a smile, referring to a famous chess opening. I smiled back.

"No defense on this one. We're going on the offensive with the Loose Lips Gambit."

"Loose Lips?"

"I'll explain later." I'd been thinking up clever ways to trap the terrorists, but I wanted to talk to Garcia before I decided to do it.

In San Salvador, we met Garcia at his palatial estate. Despite its size and luxury, the place looked like a military fortress, with broken glass embedded in the ten-foot walls encasing the compound. Armed security guards roamed the estate. Sometimes having great wealth can be a curse.

"They've called again," Garcia said after our quick introductions. "They say they'll kill him if I don't pay them immediately."

We spoke in a hallway, not the ideal place for a conversation of this nature.

"Let's sit down somewhere and work this out, okay?" I said.

Garcia nodded and led us into a dining room highlighted by a large green onyx dinner table. A pair of his top advisors were already seated, as were various family members. I wasn't expecting a crowd, and didn't appreciate it. The risk of leaks and spies rises proportionately with the number of people involved. I guessed it might not be culturally correct to request a more intimate gathering, so I let it slide. I pulled Garcia aside and spoke to him briefly.

"I'm only going to say this once. I don't trust anybody down here. You understand. Not your attorney, not your aides, not your army contacts, nobody. Your wife and family, yes. But as far as I'm concerned, anybody else in that room could be on the other side."

Garcia looked stunned. It was something that hadn't occurred to him before. He nodded as we returned to the large room.

With so many people involved, I needed to make doubly certain everyone knew I was in charge. Without asking questions, I stood and began directing the meeting. No one challenged me, which I took as a good sign.

"Okay, first things first," I opened. "Your father is safe in Miami, so right now the threats are meaningless."

"Then why doesn't Señor Garcia just tell the bastards to go to hell?" one of the aides challenged.

"Because they have time on their side," I answered. "How long can Garcia keep him and the rest of his family locked away? After a while, that'll be a fate worse than death, I don't care if he is living at the Ritz. This is his home. And the moment he comes back, the rebels will get wind of it and start the process all over again. They'll keep making threats until they either kill him, or you catch them. And if they kill him and you don't catch them, who's next? Your children? They are the ones most vulnerable."

I glanced across the room at the family members. They were terrified. The point was well taken.

"I need to get these lice out of your hair, permanently. Unless we can do that, all else is futile. Even paying them."

"That's a tough order in El Salvador," offered a well-dressed man, Garcia's attorney.

"We'll manage it," I parried, changing the subject. The last thing I wanted to do was get into a debate with a pessimistic barrister. "From this point on, I want to negotiate with the terrorists."

"Wait a minute," Garcia cut in. "Isn't that dangerous?"

"Relax," I ordered. "I know what I'm doing. I've been in these situations before. Trust me. I have a plan."

I made an effort to make friendly eye contact with the family members. They were the ones in the crosshairs, so they were the people I needed to assure the most. They also held the most sway with Garcia. The more authoritative and in control I acted, the more secure they began to feel. The thick cloud of tension hanging over the room slowly began to dissipate. Then something happened that nearly unraveled everything I'd accomplished. I wanted Garcia and his family to carry Mace for their protection, and began passing out the small personal spray cans women often carry in their purses.

"If you use it, make sure you point it in the right direction. If you don't, you could end up spraying, and disabling, yourself." I then accidentally shot a mist of Mace right into my face! It took a couple of minutes to fight off the stinging pain, wash out my eyes, and regain my senses. It wasn't a performance designed to win over converts from Garcia's suspicious aides.

"And if you do hold the can the wrong way, I've just showed you what you should do," I said with a wry smile.

There was a brief moment of silence, then everyone broke out in laughter, followed by applause. The meeting relaxed after that, which was a pleasant side effect.

I didn't want to go into my plan in front of some of Garcia's aides, so I waited until I was able to get Garcia alone before I unveiled it.

"We have to get the phone company involved," I opened.

"I already have. But they can't trace the calls. The rebels are too careful. They're calling from pay phones."

I let that pass for the time being.

"Then we'll talk them down in price just for the hell of it. We'll stall them at every turn. Remember, no one is buried in a hole somewhere, being held in a dark room, or undergoing torture, so we're in no rush from that standpoint. I told you before that time was on their side, but that was speaking long-term. Right now, because they aren't actually holding anyone, time is on our side.

"Mr. Garcia, at some point, I want you to tell them that you have pressing business in Chicago, Mexico, Brazil, wherever, then take a powder. That will buy us an entire week to try and smoke them out. The whole point, as you've no doubt picked up on by now, is to stall, stall, stall. We've got to run out the clock until we can find out who they are and put them out of business."

"Why would they even bother to negotiate?" Garcia asked.

"Because we've got what they want. They're not planning to kill an elderly man because they enjoy it. Craven as the brain-washed bastards are, even they have to blanch at that. They want the dinero. They need it! So we dangle it in front of them. Once we start haggling, they'll smell it. They'll start believing that their scheme's working and that they're going to be rich, so they'll become greedy. The key is to move the money toward them inch by inch, until that's all they can see. The closer they get to it, the more anxious they'll become. They'll be itching to rush out and grab it. That's when they'll make their mistake. And that's when we'll nab them."

He gave a wan smile.

"In order to go forward, I insist upon three things," I continued. "First and foremost, I want total control. We can only have one voice calling the shots, and that voice is mine. I can't have the police or army interfere with this."

Garcia nodded.

"If we need outside help, which we might, then I'll ask for it. Until then, it's hands off."

He nodded again.

"Secondly, we want to coordinate the phone company with some other people. Whenever we talk to these people, we'll listen for certain noises in the background."

"Noises?" Garcia said. He didn't get it, but Craig did. I saw my gifted associate nod his head.

"We know they're talking over pay phones. Outside. So, we'll create noises in certain areas of the city. Systematically. Look, they won't talk for more than about a minute, right? So, we'll have a fire truck blare its siren for sixty seconds along a certain route. A cop car along a second route. Like a grid."

"Like a grid," he slowly repeated. It was dawning on him by now.

"Yes. I can provide these things," he said.

"So every time these bastards call, we'll make specific noises all over the city and listen for them over the line. Leon here will analyze the tapes, bleed out the stuff that gets in the way and focus on background noise."

Leon gave Garcia a big smile. Garcia slowly smiled back. He was beginning to like the Loose Lips Gambit.

"There aren't that many public pay phones in San Salvador.

And these bastards aren't calling from their homes. My bet is that we'll be able to rule out three-quarters of the city. And that should give the phone company more to play with in terms of tracing their calls."

"Mr. Pena, that is an idea that never occurred to me!" His face looked more lively than before.

I grinned. "Point number three. When we nail down the caller, I want to identify the entire cell, okay? So we don't nab him. My people will follow the caller and that way we can cut off this monster's head, not just one arm. Is that clear?"

This was critical. All too often, Latin-American soldiers torture first and ask questions later, destroying any chance of gaining valuable intelligence information. I wanted to infiltrate the rebel army's operation and shut it down, before the army interrogators scrambled their brains with rifle butts.

After my experience with Salazar I wanted Garcia to be very clear about this. He agreed to keep the army out, unless we needed it.

"When do you expect the next call?" I asked.

"Tonight at eight," Garcia explained. "They gave me forty-eight hours to get the money before they went after my father."

"See!" I winked. "They're negotiating already. At eight, the game begins. We tell them their demands are too high. We won't pay a penny over eight hundred thousand!"

A weary smile cut across Garcia's lips. He was beginning to see the method to my madness.

"How are you going to explain who you are?" he asked.

"I'm not. At least, not yet. You're going to answer the phone."

"I thought you wanted to negotiate?"

"You'll do the talking. I'll supply the words."

"Are you sure . . . ?"

"I'm positive. You'll be fine. Don't worry. I'll be right there. Remember, the conversations are short. A minute or so. It's not like you're going to be on stage flapping in the wind. You'll be fine. Everything will be simple and to the point."

"Okay."

"And don't forget to call the fire department . . ."

Garcia smiled. For the first time, he felt like he was back in control. We were taking the initiative, and I knew he would get into the spirit of the deadly game. Garcia proceeded to make the necessary background noise arrangements as Leon wired up his house with extra phones so that we could listen in and tape the conversations.

The guerrillas, ever punctual, called precisely at eight. Garcia was clearly nervous, but followed the script as rehearsed. The rebel spokesperson became angry and balked at taking less money. He slammed the phone down.

"He wasn't happy," Garcia said.

"Goons like that are never happy," I joked, cutting the tension. "What's the bottom line?"

"They want the million."

"And?"

"He said he'd call back tomorrow morning at nine."

"Excellent. They've agreed to make an unscheduled call. You've started the process of negotiation. They'll be discussing your offer among themselves all evening. Some will want to play tough. Others will want to take the money and run. With that single conversation, you've sown the first seeds of discord into their camp."

By giving Garcia the credit, I was able to bolster his confidence and make him feel like he was winning, the exact thing he longed for.

"You are a clever man, Octavio," he sighed, "but this is a dangerous game."

"One I don't plan to lose. Trust me. They'll make a mistake."

Leon and I sat down and began the tedious task of sorting out the background noises on the tapes of the short conversation. Slowly but surely, we began to weed out large portions of the city.

Later on that night, I wrote down a number of excuses for Garcia to use when stalling the terrorists the next time he spoke with them. "I don't have the cash ... All my money is tied up ... The crops were bad ... I lost the money on the stock market ..." Things like that. And we also wrote down statements for Garcia to make that might elicit certain responses from the guerrillas. This would enable us to determine if Garcia had a traitor within his own camp. If Garcia said, "I was out of town for the last call," and the terrorists made a mistake of commenting that it wasn't true, then we had a traitor.

The next day, I decided to turn up the heat. When the call came, I instructed one of Garcia's aides to answer.

"Mr. Garcia is not here at the moment. He had an emergency meeting at the capital. He left word that you should call back at eight this evening."

The rebel fumed, but accepted it. What else could he do? Chop off his imaginary hostage's toe?

When I replayed the tape, I was delighted to hear a different voice. That was bad strategy on their part. No sense exposing more than one member of the cell. That told me there was obviously more than one person calling the shots in the rebel camp. The dissension may have existed even before I began playing my mind games with them. If that was true, we'd continue to fuel it.

"The 'emergency meeting' angle shows them who's boss," I explained. "A man of your stature should have more pressing concerns than a pack of rats nipping at your heels. We've set your priorities, and placed the rebels lower on the list. It's all part of the game of wits."

"What if they just say to hell with it and try to kill me or my father?"

"When they reach that point, they'll stop calling. Don't worry. They want the money. They're already spending it in their minds."

Later, Leon and I hunched over the tapes again. The fire trucks had passed through a poor area of town known to harbor a lot of revolutionaries. The sound analysis came up negative, but we had winnowed out another region of the city. After analyzing the tapes, I wrote a bolder script for Garcia. When the next call came, he went on the offensive.

"Before I pay, how can you guarantee that you won't do this to me again? That you won't strike my family again? How can you guarantee that some other faction won't come along and try the same trick? I need guarantees from you."

Surprisingly, the rebel dropped his tough-guy tone and offered the guarantees. While the pair talked, I timed them on a stopwatch. The phone company generally needed at least ninety seconds to trace a call. At exactly eighty seconds, the phone went dead.

They're good, I thought to myself. *They're using a stopwatch.*

"He said he'd call back tomorrow," Garcia relayed. "The man's getting antsy. He specifically said he's getting sick of negotiating."

"Tough shit," I said. "He ain't seen nothing yet. We'll keep the pressure up."

That evening, I studied the tapes of all the conversations. Two distinct voices were clearly identified. No big scoop on my part. In another strategic blunder, the men identified themselves separately. One gave his code name as Carlos, the other called himself Manuel. Other than that, they seemed on the ball. Both men used proper grammar, had a college-level vocabulary, and were comfortable with complex sentence constructions. They had to hail from the local university, or were educated at some other institution of higher learning. My guess was that they were local boys. Their accents and dialects fit the pattern.

I focused on the differences between the pair themselves. Carlos was cool and self-assured. Although he didn't like the delays, they didn't fluster him. Manuel, on the other hand, was nervous, extremely anxious.

"Okay, things are starting to take shape," I advised Garcia. "The fire trucks have cut out about two-thirds of the city. We can start focusing. Let's screw with them for another day, then we'll spring our trap. I'm having second thoughts about my plan to send you out of town. I think these eggs are about to crack."

"What are you going to do?" he asked.

"I'm not going to do anything. You are," I joked.

He stared at me, his eyes panicked.

I spoke calmly. "You're going to get these assholes to talk for more than ninety seconds."

"How?"

"I'll tell you tomorrow night. First, let's see what happens in the morning when you tell them you can't get the money."

Garcia looked at me in disbelief.

"Get some sleep," I laughed, excusing myself. "Tomorrow is going to be a long day."

10

EXECUTIONS

THE REBELS DIDN'T take kindly to Garcia's next attempt to devaluate their envisioned pot of gold.

"I can't get the million on such short notice," he danced. "But I can round up six hundred thousand in a few days."

Carlos and Manuel freaked. Fortunately, they couldn't rant and rave very long. The stopwatch was ticking.

Instead of going out and killing someone, the Communists displayed their anger by taking another drastic step—they increased their volume of calls. The pair phoned Garcia three more times that day, using their allotted 360 seconds to vent their spleens, threaten the universe, and try to get the figure back up into the $800,000 range.

Because of our ever-shrinking "audio grid," the rash of angry calls enabled us to direct the phone company to narrow the search area. With each call, Leon and I could hear the fire trucks more clearly. And once or twice, we thought that we heard them pass by, the telltale Doppler effect—sound drops in pitch as it moves past a stationary listener—clearly detectable. They were calling from a phone close to the university. I decided to raise the heat another crank.

I summoned everyone to a war council that evening at Garcia's estate. The billionaire's lawyers, his contact in the military, and his brother sat across the huge green onyx table from Craig and me. Leon sat behind us, more concerned with the static on the San Salvador phone lines than with strategy.

"Tomorrow is D-day," I announced. "We're going after these guys." A wave of anticipation swept over the room. I pressed on. "Mr. Garcia, Carlos is calling next, right?"

"At seven."

"He's the cool one."

"He used to be. Not so much anymore."

Garcia had not intended his response to be a joke, but it made everyone in Garcia's dining room laugh. It broke the tension.

"No, I guess not," I said. "Mind games get these high-strung types every time. When he calls, I want you to follow my script to the T, okay? You've been doing great so far, but tomorrow is ground zero. We're going to suck him into talking more than ninety seconds."

"Okay."

"We know there are two men speaking for the revolutionaries. Neither appears to be the clear-cut leader. They're probably battling over leadership right now. Sometimes they speak together. Other times only a single voice is on the line. That's where they've made their mistake. I'll explain more tomorrow."

I didn't want the military to know what I was planning just yet. They might get impatient and shoot the guy right there by the phone, before we could track him back to his nest. Craig and I already had figured out that we would have three teams of men around the university, waiting to tail the caller, as soon as the phone company completed a trace. There was no way the caller could escape my net.

I spent most of the following day mapping out Garcia's script, analyzing the tapes, and trying to keep Garcia calm.

"Since we've narrowed the area, the phone company might not need the full ninety seconds to make the trace. Still, that's what we're shooting for. We need them to go over the limit," I told him.

"How?" Garcia asked.

"We'll throw Carlos a curve, one so twisting that he'll lose his wits—and lose track of time."

The magnate's small coterie of advisors gathered at his home to wait for the final push. As the clock neared seven, the pent-up excitement in the room was like a locker room before a championship game.

Even though we'd planned and waited the entire day for Carlos's call, when the phone finally rang, it gave everyone, including me, a start. This was it, show time. I switched on my tape recorder and listened on the extension.

The Loose Lips Gambit had moved into its end game.

"Hello," Garcia said, glancing down at my script for him.

"This is Carlos."

Garcia gave me the thumbs-up. We had the right guy.

"What happened?" Garcia asked. "Any problems?"

"Problems with what? What are you talking about?"

"The delivery."

"What delivery? I'm calling to give you instructions."

Garcia acted like he didn't hear that.

"I came through on my end. Now, if you don't mind, I want my father's death sentence revoked. I want your assurance that this banditry won't happen again."

Garcia was into it now. He hardly glanced at my notes.

"What? What delivery?" Carlos's voice was high and squeaky, the way it got when he was angry or upset.

"Don't play games with me. You know what we're talking about," Garcia insisted.

"I do not know!"

"You don't know about the package? I sent it out to be delivered an hour ago. You should have it soon . . ."

"Shut up with that and just tell me what you're talking about! What package?"

It was my turn to give Garcia the thumbs-up. He was doing beautifully.

"One of my aides is dropping it off now. You were supposed to call me at six-thirty, when it was done. Why are you late?"

"When it was done? When what was done?"

Carlos's voice moved up another octave. I could sense the first hint of panic coming through. I looked at my watch. Damn, only thirty seconds gone. It seemed like forever. We had to keep him hanging. I signaled to Garcia to pour it on.

"What happened? Did something go wrong?"

"What do you mean, 'What happened'? What the hell is going on?" Carlos squeaked.

"Don't yell at me," Garcia snapped. "The six hundred thousand is on its way . . ." The guy was a born thespian. "Don't tell me you guys don't know what is going on!" he continued after a pause.

Come on, Garcia, say the magic words. Mention Manuel, I whispered to myself. *Set the hook.*

"Didn't Manuel tell you? Hell, my money might be sitting out there on the street. Some vagrant might find it!"

"What the hell are you talking about? What do you mean, 'Didn't Manuel tell me'? Tell me what? What's going on? Where is Manuel? Where is Manuel!" Carlos yelled so loud Leon winced and removed his earphones.

Garcia paused. He sighed. He stalled. He ate away the seconds.

"What's going on? You tell me! You guys are the ones who wanted the money so fast."

Garcia paused again. Seconds passed.

"Listen, I already sent the money for the pickup, just like Manuel said. I told you guys I'd have it delivered. He's on his way."

"Who told you to deliver the money?" Carlos asked. This time his voice was a full octave lower, and it dripped with suspicion.

"Who? Who the hell do you think? You, Carlos! You and your buddy Manuel."

"Manuel?"

"I believe it was him. Maybe. I don't know. I thought it was you. You or him. What's the difference? My people are probably there now with the briefcase! Jesus, I'd better stop him!"

"Who told you to do that?" Carlos ranted. "Who did you drop it off for? Who told you?"

Come on baby, stay angry, I thought. *Keep talking. Lose control. You've been duped by your pal, asshole. Can't you see the picture? Another minute, we'll have you by the balls.*

I looked at my watch. More than a minute gone. We were heading down the homestretch. The trace must about be there. I found myself unconsciously reaching for the phone that would soon ring. Then I could direct my teams in the field to start tailing the terrorist back to his nest.

"You guys called me at four today and told me where to deliver the money. I decided to go through with it and end this shit once and for all. Manuel said the six hundred thousand was enough."

"Manuel talked to you? He told you to make the drop?"

"Yeah, now that you mention it. I guess it was Manuel. I get you guys confused. Anyway, he told me to leave it in the trunk of a blue Chevrolet parked behind the library. He said that you would call at six-thirty to confirm the delivery. How come you didn't call? What went wrong?"

"When did Manuel call you?"

By now Carlos was in a complete panic. He was swallowing it. More than a minute and a half had passed. If what the phone company said was true, then they should already have had enough time to make the guy. But I wanted them to be sure.

"Come on, keep him guessing," I whispered. "Keep talking . . ."

"Hey, what's going on here?" Garcia chimed. "Didn't Manuel tell you about the pickup? Sounds to me like he didn't. Don't tell me you guys can't even . . ."

"You have to stop the delivery!" Carlos shouted, his voice so high and shrill it was almost off the scale. "Stop it right now!"

"Shut up!" Garcia yelled. He stretched the phone away from his mouth and yelled into the room. "Get Santiago on the radio. Tell him to stop the delivery!" He then returned to Carlos.

"Oh, God! The money must be there already! He's already got it. He went behind your back! Damn, you bastards aren't even honest with each other! That asshole ripped us both off. He took my six hundred thousand dollars! You better find him!"

"Shut up, old man. I don't know what's going on, but I'm sure going to find out. I'll call you back in two hours, okay? Don't tell anyone about this. And don't talk to anyone but me. Do you understand?"

"What about Manuel?"

There was no answer. The phone went dead. The rebel must have finally looked at his watch. I could only imagine his utter shock when he noticed the numbers. Almost three minutes.

We all waited for the phone to ring.

The seconds ticked by. *Come on, they had to have a trace,* I thought to myself.

Garcia's private line rang. He listened for a second and then turned to the room.

"They got him!"

Everyone in the room threw their fists in the air and cheered. Everyone but me. *They got him? Who?*

The Loose Lips Gambit had worked, all right, but I was the one checkmated.

"Senor Garcia, who got him?"

Garcia turned to me with a sheepish look.

"The army seized him. By the phone."

"What?" My heart sank. "We had a deal."

"I thought so, too. The phone company didn't tell me they were working with the army."

"Now we won't crack their cell!"

He gave a resigned shrug. "The army's got him now, Octavio, so let it go at that."

I was too pissed to let anything go. What a bunch of morons. We were primed to infiltrate their entire organization.

"Please, let me debrief him and see what he knows," I said. It was too late.

"The army's taking care of things now," one of Garcia's aides said. Yeah, right. With red-hot tongs and bootheels.

"You assholes promised me you wouldn't touch the guy!" I screamed, losing it myself.

I turned to vent some heat on Garcia, but he'd disappeared out the dining room door.

Later that night, I cought a glimpse of the terrorist, but I couldn't get near him. But Garcia's contact in the army, a colonel who never smiled at me, promised that we could debrief him. So, while Leon and the rest of the team jetted back to the States, Craig and I trooped off to our hotel to wait for an opportunity to see the kidnapper. We waited and waited for three long days, but the army shut us out.

The dour colonel gave us almost hourly briefings. "Nothing yet. But he is breaking. . . . Not yet, but he is close. Soon, my friends, he will sing. . . . He is tough, but he cannot hold on. . . ."

I could only imagine what they were doing to the terrorist. As the days passed, I feared there wouldn't be much of a rebel left to talk to. When the colonel stopped his regular briefings, I knew Carlos was either dead or close to it—and that, incredibly, he hadn't broken.

"They can't get anything out of this kid," the colonel finally admitted.

"Kid?"

"He's only twenty-two. He denied making the phone calls. Denies everything. He says it was someone else. He just walked up to the phone, and we arrested him."

"You probably tortured him an inch away from his life. Am I right?"

The larger-than-life Larry Iorizzo parties with Colombo family associate Buddy Lombardo and three others at the New York Playboy Club. (*Courtesy of the author*)

Larry Iorizzo in one of his many mug shots. At the height of his gasoline scam, he and Michael Franzese were pocketing eight million dollars per week. (*Courtesy of the author*)

The Secretary of State
of the United States of America
hereby requests all whom it may concern to permit the citizen/
national of the United States named herein to pass
without delay or hindrance and in case of need to
give all lawful aid and protection.

Le Secrétaire d'Etat
des Etats-Unis d'Amérique
prie par les présentes toutes autorités compétentes de laisser passer
le citoyen ou ressortissant des Etats-Unis titulaire du présent passeport,
sans délai ni difficulté et, en cas de besoin, de lui accorder
toute aide et protection légitimes.

Salvatore Matthew Carlino
SIGNATURE OF BEARER/SIGNATURE DU TITULAIRE

NEW YORK STATE
DRIVER LICENSE   Signature in Full (Wife use own first name)
X *Salvatore M. Carlino*
Class **5**   7/04/38 $15.00
Motorist Identification Number   Date of Birth   Date Lic. Expire
C19582 56790 666782 38   7/04/86
Height Eyes
6 0 BL   CARLINO, SALVATORE M.
              1325 FRANKLIN AVENUE
              GARDEN CITY NY   11530

              ISSUED   JUNE 7 1982
              NEW YORK STATE
              DEPT OF MOTOR VEHICLES
□ ORGAN DONOR   Commissioner of Motor Vehicles   MV-2 (6/80)

UNITED STATES OF AMERICA
PASSPORT   Type/Cat. Code of issuing / code du pays PASSPORT NO./NO DU PASSEPORT
PASSEPORT   P type   State   USA   040663040
Surname / Nom
CARLINO
Given names / Prénoms
SALVATORE MATTHEW
Nationality / Nationalité
UNITED STATES OF AMERICA
Date of birth / Date de naissance
04 JUL/JUI 38
Sex / Sexe   Place of birth / Lieu de naissance
M   NEW YORK, U.S.A.
Date of issue / Date de délivrance   Date of expiration
26 JUN/JUN 84   25 JUN/JUN 94
Authority / Autorité   Amendments/
PASSPORT AGENCY   Modifications
                                      SEE PAGE
MIAMI   24

P<USACARLINO<SALVATORE<MATTHEW<<<<<<<<<<<<<<
0406630407USA3807048M9406258<<<<<<<<<<<<<<<6

SOCIAL   SECURITY
ACCOUNT   NUMBER
124-35-4329
HAS BEEN ESTABLISHED FOR
SALVATORE M. CARLINO
Salvatore M. Carlino
FOR SOCIAL SECURITY AND TAX PURPOSES - NOT FOR IDENTIFICATION

Bureau of Vital Records   Department of Health   The City of New York

CERTIFICATION OF BIRTH

THIS IS TO CERTIFY that SALVATORE MATTHEW CARLINO

Sex M   was born in the Borough of NEW YORK CITY   City of New York on
JULY 4, 1938   according to Birth Record No. 29086713-38
filed in this Office on JULY 6, 1938

In witness whereof, the seal of the Department
of Health of the City of New York has been affixed
hereto this 9th day of FEBRUARY   1982

Irving Mellons
City Registrar

N.Y.C. M

Warning: This certification is not valid if it does not bear the raised
seal of the Department of Health. The reproduction or
alteration of this certification is prohibited by Section 3.21
of the New York City Health Code.

On the lam, Iorizzo flew to Panama using his new identity–"Salvatore Carlino." (*Courtesy of the author*)

A surveillance shot of Frankie Cestaro, an associate of Michael Franzese. He supplied Iorizzo with his fake identity. (*Courtesy of the author*)

'he American taxpayers forked out the dough for Iorizzo's posh Panama City hideaway, which vas a stone's throw from the U.S. ambassador's residence. Iorizzo allegedly paid a million ollars in cash to General Noriega to let him live in Panama and nine hundred thousand dollars or the mansion. (*Courtesy of the author*)

ABOVE LEFT: Former IRS agent Jorge Urquijo prays with President George Bush at a luncheon honoring federal undercover agents for their bravery and integrity. At the same time, the Marcianos were engineering a vindictive and spurious investigation of Urquijo because they suspected him of testifying to Congress about IRS corruption. (*Courtesy of the author*)

RIGHT: Congressional hearings disclosed that all original IRS evidence against Jordache "had been destroyed by the IRS criminal investigator who had been assigned to the Jordache tax fraud matter early in its development."

IRS SENIOR EMPLOYEE MISCONDUCT PROBLEMS

HEARINGS

BEFORE THE

COMMERCE, CONSUMER, AND MONETARY
AFFAIRS SUBCOMMITTEE

OF THE

COMMITTEE ON
GOVERNMENT OPERATIONS
HOUSE OF REPRESENTATIVES

ONE HUNDRED FIRST CONGRESS

FIRST SESSION

JULY 25, 26, AND 27, 1989

Printed for the use of the Committee on Government Operations

U.S. GOVERNMENT PRINTING OFFICE
23-404   WASHINGTON : 1989

For sale by the Superintendent of Documents, Congressional Sales Office
U.S. Government Printing Office, Washington, DC 20402

A surveillance shot of the Rasta stronghold where "Jody" was kept as a sex slave. We stormed the building shortly after this photo was taken. (*Courtesy of the author*)

The Mexico City apartment complex where the Salvadoran terrorists lived in exile, strangely enough under the protection of the Mexican government. One of the terrorists can be seen in the bottom photo. (*Courtesy of the author*)

ABOVE LEFT: My associate Sally Godfrey, aka "Kelly Grace." Sally helped on the Iorizzo and IRS cases. She is now a practicing attorney. (*Courtesy of the author*)

ABOVE RIGHT: Karen Kronman, who has a Ph.D. in psychology, has helped me on several investigations, including the Frito-Lay and Rastafarian cases. (*Courtesy of the author*)

LEFT: Another member of my team, Norma Torres. Norma helped me to infiltrate the Franzese arm of the Colombo crime family in New York. (*Courtesy of the author*)

RIGHT: My mentor and dear friend, Roger Burman, who retired from NCR to help guide me through the shoals of corporate America. (*Courtesy of the author*)

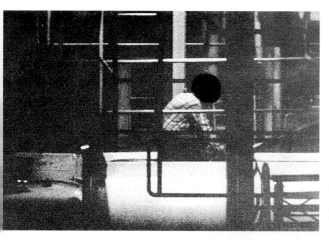

LEFT AND BELOW: A one-thousand-millimeter telephoto night shot of "Scallino's Boys" stealing from Northville. (*Courtesy of the author*)

BELOW: Scallino's headquarters the day before the raid. Note one of the tankers that Scallino threatened to use to blow up Northville's head-quarters. (*Courtesy of the author*)

Counterfeit tickets gave these kids more to scream about than rock-'n'-roll lyrics. These counterfeit tickets to popular bands were being scalped for hundreds of dollars each, and cost Ticketron millions. (*Courtesy of the author*)

The colonel wouldn't meet my gaze.

"It's time to try a different tactic. Enough torture . . ."

"What do you want?"

"I want to spend the day with him. Alone. With no interference from anyone, you included."

"You can get him to talk?"

"Yes, and I won't have to use cattle prods like the army."

Garcia quickly agreed.

The following day, Craig and I drove to the infamous Military Camp Number One—the Lubyanka Prison of El Salvador.

Instead of blackjacks and brass knuckles, my interrogation tools were simple. A briefcase. A special Uher tape recorder. And a chocolate bar.

At the main gate, the commandant of the camp, a vicious-looking colonel with beady eyes and tight chicken lips, led us into his twisted domain.

"I want a room to talk to Carlos," I said. "Alone." The colonel agreed and walked us across a drill field.

"We softened him up for you," the colonel said as he led me into the army headquarters. "He almost died on us last night, the little prick."

Inside, we walked along dim walls that dripped with the accumulated agony of a thousand dead souls. The colonel leaned over and leered at me.

"What new tricks do you Americans have there in the briefcase?" He smiled with his cold fishlike eyes, figuring I was going to torture the kid some more. "If they work on that bastard inside, let me know."

"Just papers," I answered.

He winked at me and led us down to his office. The guy must have thought I was a CIA torture expert. It was probably the only way Garcia got me in. I kept a straight face but inside I wanted to punch his beady little eyes through the back of his head.

I held my tongue.

Finally, after a few minutes, I was led to a small, dingy room decorated with two stark chairs and a table. I could see dried blood sprinkled around on the floor with swarms of flies, cockroaches, and insects of indeterminable lineage buzzing and crawling all over everything. In one corner, there appeared to be a tooth. The place reeked of vomit, urine, and fear. I grimaced, wondering what horrors had taken place in this steaming hellhole.

"You wait outside," I told Craig. "I don't want anyone from the military coming in or listening."

In retrospect, I should have suggested that my associate keep the rebel himself from coming in. The guy was in such bad shape, I recoiled in horror when I saw him.

This can't be him, I thought. *He looks fifty years old.*

The student glanced up at me through horribly blackened eyes so swollen I couldn't make out their original color. His teeth were broken off in jagged edges across the breadth of his mouth. There were inflamed bald spots on his head where clumps of hair had been yanked out.

The poor kid looked so miserable I couldn't even speak.

This young man was a murderer. But I had become used to the American way of doing things. The physical abuse of his torture was appalling. I took a deep breath and reminded myself that this guy, battered as he was, got that way because he would have slit Garcia's father's throat in a heartbeat.

My voice came back.

"My name is Octavio Pena. I was hired by Mr. Garcia to catch you. Well, I caught you, and right now, I have to admit I'm half-sorry about that. I'm sorry the army got hold of you first. What happened here is not my way."

The man sat in silence. I opened my briefcase. I saw him tense.

"Would you like some chocolate?" I asked, offering him a Milky Way bar.

He stared at the candy bar for a moment, not believing it really could be his. He probably hadn't been fed since his capture. I guessed that his hunger was even stronger than his pain.

The rebel nodded and slowly reached out a scarred and blood-encrusted hand.

"Have they given you anything to eat since you've been here?"

He shook his head.

"They haven't even let me lie down to sleep," he spat.

I made small talk as he struggled to eat the chocolate bar, which was rapidly melting in the heat. To compensate for the painfully broken teeth he was finally forced to lick the running chocolate off his mangled hands. After he finished, for whatever reason, he started opening up. He said his real name was Pablo. He was twenty-two, was a student at the university, and hated the Salvadoran government.

No shit, I thought.

"Look, Pablo, I'm not unsympathetic to your plight. The army shouldn't have done this to you. Nobody should do this to anyone, anywhere. There are countries where this could never happen, no matter what your crime was.

"However, that said, you can't kill and kidnap innocent civilians for your cause. That's wrong. That's where you crossed the line. And don't go shaking your head on me. I'm not going to beat you. You don't have to deny anything to me. That's not why I'm here. I know it was you making the calls. I have your voice on tape. We have the technology to make a definitive, voiceprint match."

"I did not make any calls. That wasn't me," he insisted, standing firm, even when I played a tape of his last call. Whatever he was, I had to admire his courage. They'd tortured him beyond human endurance, and he hadn't broken.

I chatted casually with Pablo for the next three hours, slowly befriending him. He freely talked politics and expressed his disdain for the government. I told him that when I was younger, I felt the same way about the Mexican authorities, only I expressed my displeasure in more socially acceptable ways.

"In these situations, all you can do is try to make a difference, try to change things, do what you can," I said. If that doesn't work and you can't stand it anymore, then you make a decision to live in a place where things are different. You don't add to the misery by kidnapping and killing. That never works.

"What you did was wrong, and you have to accept the responsibility for it. You've been caught. You're an unpaid soldier in a volunteer army, so you knew the risks going in, didn't you?"

Pablo nodded. I could sense him weakening. He could endure a fist to the face. What he couldn't endure was a pat on the back.

Craig arrived with a bag of cheeseburgers and fries from the local McDonald's. The sight of the cherished American fast food appeared to have a dramatic effect upon Pablo. As he ate, he began to open up another crack.

I waited for him to finish his dinner before I got down to serious business.

"Pablo, the army is going to torture you until you die—unless you talk to me. I can try to stop them, stop this madness, but only if you accept responsibility for what you did."

The young rebel wiped his swollen mouth and looked up. The food brought a trace of natural color to his bruised face, but it was too much for his traumatized body. He threw up and soiled his pants.

All of a sudden, a tear formed in the hardened rebel's eye and spilled down his cheek. My chest tightened. A lump the size of a small boulder formed in my throat. The fact that I knew he was about to crack got buried under the raw emotional moment of his weakening. I'll never forget that tear. He became human.

"Octavio. You appear to be a nice man. I'm going to tell you what you want. But they're going to kill me anyway. That's the way it is here."

"Before you say anything, I'll get Garcia to promise me that you will not be killed. On his honor. Okay? If he won't do that, then don't tell me anything."

"And you think they'll hold to that?" Pablo shook his head sadly.

"I won't come back unless I can give you my promise that you won't be killed."

I left the room. Craig came in and stood guard over Pablo while I called Garcia.

"I'm making headway with him, but before I go on, I need to know that he won't be killed. I want your word of honor as a man that he will be given a fair trial."

"You have my word," Garcia solemnly intoned.

"And he's not to be tortured anymore. Whatever he knows, I'll get. Understand?"

"Completely. No more torture."

I returned to the room.

"Okay, he gave me his word as a man that you will be given a fair trial, and that they won't lay another hand on you."

"Don't believe it."

"He's not the military. He can be trusted."

"He's worse than the military. The military is just a pawn. But either way, I'll tell you. You're not like them."

Pablo took a deep breath, then began. "I am a student at the university. My family, everybody's family, has been oppressed by the government for years. The rich rule here in El Salvador. Eleven families control this country like a feudal land, and the rest of us are serfs. We have no law, no rights, no say. Look what happened to me in here. Look at my face! This can never be reversed. This is what happens to anyone who complains. This is what we get for trying to make changes."

The young man's intensity and pathos riveted me to my seat. I understood exactly what he was saying. He could have been describing Mexico.

"Yes, I am a revolutionary, as are my comrades who took Garcia's mother. But I don't believe in Communism. Very few of us really do, only the real diehards. But America, the vaunted American democracy, supports Garcia and his kind, so we had nowhere to turn for assistance except to the Communists. We needed help, and the Soviets and Cubans were eager to provide it. They promised to help us overthrow the government. They promised us justice . . ."

"How did they train you?"

"It's all professional. The best Soviet equipment. We have six people per revolutionary cell. There was me, Manuel, and four others. This way we can't take down too many people if we get caught.

"We begin the process by walking in small groups to Guatemala to pick up Chilean or Cuban passports that are prepared for us. Then the Soviets, and sometimes the East Germans, fly us to Cuba, or Czechoslovakia, for extensive training. Plastic explosives, kidnapping tactics, how to negotiate, indoctrination, counterfeiting, forgery, how to fight, how to organize, on and on. Weaponry, everything. We are trained as soldiers preparing for a war . . ."

He paused for a moment. The confession drained him. After a few seconds, he gathered his strength and continued.

"All along, we were doing it for our country. Our people. The poor oppressed people who have nothing to hope for. No dreams. Nothing but hardship ahead of them their entire lives. We wanted to give our people hope. That's all. A reason to smile when you wake up in the morning. The ability to pursue one's ambitions. A chance to make something of ourselves. Do you know what it's like to live without hope?"

Pablo looked away. He eyes filled with water. His body began to shake. The tears came slowly first, then spilled out in deep sobs. I put my arms around him.

"It's going to be all right," I said as my own tears fell. "It's going to be okay."

Pablo's tears opened a floodgate. For the next four hours, he outlined his entire operation: He told me who was in his cell, how they planned to kidnap Garcia's father, how they kidnapped the mother, and how she died. I learned their intricate command structure, how they communicated, and what they were planning next.

When it was over, I left the rancid interrogation room as shaken as Pablo.

Deep down, Pablo was a decent kid. He had the right idea. It wasn't even his own dark side that made him bad. The Communists had taught him to hate and kill. They used his compassion for his people and turned it into something ugly.

It's sad the way some people have to grow up in this world, and how quickly others exploit them for their own causes.

My own internal conflict was tested to the extreme the following day. Garcia was so impressed with my operation that he and some other powerful magnates asked me to build an intelligence agency in Costa Rica that would assist landowners all over Central America in their battle against the Communist guerrillas plaguing their families.

"We'll pay you a million dollars a year, plus expenses," Garcia said. "You'll have the best resources and equipment money can buy."

I considered it for a while, going over the good and the bad in my head. It was a great opportunity. I'd be running my own CIA for the wealthiest men in Latin America. The work would be exciting and challenging. Stopping the spread of Communism would give me a motive I could sink my teeth into.

On the other hand, how many confused kids Pablo's age would I have to put back together after vicious interrogators like the sadistic colonel broke them? And how, for whatever reason, could I become a strong-arm agent for the wealthy landowners who kept their people in shackles?

I told Garcia that I would think about it.

I returned to New York, happy to be out of Central America. Two weeks later, Garcia came up to celebrate the destruction of Pablo's revolutionary cell.

We had dinner at Trader Vic's at the Plaza Hotel. Garcia began pressing me again to take his offer and create a private intelligence agency for his rich cohorts. I stopped eating and looked up at him.

"What happened to Pablo?" I asked casually.

"Oh, the army killed him. Executed," he said, without ever looking up from his plate of food.

I stared at Garcia for a couple of seconds, remembering his word of honor that Pablo would not be killed.

I thought about working for such a man. I thought about the million dollars per year his kind would pay me, about Roberto Salazar and René Dubois. I stared at Garcia until he looked up from his food. He swallowed and stared back at me. When I had his full attention, I spoke.

"Find someone else to help you. You did not keep your word. Señor, you have no honor." I left the restaurant.

It was so frustrating. I had accepted an assignment that I thought was right. I was fighting the good fight against all things evil. Only the evil refused to remain behind clearly drawn lines in the sand. It surrounded me.

I would never again work for a client I couldn't trust.

A TICKET TO RIDE

AFTER THE EL SALVADOR nightmare I made a dramatic change in my personal life—I married my beautiful assistant, Grace. The physical and emotional bonding helped heal the wounds of betrayal I felt after that emotional case. For a long time, I couldn't get that dingy rat-infested dungeon and Pablo's story out of my mind, but Grace helped.

Returning from my honeymoon refreshed and renewed, I poured myself into managing my business, now a multimillion-dollar corporation. Keeping track of the business kept my mind off of El Salvador, but I needed another good case. Fortunately, one came along quickly. It pointed me toward another facet of American business riddled with massive corruption, one the average person might not suspect was so lucrative for the criminals involved.

I received a call from Ticketron, the concert ticket distribution giant that was a division of Control Data. Ticketron was having a terrible problem with counterfeiting. Thousands and thousands of bogus tickets were being printed and sold to various rock-and-roll, country, and jazz concerts. This resulted in ugly scenes as excited fans arrived at an arena only to find someone else, someone else with a valid ticket, in his or her seat.

"The problem is so bad at Madison Square Garden here in New York that the management has to set aside a special section for people with duplicate tickets," Ticketron president Bill Schmitt explained in his spacious New York office. With a magnificent view of midtown Manhattan as a backdrop, Schmitt ended his briefing in exasperation. "If we don't get to the bottom of this, we may lose our contracts."

Schmitt added that at concerts with general admission seating—meaning first come, first served—it was even easier for the counterfeiters to operate. Once through the doors, the fans could sit anywhere, avoiding the problem of people fighting over seats.

That worked okay if a concert wasn't sold out. However, the greedy counterfeiters started overselling arenas by up to ten thousand people. The overflow crowds packed the halls from wall to wall, jamming the aisles and flooding the concession areas.

The arena managers and fire marshals were not too pleased.

"Do you have examples of the counterfeit tickets?" I asked.

Schmitt threw up his arms.

"That's the strange part. We can't tell the difference! At first, we thought it was a glitch in our own computers. The duplicates are that good. To answer your question, I don't have a confirmed counterfeit to show you."

I raised my eyebrows. Hundreds of thousands of phony concert tickets were being knocked off, and these guys didn't have an example of a single one? No wonder they needed help.

"How big is this? How much money are we talking about?"

"Well, if scalpers sold an extra ten thousand tickets to a primo concert at fifty dollars a shot—and these guys aren't duplicating the bad seats—you figure it out. Our managers say it's happening all over the country. Most of our best concerts are going on overbooked. It's becoming a real mess."

"I'll bet," I said, doing the math. Someone was grossing up to five hundred grand *per concert!* And Ticketron booked tickets for dozens and dozens of concerts.

My associates and I spent the next four days learning the inner workings of the concert ticket business. It's amazing how lucrative this feeder industry is. Most of the Ticketron employees couldn't bang a steady beat with two pencils on their desk, yet the company was raking in tens of millions from the fat service fees they tack on to the tickets they supplied. Now I understood why someone would want to target them. This was a multimillion-dollar scam, one of the biggest I'd ever seen.

After getting the background on the legal operation, I turned my attention to the illegal one. With most criminal conspiracies, there's always a weak link somewhere along the print-and-run chain. In this case, it wasn't hard to spot the vulnerable link. It was my guess that the scalpers themselves, the point men in the illegal operation, weren't the most loyal of employees for whoever was behind it all.

If I could infiltrate the scalpers, I could trace the operation back to the source—the print shop manufacturing the phony tickets.

I targeted an upcoming ZZ Top concert in Waterbury, Connecticut, for my first stab at uncovering the scam. I selected the medium-sized city because I felt the scalpers there might not be as hardened as the ones that operate around Madison Square Garden in New York.

I also bet that the local police would be more cooperative. In New York, beleaguered cops have bigger problems to worry about than scalpers. Plus, some might possibly be on the scalpers' payroll. In Waterbury, the less cynical police might relish the opportunity to break a major counterfeiting ring.

That proved to be a good guess. The Waterbury police and the prosecutor we were working with readily agreed to assist me in flushing out and arresting the scalpers.

Prior to the concert, I had a pair of associates linger outside the arena and pinpoint the most prominent scalpers, the guys who waved around fans of tickets so large that they looked like Japanese geisha girls. My associates then directed the police to the fan dancers, who were promptly arrested and dragged down to the local jail.

"We've got three birds on ice." My associate called me at my office, relaying the news.

Grace and I sped up to Waterbury for the next phase of the operation. I huddled with the police and prosecutor and received their permission to offer a deal to the scalpers for their cooperation.

After a brief conversation with the hot ticket trio, I decided to focus my efforts on a tall, smooth-talking African-American who appeared to be their ringleader. This bearded dandy struck me as the kind of guy whose interests would be limited to one goal—saving his well-dressed hide.

"Jerome, let me lay it out for you," I opened. "I work for Ticketron. You've been illegally scalping their tickets. For that, you're going down. You'll do three, maybe four years. However . . ." I paused to dramatize the pitch. ". . . if you cooperate with me, then I've been authorized to guarantee that you won't spend a minute in jail."

Jerome shook his head. "No way, my man. Ain't doing no deals. Ain't bitin' the hand."

I understood his colorfully expressed sentiments. From the look of his sartorial splendor, he was making some serious cash—tax-free—from scalping. He wasn't about to kill the goose laying the golden eggs. Not unless he was squeezed.

"Think it over, Jerome. A handsome fella like you doesn't belong in some stinking jail, keeping your back to the wall, you know what I mean? Here's my card. I'm sure you'll make bail, but I want you to know that I'm going to hound you at every concert from here to China. Life as you know it is over."

He looked at me with a stony expression.

"Call me when you come to your senses," I continued. "If you decide to help me in this little matter, we can make it work so you won't have to sacrifice your livelihood. I don't want to bust you. I don't even want to mess up your action. I just want some insight into your world. I want you to teach me the tricks of the trade. How you scalp. What the process is. Do you understand?"

Jerome continued to stare at me in defiant silence.

Five days later, he called me at my Pan Am Building office. "Pena, if you wanna rap, I'll be at Fifth Avenue and Forty-second Street in ten minutes. Bring your ride, nothing else. No tape recorders. No buddies. Just you. Got it?"

He was smooth. Although there was an element of danger to his request, I was too curious to pass it up. I hopped into my "ride" and made it to the historic intersection with time to spare. My scalping guru, dressed in a fancy silk suit, was waiting.

Jerome ducked into my car at the light.

After reintroducing ourselves, he asked me to circle around for a while and then head for 12th Avenue on the west side of Manhattan. I guessed that he wanted to make sure he wasn't being tailed.

When we arrived at 12th, he motioned for me to pull over.

"No offense, but I've got to frisk you for ears."

"No offense taken," I said, opening my jacket. I let him see the .38 nestled under my left arm, and made sure he didn't get near it while he looked for wires.

After patting me down and searching through the car, Jerome was ready to talk turkey.

"I'll help you, but I can't be singled out for special treatment in Waterbury, you dig? All three of us have to be sprung. I can't be the Lone Ranger, or people'll know I'm snitchin'."

Jerome continued to impress me with his street smarts.

"That shouldn't be a problem. But you have to give me something, something useful. What do you have to offer?"

"For starters, how about I tell you about the folks at your own crib who are giving us the goods?"

I tried to suppress my surprise. That's why Ticketron's security couldn't produce a single phony ticket. There weren't any! This was an inside job.

"Hey, we already know about those guys," I bluffed.

"You know about Jimmy? And Pete in the computer room?" Jerome spilled.

"Sure, Jimmy's been taking orders and supplying them. Pete does the printing," I deduced.

"You got it! I don't have no need for counterfeits. There's fake stuff out there, sure, but I'm hooked into the real thing. If you know about that, then you don't need me," he sighed.

"Maybe not. I appreciate it that you're trying to help. There are some details we could use. Let me see if I can keep your deal together."

I drove Jerome to the garage in the Pan Am Building. Together we caught an elevator to my office. There, Jerome laid it all out for me.

"We keep track of concerts all over the U.S., especially those with unrestricted seating because those are the easiest to scam and they cause the least amount of problems. If a concert isn't sold out, nobody knows it happened at all. The extra marks just filter in with the legitimates and everything is cool.

"Once we target a concert, we call Pete in the computer department at Ticketron and place our orders. Jimmy usually did the printing. He'd whip off an extra thousand tickets or so, and sell them to us for five to ten dollars a shot. Then we hustle the concerts and hawk the 'board' for twenty to one hundred dollars per, depending on how hot the band is." I could tell Jerome relished rehashing this. Most thieves do: They're as proud of their schemes as any legit businessman is of his success.

"We tried to do it in small doses so nobody would notice. You know, keep the scam going forever. Everybody makin' good bread. I guess we weren't small enough."

"How much money do you make a year doing this?"

Jerome paused and smiled.

"Me? Personally? You ain't gonna believe it."

"Try me."

"This is between you and I, right? No IRS fools, okay?"

"No IRS."

"I scratch out somewhere in the neighborhood of two hundred and fifty to five hundred thousand per year. That includes all my scalping activities, not just the 'Tron."

"Whewwwwww!" I exclaimed. "That's a nice neighborhood!"

No wonder Jerome was so well-dressed. He made more money than 99 percent of the people in the whole world! Come to think of it, he made more money than 90 percent of all the corporate executives in the United States.

"Well, Jerome," I said. "You're gonna make a little less this year. But at least you'll be free."

"Freedom costs," he said philosophically.

"That it does," I agreed.

I reported my findings to Bill Schmitt at Ticketron. To avoid embarrassment, the company chose not to prosecute Pete and Jimmy, but based on the signed confessions I got out of them, they were summarily fired.

Jerome got his deal and faded back into the streets—the highly lucrative streets, as it turned out. Something told me, however, that our paths would cross again.

Sure enough, three months later, Ticketron called me again.

"This time, it's got to be counterfeiting," the general counsel explained. "People are showing up for reserved and general admission seating with identical tickets printed on different paper. It doesn't look like an inside job, thankfully. But whatever it is, it's worse than before. We're experiencing this all over the country."

I returned to my office and immediately dialed my pal Jerome, trying to catch him at one of his numerous residences. After all, he'd hinted at counterfeiting operations during our first encounter.

Jerome shared a bizarre personal trait with the subject of another of my investigations, Mafia money man Lawrence Iorizzo. Like the larger-than-life Iorizzo, Jerome felt the need to have two wives. Jerome was smart enough to keep an entire continent between them. Wife Number One was in New York, while Wife Two was stashed in sunny L.A.

I tracked Jerome down in New York, where he was sponsoring an inner-city youth basketball tournament with his illicit gains.

"Jerome, how's it goin'?"

"It was goin' good before you called," he joked. "Now I'm not so sure."

"I need your help again."

"Oh no, man! You done cut into my pie big-time already. I may have to shuck one of my ladies . . ."

"Nah, you'll be okay. I'll make it worth your while."

"Now you're talking. What's the problem?"

"Real counterfeiters this time. They're working both the reserved seating and general admission circuit."

"I don't do counterfeits, man, I told you."

"Jerome, if you don't do fakes, then how are you surviving these days?"

He smiled and explained his new modus operandi. At most general admission rock concerts, particularly at certain venues, he would get used tickets from the cops assigned to the stadium.

"Cops?" I exclaimed.

"Sure. They're the middlemen. We pay them to get tickets from the ticket takers after they'd been collected from the people comin' in. The dudes takin' the tickets forget to rip 'em up. They hand 'em over to the pigs on my payroll, and we resell them."

"You're unbelievable. Cops?" He laughed while I continued with my pitch. "Okay, you don't do counterfeits, but you're a known player, so maybe you can help smoke them out."

"Maybe. What's in it for me?"

"Same as before, you get to keep the bread from all the preliminary deals you set up. Plus, anybody grabs you, I'll put in a good word with the cops. How's that sound?"

"Sounds like I may need a new wife. Chicago is pretty this time of year."

I didn't doubt for a minute that Jerome could juggle three wives. And I knew something else. He may have been a big-time criminal, but with Jerome the thrill was in the deception, the excitement of the deal. I knew he'd come through for me. He was having too much fun playing double agent.

Jerome put out the word that he wanted to branch out into the counterfeit general admission seat business. Within a week, he was contacted by a "salesman" for an outfit based somewhere on the East Coast. Jerome explained he intended to set up a major distribution operation. The "salesman" had already checked out Jerome and found him to be a big-timer in the scalping business. He readily agreed to be his supplier.

"How many can you get me?" Jerome asked.

"How many do you need?" the salesman laughed.

When Jerome reported the conversation, I knew we were on to something huge. The well-hidden, highly insulated printing outfit was a multimillion-dollar organized crime operation—and my man Jerome was now on the inside.

Ticketron decided that the counterfeiters were too big for them to handle internally. They decided, at Craig's and my urging, that it was time to bring in the FBI and the U.S. Attorney. The government was happy to add their muscle to the investigation. That's not surprising. The two publicity-conscious law enforcement agencies like nothing better than to have a "sexy" case—as they like to call them—handed to them on a platter.

For the next two weeks, Jerome baited the hook by requesting large ticket orders for concerts from New York to Los Angeles. I huddled with the FBI so we could lay down a perfect criminal conspiracy case for the U.S. Attorney, one that would lead to a slam dunk in court.

"We want a clean sweep on this one," my FBI contact, Greg Gordon, told me. "We need to bag them all, from the couriers flying the tickets around the country to the print shop owners masterminding the ring. Everybody goes down, top to bottom."

"My feelings exactly."

"Can you trust your informant? Is he cool?"

"I think so. He's been stand-up so far. And they don't come cooler than this guy."

Gordon and his partner, another clean-cut, aggressive FBI special agent by the name of Bob Harris, specifically asked about Jerome because they knew that the dapper scalper would have to play a bigger role if we were going to trace the operation back to the ringleaders. I was confident that he could handle it. To be sure, we had a meeting at The Copter Club restaurant in the Pan Am Building shortly after he jetted back to New York and Wife Numero Uno.

"The FBI wants to nail the entire organization. You're going to have to get inside deeper and determine where these admission slips are originating."

"Whatever you say. This is kinda fun, in a mean green kinda way. Damn, I wish I knew about these guys before I met you."

I was right about Jerome. He thrived on the excitement of it all.

"Okay, here's the story. On your next major order, tell the contact that you want to do the exchange in Penn Station in Manhattan. We'll have to wire you for the drop. Then we'll take it from there. Can you handle that?"

"Just make sure the bug matches my threads," he laughed.

"I'll try."

"You gonna tail the mule back home?"

"That's the plan."

"Might be a long way."

"We'll follow them to the ends of the earth if that's what it takes."

Jerome got to work. He phoned in an order for 5,000 tickets to a big stadium concert in Chicago. As per my instructions, he arranged for the buy to occur at Gate 16 downstairs in Pennsylvania Station before the afternoon rush hour. That was a mistake.

The exchange went as planned. Jerome forked over a cash deposit, and the "mule," a casually dressed African-American man, handed him a small box stuffed with freshly printed tickets worth up to $500,000 on the scalping market.

Jerome sauntered out of the train station and presented me with the tape. I popped it into a recorder and heard . . . nothing but the roar of the trains combined with the garbled voices of commuters and train announcements. And it wasn't even rush hour!

I kicked myself for that one. Bad choice of locations for a taped conversation. We'd have to set up another buy in a quieter spot. Vermont would be a good choice. The New York din is just about inaudible up there.

Thankfully, the second, most important part of the plan went off without a hitch. After the exchange, several of my associates placed the mule under surveillance. They followed him onto a Washington-bound Metroliner and rode the rails all the way to Philadelphia. Once in the famed City of Brotherly Love, the clueless courier took a cab to a business in a seedy part of town.

As chance would have it, the place was a print shop.

That was a break. The courier could have gone to a hundred

different places after the drop. To my good fortune, he flew like a homing pigeon right back to his criminal nest and handed over Jerome's money.

I relayed the information to the FBI special agents, Harris and Gordon. They immediately rented an apartment across the street from the printer and placed it under tight surveillance.

"Jerome, I've got good news and bad news," I advised.

"Man, when are you gonna leave me alone?"

"The good news is the courier led us right to the printer."

"That's what you wanted. Now lay it on me . . ."

"The bad news is that your tape is no good . . ."

"Too noisy, huh?"

"Yeah. Next time, take the guy into the john or something. Get away from the trains and all the commuters."

Jerome took my instructions to heart. Two weeks later, he arranged another drop. This time, he dragged the mule into the men's room. The pair sat side by side and did their business, both literally and figuratively. The tapes were crystal clear—too clear. The conversation was punctuated by the bodily functions of the two men.

"Jerome! A federal judge and jury is going to hear you, live on Memorex, taking a nasty dump!"

"Can you tell us apart?" Jerome laughed.

"I don't know. Which one of you ate beans and rice?"

"Not me, I'm into soul food."

"Who flushed first?"

"He did!"

"I'll be sure to note that as Exhibit Number One."

I thought we had the case nailed. We were able to trace the tickets from shop to drop, with taped evidence to back it up. However, the FBI and U.S. Attorney's office wanted to hammer it down even tighter. They wanted to trace the chain in reverse, meaning they wanted Jerome to make his request, and then capture the courier placing the order in Philly. That way, they'd have the crooks coming and going.

"Can you arrange it?" one of the agents asked.

"I'll take care of it," I said. I got on the phone to Jerome.

"One more little favor and we should be done with this," I explained to the suave street shark. "The tape was great, but now we want to go after the whole enchilada." Luckily for the FBI, Jerome was still game.

The next morning, Jerome phoned the counterfeiter's "West Coast sales executive" in Los Angeles and said he was sending a detailed written order for tickets covering a series of upcoming concerts in the spacious Rose Bowl. The list was coming in an American Airlines courier pouch delivered by an undercover FBI agent.

The long-distance request was made so we could show the court the coast-to-coast scope of the vast criminal operation, and to slap the crooks with a heavier felony count for operating interstate.

Everything went as planned. The salesman, as predicted, caught a jet to Philadelphia to deliver the huge request in person.

We tailed the salesman the whole way. Just before he entered the print shop, I signaled for the final phase of the operation to kick in. It was time for Jerome to step aside and let someone else have some fun. That someone was Mary Louise Rogers.

Mary Louise was a trusted associate who had a knack for getting into places without attracting attention. Actually, she attracted a lot of attention, she just didn't arouse suspicion. The diminutive, button-cute operative could choose from a thousand different personas to fit the occasion.

After I'd briefed her, she skipped into the print shop just ahead of the L.A. "salesman." She was dressed like a sixties flower child, complete with a tie-died blouse, sandals, and a big floppy hat. She also carried a large woven bag overflowing with bandannas, flowers, secondhand clothing, and all kinds of other stuff. Buried beneath the pile was a high-powered microphone and transmitter.

I was across the street monitoring her signals, surrounded by FBI agents.

"Peace and love to you all!" she greeted the African-American man behind the counter, flashing a two-fingered, V-shaped peace sign. "I'm marrying a brother next month, and he told me about your print shop. Do you think you could print our wedding invitations?"

As an added effect, the tiny white lady then raised her petite pink fist in a Black Power salute.

After recovering from the odd sight, the proprietor agreed to take the job. As Mary Louise perused the print style books, the L.A. salesman rolled in.

"Here's Jerome's latest order. It's a big one," he said for all the world to hear. "He's blanketing the whole coast with this one . . ."

I took off my headphones and shook the FBI agents' hands. We'd slammed the door on this outfit. Even F. Lee Bailey couldn't get them off now.

In short order, the FBI fanned out across the country, dropped a net over all the players, and shut down the entire operation. Five months later, faced with the overwhelming evidence I'd gathered (with a big assist from Jerome), they all pleaded guilty and were given stiff jail terms.

Ticketron continued to grow, their huge contracts safe for the time being.

And the bands played on.

Ticketron had more cases for me after that, but none of them could measure up to what happened a few weeks after we nailed the counterfeiters. My associate Craig Anderson, who had helped me in El Salvador, showed me that even someone as careful as I try to be can be hoodwinked.

Grace and I developed a friendship with the sharp legal strategist and his Asian girlfriend. I'd learned by now to distrust almost all attorneys, but because of Craig's quick mind and unorthodox solutions to thorny problems, I soon began to wholeheartedly recommend him to many of my clients.

When the president of Ticketron called with a complicated legal problem, I didn't hesitate to recommend Craig. "I have just the man for you," I said. "I've worked with this attorney who possesses the most brilliant legal mind I've ever come across. He'll be able to straighten this out for you in no time."

Ticketron gave him a $50,000 retainer and put him on the case. A month later, I received a call from the ticket seller's president.

"I'd like to thank you for recommending Craig. We were stymied there, and he came up with an angle no one even thought of. It won the day! He did a hell of a job. We're going to keep him on."

"Great," I said. "You won't regret it."

After thinking long and hard about it, I decided to team up with this rising legal superstar. Even though I'd turned down Ramon Garcia and his billionaire buddies in Central America, the idea of a private intelligence agency was one I'd been mulling over ever since El Salvador. I wanted to share my success with my loyal friends, so I proposed to start an investigative outfit called The

Center for Counter Intelligence (CCI). CCI's profits would be split three ways: a third for The Lynch Company—which I owned 35 percent of—a third for Leon, the electronics whiz, and the last third for Craig, who would serve as treasurer under me.

CCI immediately took off. In the first six months, we helped solve some dicey cases and raked in $100,000 in billings. That's when the problems began. Although we continued to dine and socialize, Craig made no further mention of our joint effort.

As treasurer, he was supposed to file monthly finance reports. Three months passed without a word about it from the guy. But hey, he was my buddy, so I didn't say anything, figuring he'd get around to the reports when he could.

Another three months passed. Not a peep about CCI. When I finally asked him, he begged off, saying his legal caseload was heavy and he'd get "right on it next week."

After a few "next weeks" came and went, I decided to check on the account myself. There was only $16,000 left! The missing $84,000 translated into some serious expenses.

The drained bank account raised my suspicions. It pained me to suspect Craig or go behind his back, but something told me a full check on my pal's credentials might be in order.

I couldn't believe it when the paperwork arrived.

"Are you sure this is the right guy?" I asked my associate, asking him to double-check.

"It's him. Look at the picture."

Digging through the file, I found a police mug shot. It was not the suave, debonair attorney I'd dined with so often, but it was definitely Craig.

My pal and business partner had a rap sheet that would crack a smile on the face of even the most hardened con down at Riker's Island. He'd been arrested and jailed eight times, all for misrepresenting himself as an attorney.

I sat stunned in my chair for the next half-hour, replaying all the images of the good times Grace and I had shared with Craig and his girlfriend—all the times Craig gave me advice that turned out to be right on the money. Only now it wasn't my handsome pal the legal eagle and his date that flickered through my mind, but a prison-hardened con man and his moll.

Here I was, Mr. Crack-a-Million-Dollar-a-Case investigator, taken in by a true-blue, bona fide ... phony! I'd smoked out and outsmarted the most ingenious white-collar criminals in some of the biggest corporations in America, and yet here I was, snookered by a slick street shark!

When I emerged from my surprise and anger, I laughed and shook my head. The guy had chutzpah, that's for sure. But when I stopped laughing, I realized what kind of damage this guy could do. I jumped on the phone and called an emergency meeting with the president of Ticketron. I walked into his huge office and handed him the file.

"What?" he exclaimed. "Craig's an impostor? And he's so damn good! He's the best attorney we've ever had. Got him on a case right now! What should I do?"

"I don't know. I have a problem myself. We're in business together," I said with a rueful smile.

"This is crazy. I wouldn't have suspected him in a million years."

"You and me both. But I take full responsibility. I made the recommendation . . ."

"That's okay," he said, waving off my mea culpa. "These things happen."

"You're going to have to deal with it as soon as possible," I advised. "Craig could be putting your corporation in jeopardy. There could be all kinds of legal problems in having your firm represented by a bogus attorney. You're going to have to get someone else."

"Yeah, I guess so."

We eventually decided to let Craig finish the case he was working on before Ticketron cut him loose. Naturally, he won it.

Unlike Ticketron, I didn't have the desire, or the patience, to wait. I marched into Craig's bustling law firm and dropped the file on his desk.

"Hey, Octavio, what's cooking?" he said, grinning up at me. His ultra-bright smile vanished the moment he saw the first page.

"I was wondering when you were going to discover this," he said sheepishly.

"If you were wondering that, why'd you do it?" I asked him. He averted his eyes and hung his head in what appeared to be genuine shame.

"I'm sorry. You may not believe it, but I really am."

"Look, if you would have just leveled with me, things could have been different. Whoever, whatever you are, your talent and ability is real. But how could you let me compromise myself with my clients by recommending you? You put my business at risk. My word, my reputation is the most important thing I have, Craig. I can't forgive that kind of betrayal."

"I'm sorry."

"I am too, Craig."

With that, I stormed out of his office, never to see him again. To his credit, he returned all the money to the account the next day.

I was too pissed off to probe any further or find out what the deal was with Craig. He probably went to law school, but either dropped out, ran short of tuition money, couldn't pass the bar after graduation, or whatever. Then again, for all I knew, he may not have even graduated from high school.

I don't know what happened to Craig after that, but he's probably still out there somewhere, hanging out a shingle and dazzling satisfied clients with his legal brilliance. To this day I miss his advice. Despite his duplicity, he was probably the most honest attorney I've ever worked with.

THE JOURNEY NORTH

Throughout the previous chapters, I've made reference to various friends and associates around the world who possess highly specialized investigative skills. I've also mentioned trusted contacts inside the CIA and various other international intelligence agencies. These operatives, in many instances, proved to be critical cogs in the successful completion of my most memorable cases. How, one might ask, did I come to know these interesting characters?

I was born in Mexico City in 1941. Although we weren't rich, my father, Gabriel, was a prominent government attorney who at one time worked for the Chief Justice of the Mexican Supreme Court. Both my grandfather, Rafael Garcia Pena, and great-grandfather, Angel Garcia Pena, were attorneys who distinguished themselves as honorable men in a country that isn't noted for its strict adherence to the law. They were descendants of the original Spanish conquistadors, and not only carried those dignified bearings with them throughout their lives, but instilled them into generation after generation of Penas.

Despite my father's position and influence, we weren't by any means one of Mexico's ruling families. Government attorneys like my father are paid a good wage that enables them to lead a decent middle-class life. My father, as his father before him, did not inherit or buy his position with the government. He earned it through hard work and ability, qualities he emphasized with his children.

My mother, Ruth, had an equally colorful background. She was born in Mexico to an Irish-American father and a Mexican mother. My grandfather Richard Ray came to Mexico as an employee of an American mining company.

Mom and Dad made for an interesting blend. My family—there were five of us, three brothers and two sisters—is equal parts Mexican, American, Spanish, and Irish. For me, like many Mexicans, it was the stories of the magical country north of the border that I found to be the most enchanting. America, the fabled "land of the free," was said to be a stark contrast to the venality and arbitrary brutality of Mexico.

But America could have been on another planet as far as my family was concerned. We were Mexicans, take it or leave it, and my father never expressed any interest in pulling up stakes and going for the gold on the new frontier.

Because my father knew that the surrounding society wasn't too dependent on the rule of law, he raised his five children with a strict Catholic hand. As I grew older, however, the contrast between my internal family values and the external influences of a country spinning madly out of control began to tear at me.

At school, I was a good student (my father constantly drilled the following lesson into our heads: "The most important thing in life is what you put in your head"), but I was never held in the same esteem as my richer classmates. There was a clear-cut caste system in effect at the Instituto Patria, one that I found demeaning. Unlike the rich kids' fathers, my father couldn't make large contributions to the Jesuits at the school, contributions designed to boost grades and purchase special favors for their children.

One day, tired of being treated like a second-class student, I confronted my father.

"Let me tell you a story," he said after sitting me down in his spartan office one afternoon after I returned home from school. "When I was working for the Chief Justice, some lawyers introduced themselves to me one afternoon as I was leaving the office. They represented a large American company in Mexico, and they wanted me to influence the justices. There was a decision they wanted passed. They felt the decision would help their business interests. They offered me a lot of money to assist them. And you know what I did?"

"You refused."

"I refused. But the story doesn't end there. These attorneys eventually went right to the judges with their offer. My boss asked me to change the decision. I knew what had happened, so I refused again."

"You were doing a lot of refusing."

"I guess so," he laughed. "But this time, I not only refused, I resigned. I couldn't work for the man anymore. Do you understand what I'm telling you here?"

"That I should refuse to go to school?" I said with a twinkle in my eye.

"No," he said. "It was wrong to take the money from the Americans. And it was wrong to look the other way when my boss did it. Just like it's wrong for the fathers of those other boys at school to pay so their children can receive awards and privileges they didn't earn, awards and privileges that you deserve. But that's life here in Mexico. Either you succumb to it and lose your soul, or you fight it and stay true to yourself. Always remember, when you cheat someone, you cheat yourself worse."

I knew my dad was right, but being right can sure be frustrating, especially for a kid who keeps getting the short end of the stick.

A family upheaval soon pushed the problems of Mexico into the background. My parents decided to divorce, a rarity at the time among Mexican Catholics. On top of everything else, the Mexican elite can be very morally judgmental when it comes to marriage. Being the child of a broken home was yet another burden to carry on my young shoulders.

In a court ruling that would have made King Solomon wince, my father was given custody of the three boys while my mother kept my two sisters. Once in total control of my fate, Dad yanked me from the Jesuit school and tossed me into the concrete jungle of the rough-and-tumble Mexican public school system. "El Jefe," as we called Dad, wanted to toughen me up.

Now, instead of being a poor boy in a rich boy's school, I was the rich kid in the raw world of a Mexican public school. Secundaria Numero Tres—as it was called—was populated by the off-spring of the urban middle and angry lower classes. I was taunted and goaded into fights nearly every day. My father got his wish. It was sink or swim, survival of the fittest. I can't remember how many bloody noses and black eyes I got.

Yet, looking back, I have to hand it to my father. The hard-knocks education I received was one I've never forgotten. I learned to fight back until I became pretty good with my fists. And as I fought, I began to realize that in this violent environment, survival was based upon the strength of one's character, the mettle in a person's backbone, the power in one's punches, and the development of a cunning street intelligence.

Ironically, a person was judged at this school based upon his own actions and abilities—the Darwinian equal opportunity I had sought at my coddled rich-boy school.

By graduation, I'd been exposed to the entire spectrum of Mexican society, a unique educational experience among Mexicans, who tend to stay among their own. As I matured, I respected my father more for turning away from the soul-destroying, corrupt lifestyle that could have afforded us the same luxuries our Polanco neighbors enjoyed—chauffeurs, swimming pools, fashionable clothing, fancy cars, and all the other materialistic toys money can buy. I began to understand why my public school cohorts wanted to clean my clock every day because of the few things I did have.

When I was seventeen, and ready to go out on my own to college, El Jefe sat me down again.

"Octavio, it's time to educate you about your country. It's not a pleasant story."

"Why?"

"We live in a land thoroughly corroded by corruption. We only have one real political party, the PRI (Partido Revolucionario Institucional), and they control the economy. Every six years, the sitting president selects a new president. The president's basic function is to give jobs and government contracts to his buddies in the business world. There is no political opposition, unless you count the Communist insurgents, and they're very weak."

My father continued to put words to many of the things I'd witnessed but didn't yet understand.

"We have a poisoned society. There's nothing remotely democratic about it. What we need here is the rule of a just law. That's the only way we can save Mexico. That's why I want you to study law, as your grandfather and great-grandfather did before you. Our family has always depended upon and acted upon the rule of law."

Instead, I went to college, got my degree, and enrolled in law school like a dutiful Pena male.

"Remember, Octavio," my dad beamed. "A law practice represents one of the few ways to achieve legitimate prestige in our society."

All well and good, only I didn't want to become an attorney! I wanted to do something different than my forefathers. I wanted it to be exciting. And I wanted it to be far from Mexico.

I longed for that grandiose, yet unspecific goal enough to do everything but stand up to my father. Off to law school I trudged, studying torts, courts, and reports—being bored out of my gourd. Outside the classroom, however, it was a different story. I fell in with a crowd of upperclassmen and tagged along to their parties, cafes, and restaurants. One evening, at one of these hangouts, something happened that changed my life.

A group of us went to a cafe noted for spirited political debates. At the time, many Mexican university students were inflamed with the brand of left-wing revolutionary rhetoric that infuses college campuses throughout the world. I didn't agree with the Communist plan to cure Mexico's ills, but I enjoyed the debate. At the cafe that evening, the speeches, arguments, and vitriol were louder and more passionate than ever before.

"Castro is a swine," spat a young man with a different accent. "He will be worse than Batista!"

"No, you're wrong. Castro cleaned up the corrupt, capitalist, pro-American leeches who were sucking the blood out of the Cuban people!" countered a young Mexican.

The argument escalated into a shouting match. The radical leftist crowd far outnumbered the anti-Castro student, who turned out to be a Cuban recently displaced by Castro's victory.

I stayed out of it, but found myself agreeing with the Cuban. And I liked the guy. He refused to back down an inch despite the flack he was catching from all sides. He would have survived Secundaria Numero Tres, that's for sure.

When things cooled, I took the opportunity to introduce myself.

"Hi, my name is Octavio. Don't listen to them," I said, jerking my thumb toward the ranting leftists. "I'm with you."

The student smiled and took me aside.

"You and a lot of others, my friend. My name is Martin. Glad to meet you," he said, offering me his hand.

Martin and I quickly became tight. He brought me home to

dine on black beans and rice and meet his family, an interesting group. His father and two older brothers spit anti-Castro venom with every breath. But they weren't just dissatisfied expats looking for a sympathetic ear.

Martin and his brothers introduced me into the quickly growing colony of anti-Castro Cuban exiles. I soon found myself attending secret meetings of counterrevolutionaries who were diligently planning to go on the offensive against the hated Cuban dictator.

Despite being an outsider, I found these meetings exciting. Planning a counterrevolution sure beat law school. By the time one of Martin's brothers, known as "El Cubano," asked me to join them in the good fight, I was more than ready to sign on.

My initial assignments were all the same. I was dispatched to various locations around the city to shadow Cuban exiles suspected of being double agents for Fidel Castro. I was then to report their activities to El Cubano. I didn't even know what activities I should be watching for, and El Cubano didn't feel the need to tell me. Still, I found the assignment extremely exciting and worked at it with a youthful fervor that probably would have earned me straight A's if I'd stayed in school. I gave detailed reports of my assigned targets' comings and goings, and even went as far as getting close enough to overhear bits and pieces of their conversations.

One day, El Cubano summoned me to meet him in front of Mexico City's Hilton Hotel. The first thing I noticed when he arrived was that he was carrying bundles of expensive silk stockings.

"What are those for?"

"Come with me. You'll find out."

We strolled into the hotel's lobby and approached the hotel telephone switchboard. After a brief moment of finagling, El Cubano ushered me inside the room. I watched in amazement as he greeted several female operators with hugs and kisses, then showered them with the gifts. He chatted for a while, then promised to be back with more goodies.

"Okay, are you trying to teach me how to pick up women?" I asked. El Cubano laughed at my naivete.

"If you want to watch people, the best way to keep an eye on them in a hotel is to get the staff to do it for you. And you can't bully these people into doing what you want. You have to charm them. If you want to know if someone has been in your room, leave a nice tip and a nice word for the hotel maid. That's because they know everything that goes on. Understand?"

"I'm starting to. So why here, at this hotel?"

"Upstairs in Room 1260 there's a nest of Fidel's dirty spies. Now, thanks to my giving personality, I have access to their telephone conversations, hard records of their calls, and I know what their messages are and who they're from. With that information, I can determine who's a friend, and who's a pig spy."

We walked in silence for a while down the boulevard, enjoying the evening. When we reached a small park, El Cubano stopped me.

"Octavio, you've done a good job for us in Mexico City. I've thought a lot about you, and talked to some people I know. How would you like to work in the United States? In Miami?"

How would I? Getting to America had been my dream since I was a boy, when I'd hopped a bus to El Paso, Texas, and tried to enlist in the Marine Corps at the ripe age of fifteen. (They kicked me right back to Mexico!)

El Cubano's offer was almost too good to be true. I'd be given what had to be an exciting job, I'd get out of Mexico, and I could kiss law school *adios*!

"I'll consider it," I downplayed, trying not to appear overly excited.

Over the next two months, as I prepared for my departure, I began to look at El Cubano with new eyes. He appeared far too intelligent and skilled for his age and background, and his operation was well financed. He had to be getting help somewhere. That somewhere was probably the famous American CIA, *La Compañía*, as it's called. (The letters "Cia" are the Mexican equivalent of Inc. or Ltd., signifying a corporation, and hence the name for the American intelligence outfit.)

The more they trained me, the more I became convinced that El Cubano had a very rich uncle—Uncle Sam. This was no on-the-fly operation. Everything followed a precisely mapped-out pattern. I was told that my departure from Mexico would have to be a dead-of-night kind of thing, and I wasn't to tell anyone, not even my family. The plan was for me to simply vanish from Mexico and resurface in Miami.

"It's time," El Cubano whispered one evening. I felt chills shoot through my body as I waited for his next words. "You'll be leaving soon. Are you ready?"

"Yes!" I gulped.

"I assume you're curious about what you'll be doing there?"

"It has crossed my mind."

"Okay, my associate here is going to lay it out for you," he said, tossing the ball to a Cuban pilot who was part of our group.

"As I'm sure you already suspect, you'll be assisting the CIA in Miami," the pilot began. "You won't be working directly for *La Compañía*, but you'll be on salary.

"You'll pose as an anticommunist Mexican student who wants to join the Cuban anti-Castro movement . . ."

"That shouldn't be difficult," I smiled, knowing how close to the truth that really was.

"It gets tougher," the pilot laughed. "You'll be linking up with those planning to violently overthrow Castro so we exiles can return to our homes and businesses. What you'll do is just listen to these people. See what they do, who they meet. We are very worried that Castro's worms have infiltrated Miami's expatriate community and are undermining the counterrevolution. You're going to help us determine if our fears are correct."

"What do I look for?"

"Anything. Everything. Don't worry about specifics. Just tell us what you see and hear, and we'll know what to do from there."

The constant evasiveness annoyed me, but I had visions of Miami dancing in my head, so I didn't protest.

"I'll give you the number of your control contact in Miami," the pilot added. "You'll report to him and call in on a prearranged schedule."

I felt a bit uneasy as I walked home that evening. This wasn't what I expected. I would be left in the dark, as usual, and I'd have to report to some mysterious control. I didn't like the sound of that. The word *control* carried sinister implications.

Then again, it was logical I'd have to report to someone. And Miami was calling! No little nagging doubts were going to stop me from going to the land of the free.

America would indeed prove to be glorious, but my job as a spy turned out to be psychologically grinding, rife with danger, and far less glamorous than I had envisioned.

I had little trouble joining the rebels in Miami and getting to know their leaders. The Cubans dubbed me "Mexico" and welcomed me into their circle. We received combat training in CIA-operated camps in the Florida Everglades and in Nicaragua. Twice I went on exciting missions inside Cuba itself. We landed on the northern coast and delivered guns to the underground operating in the country.

Still, what grated on me were the layers of secrecy on my own side. My control, an exacting, tight-lipped, middle-aged macho bureaucrat with dark hair and a darker tan, never offered an iota more than the minimum he felt I needed to know. I understood that this was because of security, but there comes a time when a person should be trusted. The closemouthed nature of The Company greatly offended my personal sense of honor.

A couple of months into my Miami adventure, I was called in and handed my first long-term undercover assignment.

"We want you to get close to this man," my control said, pointing to some photographs he had spread across his spartan desk. "His name is Luis. He used to be a commander in the Cuban rebel army with Fidel. He was the same rank as Fidel, and he's about the same age."

"What do I look for?"

"You know what to do," the control answered brusquely.

Great. Another blind, wild Cuban goose chase.

I spent the next nine months eating, breathing, and practically living with the respected Cuban commander. We became so close that he treated me like a surrogate son. I knew him inside out— when he felt lonely, when he made love to his wife, when his hopes for returning to Cuba peaked and when they waned.

As the weeks passed and our personal bond tightened, I started to hate myself for what I was doing—whatever the hell that was!

Luis and his wife, Tita, were honorable people whom I grew to admire and respect. Unlike many other Cuban exiles, he wasn't driven by power or money. He had a single goal: kick Castro's double-dealing, Soviet-supported butt out of Cuba!

The more I got to know Luis, the more I hated reporting on his activities. I began to feel that I was betraying his trust. At night, I could hear my father's words about honor and integrity bouncing around my head. For the first time, they really meant something to me.

I learned then what most covert operatives eventually come to realize: Once you go under, you begin to sympathize with the target. That was especially true in my case, since my target didn't appear to have any flaws or undesirable traits. If Luis was a Castro spy, then it was time for me to hightail it back to law school, because I was the dumbest man on the planet.

After nine months, I couldn't stand it anymore. The daily pressure of my personal betrayal of Luis was becoming unbearable. I was either going to quit, confess to Luis what I was doing, or both. I couldn't deal with the confession, so I decided to quit. I told my control to essentially "take this job and shove it" and hitched a ride to New York with a friend.

(I'd left Luis in the lurch, and that ate at me. I wouldn't be able to live with myself until I made things right. I returned to Miami to talk to Luis several years later, only to find that it was too late. Luis had been killed in a raid against Castro while delivering arms in the northern part of Cuba.)

The long year working undercover acted to temper me. It stripped away my illusions about espionage in general, and the CIA in particular. Spying was a dirty business. To carry it off, you have to believe strongly in what you are doing, in yourself, and be absolutely certain that you're working for the good guys.

I also learned how not to handle operatives. Undercover agents must be groomed for their specific functions, treated with respect during and afterward, and carefully observed for cracks in their psyche and other signs of stress. It's a tough job, and many can't take the long-term pressure.

These were the areas where I felt the CIA failed, and failed badly.

Despite my disillusionment with the spy business, there was one giant plus to my experience—being in the good ol' USA. Now that was everything, and more, than I expected it would be.

This feeling crystallized one day outside Miami when I saw the flashing bubblegum lights of a police car in my rearview mirror. My mouth became dry and my heart pounded. I began to fumble for money in my pants pocket, wondering how much I'd have to pay to keep from being thrown in jail.

"I see you're a Mexican national," the smiling officer said after checking my license. "I'll give you a break this time, but slow down."

That was it! No bribe. No ticket. No being dragged kicking and screaming to the jailhouse.

"What a great country!" I exclaimed as I motored on my way. I had more rights in the United States as a faceless immigrant than I did in Mexico as the son of a Supreme Court attorney!

All this reverberated in my mind as I made plans to return home to Mexico. My life was at a crossroads in every sense of the word, personally, professionally, geographically, and educationally.

Back home, I wasn't sure what I wanted to do, but I knew what I didn't want. No more law school, spying, controls spoon-feeding me tiny nuggets of information, classes of any kind, or living the life my father wanted. It was time to be my own man.

Without the law degree, however, that wasn't going to be easy. Good jobs are hard to come by in Mexico, and any shortcoming gets you quickly weeded out. The only chance I had at independence and success was to start my own business.

The food service industry intrigued me, so I started there. Using the money I'd saved from the CIA, I founded a company called Capormex, with Roberto "Chaparrin" Hidalgo, a friend I'd met in New York. The business consisted of small coffee carts laden with coffee, pastries, sandwiches, beverages, cigarettes, and other sundries that we had someone wheel around office buildings. It was a bit of a comedown from being a CIA spy, but at least I was my own boss. Or so I thought.

Capormex quickly grew in scope and service. I went from one cart in one building to four operating in several. I hired several sunny-faced young people to cheerfully push the carts up and down the floors. For a while, things were good. The profits were healthy, and I was truly my own man, beholden to no one.

It didn't last. Coca-Cola Mexico was the largest tenant in the biggest building we serviced. One day, one of their men came down and told me nicely that they would appreciate it if I would only sell Coca-Cola products inside the building. I had contracts with other food vendors, so I refused. The man insisted. I insisted right back. Within a week, my contract for the building was terminated! Coca-Cola snapped its fat fingers and we were bounced out on the street.

I seethed from the injustice of it all. But when I cooled down, I had the sense to realize that I was sometimes my own worst enemy. My obstinate pride and my inability to play the game by Mexican rules led to my downfall.

Thinking that things might be different outside the urban jungle of Mexico City, I sold the food cart business and ventured out to Cuernavaca, the capital of the state of Morelos in south central Mexico, and a popular resort area for the well-heeled, including a large contingent of American retirees. In Cuernavaca, my upbringing and general education helped me snag a coveted position as a motor oil distributor for Esso. As the cliché goes, what I lacked in experience I made up for in hustle, energy, and tenacity. It was a good career-track job, one that allowed me to advance up the ladder if I worked hard and kept my nose clean. It could provide a lifetime of security. It also bored me out of my mind.

Worse still, even out in the country—miles from the capital—nothing changed. The poison of corruption touched all facets of Mexican life. Every gas dealer in every one-horse town wanted a kickback. Every distributor lusted for action on the side. The local police needed their palms greased to guard our oil trucks—or else. The tax assessor, electrician, trucker, phone installer, and pump jockey demanded under-the-table deals.

Everything was just as my father had described, not just in Mexico City, but from one end of the country to the other. And no matter how often it happened, how many palms I greased and kickbacks I was forced to pay, it still turned my stomach. Wrong is wrong, even if everybody is doing it.

I thought back to my father's most compelling advice. He warned me never to desensitize myself to the corruption.

"Once you do that, you're lost," he admonished. "Always fight it."

That's why he was so adamant about my becoming an attorney. It was the only profession in which he felt someone in Mexico without political connections could actually thrive. Not that attorneys themselves aren't corrupt. As everyone knows, they're often the worst offenders. It was just that in the legal profession, it wasn't necessary to be corrupt to eke out a decent living. (Even though I didn't become an attorney, my younger brother Gabriel did, and is a partner in the Mexican firm Garcia Pena y Gutierrez, carrying on the Pena tradition.)

One afternoon, my feelings about Mexico reached the breaking point. Driving to Mexico City for a sales trip, I was pulled over by the "Fiscal Police." This is the equivalent of the IRS, only they take a more active posture in Mexico. The financial cops wanted to check to see if I had paid my automobile taxes. What they really wanted was a bribe. If I refused, they'd make up some lame excuse and confiscate my car—like they've done to thousands of defenseless motorists for countless years

When the officers walked up to the window, I brightened for a moment. I had gone to school with one of them. Maybe he'd let me off the hook!

Yeah, and maybe Coca-Cola would now let me sell Pepsi in its offices. My old pal was the one who put on the squeeze.

"If you don't have the cash," he said, "I'll take a check." A check!

I immediately grabbed a pen and wrote out the three-figure bribe. As I scribbled, all I could think about was the smiling cop in Miami who let me slide without even a ticket.

The next day, I marched into the U.S. Embassy and filed for residency in the United States. It was time to leave Mexico for good.

LIFE, DEATH, AND REBIRTH

I ARRIVED IN NEW YORK hoping to fulfill an old dream I had of opening a restaurant. Unlike a lot of recent immigrants, I was pretty close to achieving it. The CIA, Capormex, and Esso all paid well, and I lived modestly, so I had been able to save some money. It wasn't quite enough to fulfill my dream immediately, but it was a good start. I'd have to get a job first and save some more.

The question was, what kind of job? I certainly had a unique résumé for a twenty-five-year-old. I'd worked undercover for the CIA, participated in covert missions inside Cuba, owned a small food service company, and sold oil for Esso. As diverse as it was, I couldn't find anyone looking for a person with those eclectic skills in the want ads.

But I did find something in the *New York Times* that sounded intriguing.

"New York investigative firm seeks part-time undercover operatives. Good pay. Interested parties should call 212-687-8726."[*]

My first reaction was, "Part-time? Who are they kidding?"

---

[*]This number is still listed to Lynch International—the name of my company after I bought out Lynch's East Coast operations.

Undercover agents usually work twenty-four hours a day. When you go "under" you stay under. You don't punch a clock and shift back and forth from drug dealer to church deacon.

I shook my head and moved down the reams of classifieds, wondering which tiny ad was destined to alter the course of my life. Nothing struck me. My eyes kept going back to the investigator position. Given the paucity of other opportunities, it looked more and more interesting. And I wanted that restaurant. Finally, I picked up the phone and called.

The receptionist identified the firm as "The John T. Lynch Company" and boasted that it was the largest private investigative group in America. That piqued my interest. By the time the office manager came to the phone, I was warming up to the position.

"No offense, but I don't think a person your age who speaks English with a heavy Mexican accent is what we are looking for," the manager curtly said.

I wasn't about to be blown off that easily.

"I've worked undercover for the CIA, and I've had experience infiltrating organizations. Maybe you should reconsider?"

There was a brief pause.

"If that's true, maybe I should. Why don't you come by?"

I met the reluctant manager, Gerry Clarke, that same afternoon at his office inside the Pan Am Building. After discussing my experiences in Mexico, Miami, and Cuba, something odd happened. Clarke sat back and began to share some of his own adventures as a former military intelligence officer and FBI agent.

The minute he started spinning war stories and treating me like a trusted comrade, I knew I was in.

"When can you start?" he said, extending his hand.

"When do you need me?"

"Tomorrow."

"I'll be here."

Things proceeded quickly after that. Clarke put me right to work on an undercover assignment. The 3M paper products factory in Newark was experiencing a sticky problem. Hundreds of gigantic ten-foot rolls of Scotch tape were marching like tin soldiers out of their warehouse every month.

Anyone pinching something that big and cumbersome must have had a smooth and knowledgeable operation. I couldn't even imagine where a thief could fence a ten-foot roll of tape. Whoever was responsible was well versed in that specific market niche. That meant it was an inside job.

After some rapid-fire training, I materialized at the 3-M factory as a graveyard shift forklift driver. The manager wanted to introduce me to his informant inside the warehouse, one of the night-time janitors, but I begged off. I wanted to remain anonymous and reach my own conclusions. Without really knowing it, I was already practicing a cardinal rule of intelligence work: You can't trust other people's info—even the guy who hired you. You have to get your own take on the situation.

Perched in my little yellow truck, I kept my eyes open while loading and unloading various shipping crates. (My Spanish helped to break the ice with several night shift workers.) From the first night, I could sense that something strange was going on. Workers appeared and disappeared at regular intervals.

By the third night, I noticed that the vanishing acts began when the janitor arrived. It appeared as though the manager's big informant was the key. Ducking behind the boxes and pallets, I shadowed the man while keeping an eye on some of the more suspicious laborers. Aside from being laggard in their duties, their only unusual activity was that they spent an inordinate amount of time shooting the breeze with the garbage truck drivers.

The following night, I realized why. Hiding between some bulky wooden crates, I watched the janitor and his cohorts load two massive rolls of tape into an open bin garbage truck.

"No wonder 3-M couldn't stop this. The informant has his big paws in the till," I thought, marveling at the never-ending ingenuity of thieves. "They throw out the good with the bad!"

The janitor taught me a lesson that has stayed with me through more than twenty-five years of undercover work: The most likely suspects are the people on the inside, more often than not the very security people who are supposed to protect their companies!

Back across the border in upscale Manhattan, Mr. Clarke was impressed with my quick resolution of the Scotch tape caper.

"You have a very valuable intangible," he complimented. "You're cool undercover. That's something we can't teach."

Clarke backed up his praise by offering a full-time position. Despite the fact that I enjoyed catching bad guys, I held him off for nearly three years, preferring to work part-time while staying focused on opening the restaurant. That proved to be an elusive dream. Manhattan was going through a real estate explosion. Rents and start-up business expenses were skyrocketing. The harder I worked, the farther behind I was getting.

It didn't take a genius to figure out that I was rowing upstream, losing ground with every furious paddle. I was caught in a real estate whirlwind that wasn't about to slow down.

After a few more part-time undercover operations, I finally relented and went to work for the Lynch Company full-time. Initially, life as a full-time sleuth was pretty dismal. Instead of being able to pick and choose interesting cases as a part-timer, I now had to occupy a full day, five days a week. That led to mundane tasks like picking up VIPs at airports, following people around downtown, or gathering background research at the library.

Mostly, I waited for clients to call.

Boredom set in. It sure didn't have the excitement of wading through inlets along the Cuban coast to bring guns in, or the psychological risks of infiltrating the anti-Castro zealots in Miami. I began to wonder if maybe I had made a mistake. I had a choice. Either I bailed out, or I needed to find a way to make my job interesting.

One day, as I sat in the Pan Am Building and looked over the vista of midtown Manhattan, it dawned on me. Why not treat my job like it was any other business? I started doing something that's almost unheard of in the investigative industry. I began coldcalling potential clients, as if I were a salesman. All the old techniques from my first foray into business selling coffee and rolls in Mexico City came back to me.

"Hi," I'd say, walking into their offices. "My name is Octavio Pena from the John T. Lynch Company, the largest private investigative firm in America. I was wondering if you have any corporate security problems you'd like us to solve?"

Most executives were either startled or amused by my approach, but a few were intrigued. If anyone did have a problem that was eating away at their bottom line, my call hit home.

Borden was one of the first to respond to my boiler-room technique. The international milk and ice cream company was having trouble keeping their office equipment nailed down. The president took me up on my unsolicited offer and hired us to find out what was going on. What was going on was that the employees were looting the place like locusts, all with the help of Borden's lax, and mostly unqualified, security guards. (Proving again what would become an axiom to me: Check the "watchers" first.) After ferreting out the cancer, the grateful Borden president asked me to clean up his security operation.

I handled that assignment by replacing the mostly untrained and uneducated—therefore easily tempted—security guards with workers from the vast pool of recent immigrants. The eager newcomers were willing to put in long hours, were unwilling to risk their status in America by doing anything dishonest, and were usually more intelligent than most entry-level employees. Many of the immigrants had been professionals in their own countries, and were waiting to meet America's rigid educational and licensing requirements before they could qualify to practice their chosen professions. (A foreign doctor or lawyer can't just hop off the boat and set up a shingle in America. The recertification schooling alone is substantial. In many cases, they have to start from scratch.)

In addition, all immigrants must clear the Department of Immigration and Naturalization's criminal record investigation, which meant that the government was performing the tedious and expensive background checks for me.

My Statue of Liberty strategy succeeded beyond my wildest expectations. The news of Borden's innovative security operation spread like wildfire. Soon other large companies were calling me to similarly overhaul their decaying internal security. During the next six months, I rebuilt the protective branches of a half-dozen major firms, including PepsiCo, and raked in more than $1 million in billings for Lynch.

That's when I realized that investigative work was a business, just like any other, and should be treated as such.

I think John Lynch realized it, too. He soon rewarded me with a 10 percent ownership in the company (a figure that would jump to 35 percent over the years before I bought Lynch out completely in 1985). Within a few months of taking the job, I was making my fortune helping American companies battle the encroachment of the very thing I hated so much about Mexico—rampant social, moral, and corporate corruption.

The best part was that I got to hire a secretary. Once again I relied on the *New York Times* classifieds. And once again, the tiny print changed my life.

Grace Marvilli, an adventurous eighteen-year-old from Queens with light brown hair and dark, alluring eyes, was one of the scores of hopefuls who responded to my ad. Although she was inexperienced, her youthful exuberance and zest pushed her slim résumé to the top.

I had so much confidence in Grace's innate abilities that I got her involved in a tense undercover operation during her first week. The wife and toddler son of a Chinese restaurant magnate had been kidnapped. He suspected that it was one of his main business rivals, but wasn't sure. His attorney called me.

"We want, above all else, the safe return of his wife and child," the attorney explained. "Secondly, we want to know who's behind this."

The restaurant owner, Mr. Chen, filled me in on the person he thought was responsible, an apparently shady player in the garment industry named Wu Fong. That meant the kidnapping appeared to be more financially motivated than professional. Food and clothing aren't directly competitive, at least in my experience. However, business interests in Chinatown are often strangely interwoven, so there may have been a deeper connection. Regardless, the inner workings of Chinatown's economy, or these two men's personal history, weren't my concern.

Freeing his family was.

"When are you expecting his next call?" I asked.

"Tonight at ten. They're going to give the instructions for the money. Let me talk to my wife."

I didn't have much time. I had to come up with a plan immediately. The safe return of Mr. Chen's family depended on it.

I contacted the suspect, pretended to be a Mexican businessman, and offered him a killer deal to export his sweatshop clothing to Mexico. That naturally got his attention. I pushed him under a pretext that I had to have dinner with him that evening.

"Grace, I know you've only been here a week, but would you like a firsthand taste of what we do?"

"Sure! What?"

"I'm trying to infiltrate a kidnapping ring. I need a dinner date."

"Kidnappers?" she said, suddenly less eager.

"Don't worry. It'll be okay. This isn't the dangerous part. That comes later."

"Okay! What do I do?"

"Just act dumb and look great," I laughed. "You know, like a gangster's moll."

"A doll?"

"No. Moll. You'll learn."

The dinner date turned out to be edgier than I anticipated. From the moment the man and his crew strolled in, I knew that shirts and blouses weren't their main interest. I also knew why their reach extended into my client's restaurant—and into his house.

Wu Fong was a "Tong"—a member of the Chinese Mafia. That explained why the restaurant tycoon's mouthpiece came to me instead of the police. The Tong can be nasty to deal with.

In true gangster style, Fong, a tough, muscular man, ordered big, talked bigger, and ate heartily. It never ceases to amaze me how similar all these organized crime guys are, regardless of ethnicity: fancy suits, sleek cars, beautiful women, macho, tough-guy postures, obvious, I'm-a-crook-so-don't-mess-with-me stances.

Among the delicacies Mr. Fong ordered were racks of oysters on the half-shell, which he insisted that we eat. I was used to them, and I slurped a few down. Grace was foreign to the pleasure of the raw, slimy shellfish. This was her first test under fire. She held her nose and gulped, hiding her revulsion.

That scored big points with me. The lady was a trooper.

After dinner, the group retreated to a room I had rented at the Americana Hotel on Seventh Avenue. When I excused myself to go to the bathroom, the muscular Chinese mobster made his move.

"You're a pretty woman. Whatever he's paying you for tonight, I'll pay you twice!"

It was another lesson in gangsterology. In their eyes, every woman's either a whore or a gold-digging opportunist—and most of all property to be bought, sold, and controlled.

At the time, it was a lesson that shot way over Grace's teenage head. She thought he was in the market for a new secretary.

"Let's go out somewhere and party," I suggested, picking up on the uneasiness as I exited the lavatory. I didn't want Fong to think Grace was part of my offering, and I needed to stall for time.

We alighted at the Hawaii Kai, a tropically decorated night spot near the hotel. Although Mr. Fong appeared to be having a fine time, he continually glanced at his watch.

"Are you on a schedule?" I asked.

"I do have another pressing appointment," he said. "We'll talk business tomorrow."

It was 9:30 P.M. I wondered what kind of pressing appointment he had that late in the evening. Why would he suddenly withdraw from what could be a highly lucrative new partnership before we really had a chance to get down to brass tacks? Perhaps he had to make a million-dollar extortion call.

"He's gotta be our guy," I whispered to Grace.

Anticipating such a departure, I had arranged to have the Chinese gangster followed the moment he left the bar. He was tracked to an apartment building in Queens.

"He got off on the fifth floor," my associate reported.

Grace and I hightailed it to Queens. We entered a building across the street, climbed out on the roof, and scoured the fifth-floor windows with binoculars. Sure enough, I spotted a Chinese woman and small child who fit the description of the restaurateur's wife and son.

When I informed Mr. Chen, he was adamant that we not involve the police. That wasn't surprising. He wanted his wife back with minimal cause for retribution from the Tong.

Mr. Chen arrived shortly thereafter. We confronted the outnumbered Tong henchmen and let Chen work out the details of the exchange with his surprised countryman. As Chen predicted, Wu Fong the Tong was silently appreciative that we didn't call the SWAT team on him. He turned the traumatized woman and child over without a fight.

"Wow, that was exciting!" Grace said afterward. "I'd like to go on more operations."

"You handled yourself well tonight," I praised her. "I won't hesitate to use you again."

I didn't hesitate to do a lot of things with Grace. We spent hundreds of hours together posing as lovers, tailing people, investigating crimes, and handling the security guards. I increased her responsibilities to the point where she ended up managing Lynch's entire 250-employee security guard operation.

Our mutual romantic attraction led us to the marriage altar in 1975. We've been inseparable ever since.

That, however, is getting ahead of things. When I first hired Grace, the security side of Lynch's operation was expanding rapidly. It became so profitable that the company's New York headquarters was billing nearly as much as all the branch offices combined. True to my maxim that the investigative business has to operate like any other, most of my time was consumed with management functions, including financial analysis, accounting, and operations. I was learning vast amounts, gaining valuable insights into the business world.

Soon Grace and I were overseeing 300 employees, along with managing—to some degree—the 200 to 300 investigations that poured into Lynch's offices nationwide. I continued my concept of hiring refugees and recent immigrants as security guards, and built one of the most professional and trusted forces in the industry. Six years after emigrating from Mexico, my life, on the surface, seemed perfect. In addition to the guards and the investigations, I owned a steak house in Manhattan, had a great apartment in New York, drove a fancy new car, and was about to fulfill my dream of becoming an American citizen. I had also just started seriously romancing my future wife. And yet something wasn't in synch.

Making a lot of money is fine, but it began to leave me feeling restless. Success, as they say, can be its own worst enemy. After considerable self-evaluation, I concluded that what was missing from my life was a sense of challenge. I needed more action and less pencil-pushing. I wanted bigger, more exciting cases, where I could match wits with the smartest criminals in the world. I wanted to redefine what I was doing, and take it to the next level. The term "private detective" always gave me pause. To me, it evoked the seedy image of a man reeking of stale cigarettes and coffee, wrapped in a rumpled overcoat, padding his bill with bogus hourly billings, and tailing an unfaithful wife or husband.

In short, I wanted to tackle big, intractable problems, the kind of problems that no one else could solve.

Sometimes you should count your blessings and be careful what you wish for, because that's when fate tossed me the biggest challenge of my life.

I was mulling over my dissatisfaction one cold winter night as I sped south from New York to an early morning meeting with Frank Rizzo, the famed Philadelphia police chief. I needed to brief the tough cop about a sting operation I'd set up in the City of Brotherly Love to catch some thieves who were stealing millions of gallons of milk and ice cream from Borden. After spending a tiresome evening managing my restaurant, I elected to drive to Philadelphia without any sleep.

The trip from New York gave me a chance to think about the changes I wanted to make. As I rode through the night, taking the long way to Philly, my mind wandered. My last memory of that early morning was passing Allentown, Pennsylvania, the bleak steel town singer Billy Joel would later immortalize. I started nodding off. That's when I made the stupidest mistake of my life. Instead of pulling over to catch a few winks, I tried to bull my way through.

No go. I fell dead asleep at the wheel inside a 2,000-pound needle-nosed Jaguar XKE sports coupe hurtling down a dark highway.

I have no memory of the horrible squeal as the Jag spun out of control, or the thunderous crunch as a truck smashed into it. The truck's driver, the ultimate Good Samaritan, ran over and held my head while I lay bleeding and broken in the twisted wreckage.

"Don't worry, help is on the way!" I heard the driver say as I struggled with consciousness. "Hold on! Come on, you're gonna be all right." The guy repeated the words "hold on" over and over as he sat next to me, clutching my chest with his arm. Glancing down across my body, I saw a sea of red, then passed out.

While unconscious, I began to drown in my own blood. I would have died if not for the extraordinary efforts of the truck driver. Realizing I was choking to death, he whipped out a penknife and sliced a hole in my neck so I could breathe. How he had the knowledge, wherewithal, and sheer guts to do that, I don't know, but it saved my life. (After the accident I tried to track down my Good Samaritan, but he wished to remain anonymous. I respected his wishes, but if he is reading this book, here's a belated thank-you.)

At the hospital, the roll call of my injuries was not pretty. I had a ruptured spleen, a fractured skull, a broken jaw, five broken ribs, a punctured lung, and a badly shattered left arm.

Suddenly the pain vanished and I felt an odd, peaceful sensation. I glanced down and saw an orderly wheeling a person into the operating room. Looking closer, I realized that it was me! Somehow my spirit had left my body. I watched with fascination as the doctors cut the blood-soaked clothes from my mangled torso, which seemed to lie a few feet below me.

"We're losing him," I heard someone say. "We're losing him. No! No! He's gone!"

I was bathed in such tranquillity that the disquieting statement didn't faze me. The weird sense of serenity continued as I watched the nurses and doctors frantically attempt to revive my body. Soon I began to feel another presence in the room, floating near me. I was aware enough to remember that the date was December 12th, the Feast day of the Virgin of Guadalupe, the patron saint of Mexico. I knew that it was her presence I felt, and that she would protect me.

I watched the doctors and nurses jam tubes into my mouth and work feverishly on my broken frame. As they did, my spiritual awareness began to fade until I blacked out. The last thing I felt as my soul returned to my body was the comforting glow of the Virgin of Guadalupe.

My initial thought upon awakening several days later was that I was paralyzed. That was followed by the first of a series of horrible shocks. I tried to call someone, but the air just whistled out of my throat!

I had no idea what was going on, just that I couldn't move or talk. Thankfully, a doctor soon appeared.

"Here, put your finger over the hole in your neck, like this," he instructed, taking my hand. With the tracheotomy opening covered, I found my voice.

"What, what happened to me? What's wrong? Am I paralyzed?"

"No, you're going to be okay," the doctor smiled. "You were in an automobile accident. We were worried there for a while, but you pulled through. The worst injury is to your left arm. The bones were shattered and you may have some severe nerve damage. You might not be able to use it again."

I instantly tried to move the damaged appendage, but couldn't. Even though that was a frightening feeling, I felt a strange sense of confidence and determination.

"I'll be okay," I announced to the doctor. "I'll get everything working back to normal."

"I'm sure you will," the doctor said, chuckling. "We also thought you might have some brain damage, but I can see that doesn't appear to be the case."

My impatience to heal, however, resulted in the first postaccident disaster. Anxious to get out of the hospital and rocket down the road to recovery, I was discharged over my doctors' protests and immediately developed pneumonia. I promised the doctors, and myself, that I'd try to take it slower.

The recovery was indeed slow, and painful as well. The doctors had to rebreak my jaw and graft over the tracheotomy incision so I could get my voice back.

When it came to the arm, however, the doctors couldn't offer much hope. They advised me to learn to live with it, or, to be more precise, without it.

That was not acceptable. I'd been looking for a challenge, and my left arm became it. After several "no's" from pessimistic doctors all along the East Coast, I finally found one courageous enough to tackle the extensive repair job. Dr. Jacob Katz, Director of Orthopedics at Mount Sinai Hospital in New York, was the kind of confident, never-say-die optimist that's a breath of fresh air in any profession. He agreed to fortify the shattered bones with pins and screws, and perform the delicate microsurgery that could spur the regeneration of the damaged nerves.

"I can give you a start," he explained. "But the rest will be up to you. The rehabilitation and your willpower are the key."

A start was all I needed. Aside from the extensive exercise program, I forced myself to do everything with my weakened left arm. I drove with it, wrote with it, and even learned to shoot with it. There were ups and downs, but eventually, after nine months, it stabilized at 95 percent of my original strength and mobility.

More importantly, the physical reclamation led to a mental and professional metamorphosis. The accident and near-death experience gave me the courage to steer a new course for my career. I stopped charging by the hour, instead insisting upon a minimum retainer whether I worked one or forty hours, and a large bonus if a case was successfully resolved. This infused me with a winner-take-all mentality that pumped new life into my assignments. At the same time, I realized that in order to reel in the really big cases, I had to refine my professional presentation even more than I already had, and learn the nuances of the American business world. For that, I needed help.

I searched for a mentor with experience in the upper levels of the corporate world. He or she would become my personal advisor and assist me in my quest to move up the investigative ladder.

I'd struck gold twice with the *New York Times* classifieds, securing a great job and greater soon-to-be wife, so it was no surprise that I cast my fate with the small print again. "Successful emigre businessman seeks mentor to help him deepen his understanding of the American corporate world . . ." began my call for assistance.

Among the fifty or so responses to my "Help Wanted" ad was a terse letter from a man named Roger Burman. He stated that he had retired from a Fortune 100 company and was looking for something to do. His simple presentation wasn't nearly as fancy as the others, but I kept going back to it. I called him in, even though I was all set to hire someone else.

I was unimpressed with him at first glance. Although impeccably dressed, the tall, slender older man seemed positively ancient to a thirty-year-old like myself. However, the more he spoke, the more the negative physical images began to recede. He exuded the quiet confidence of a lifetime of success, and carried himself without the flash and swagger of a more insecure younger man.

His most distinguishing features were his eyes. They radiated a personal warmth that I responded to.

Mr. Burman casually explained that he had retired as an executive VP of NCR, the cash register company, ten years earlier and was tired of playing golf and traveling. We had something in common. He also needed a challenge.

"So, what can I do for you?" he asked, taking the initiative.

"As you can see, I'm a foreigner," I responded. "I've been in this country for nearly a decade, but there are so many things I don't know about life here. I need an advisor to help me with the subtleties of the American business culture. I know how to make money. I know how to flush out the rats gnawing away at a company. I know I can expand Lynch's New York offices. But I need to learn how to better communicate with people. How to groom accounts, so I can take myself to the next level."

The older man nodded as if his understanding went beyond the surface of what I was struggling to say.

"I would like to see your client list, see what kind of people you're dealing with and the businesses they're in," he said. "I also need to get a sense of who you are and what you stand for. If I decide to work with you, I won't be a salesman. Don't expect me to introduce you to my friends and business associates. I don't want to be used that way."

"Agreed on all counts."

He was blunt, but I liked that. I wanted someone who wouldn't pull punches, someone who'd stand up to me and tell me I was wrong, even if it might cost him his job. Burman was that man.

My new mentor came aboard. Each weekday, Burman would take the train from his twenty-acre estate in Chappaqua, New York, where he lived with his wife, Christabel, hop the escalator at Grand Central Station, and arrive at my office before 8:00 A.M. We'd spend the next few hours hashing out the problems that I was expected to face that day. We may have been the Odd Couple—a young Mexican émigré and a wizened successful WASP—but by the end of the first month, we'd bonded beyond that of a boss and employee. Roger Burman became like a second father to me, a spiritual guide who helped me navigate the muddy waters of corporate security. Roger even sponsored me to become a Rotarian and wanted me to join the Union League Club in Manhattan, an exclusive enclave of top industrialists.

Burman was rarely overtly critical. Instead, he used anecdotes and stories from his past to illustrate the points he wanted to make. He was a walking encyclopedia of American business, knowing and having forgotten more about the hidden pitfalls of corporate battle than most people learn in a lifetime. I listened to him like a child sitting at his beloved father's knee.

"Only work with people you trust," he advised. "Remember, a business relationship is, in every sense, a relationship. It's just like the one you have with your wife, your father, or a cherished friend. It must be cultivated and protected. Don't be impatient. It took us thirty years to get NCR to the point where it was a big success.

"Above everything else, never trust an attorney unless you're a personal friend, and then you shouldn't use him anyway. Attorneys are businessmen, just like us. They exist to make money, as much as they can grab. The difference is, they travel in a whole different world where everything is upside down. If their profits are down, they'll create problems to solve. And you can count on them to turn small problems into big ones, because that's how they get rich."

That was certainly different from what my father had taught me in Mexico. But from my growing experiences with the army of lawyers I had dealt with in New York, I knew Burman was right.

"Most of all, remember, unlike any other profession, attorneys profit from failure. They win when they lose, or when their client loses. The more setbacks they encounter, the more money they make. If they can turn a small problem into years of defeat, of rejected motions, botched trials, and fruitless appeal upon appeal, they laugh all the way to the bank."

A harsh indictment, but he was speaking from forty years of bitter experience.

Burman was especially helpful in the areas where I was weak: writing letters to corporate presidents, and drafting reports. I was stronger when it came to personal presentations, but he still offered suggestions aimed at improving my style. The only area where he really couldn't help was in the nitty-gritty of going undercover. I had to rely on natural instincts and planning there. Fortunately, my instincts were good. In essence, I could boat the fish once they were hooked. I needed Burman to help me choose the right bait.

"Let these companies know that you don't just provide guards. You solve problems. Big problems. Who are you handling the security for now? PepsiCo, Borden, Citibank, Prudential, Jersey Bell, Norcross Industries, some big law firms? . . . Make sure they know that you're not just another security guard manager and private investigator. A PI is a peeping Tom. These people need to know about the way you handled the Chinatown kidnapping and the PepsiCo bottling thefts. That's the direction you should go. Leave the penny-ante stuff to underlings and concentrate on the larger cases.

"If a company is losing two, three million dollars a year in stolen merchandise, they'll pay, and pay big, to stop it. You should be charging a lot more for what you do."

I liked the sound of that!

"If a company is in a heated legal battle and they can't figure out why they keep losing, don't you think they'd rather pay you a fifty-thousand-dollar bonus after you corrected the problem than dump one hundred thousand dollars up front to some law firm before the case even goes to trial?" From that point on, I decided that all my billing would be done on a fee-plus-bonus basis. That alone separated me from every other investigative firm I knew of. It put the pressure on me to succeed.

The older man was on a roll, so I let him continue. By the time he finished, I was ready to leave behind the lucrative but unfulfilling world of security guards and nickel-and-dime investigations, and jump headfirst into the dangerous world of organized crime and billion-dollar corporate theft.

I've never looked back.

A PIPE FULL
OF HOT CASH

A FEW YEARS AFTER his troubles with the mob, my old pal at Northville Industries, Harold Bernstein, called about what he thought would be a small information-gathering task. I met with the suave executive over dinner at a restaurant on Manhattan's East Side. While he picked at his steamed rice and vegetables, Bernstein outlined a potential problem.

Northville had just finished building a $200 million oil pipeline across the isthmus of Panama. The burnished pipes enabled companies to pump their product from the Alaska oil fields to the gas-gobbling American East Coast without having to lumber small tankers through the aging Panama Canal. Most of today's huge supertankers don't even fit in the canal.

"The project went 50 percent over budget," Bernstein explained. "That's not really unusual because of the normal change orders and cost overruns of a job this size. I wasn't worried much about it until I went to the grand opening party in Panama City. A Panamanian engineer took me aside and told me that the construction companies may have bilked us out of a lot of money."

"Which companies?"

"This guy said all of them," Bernstein laughed, "from the smallest Panamanian subcontractor to the big American company overseeing the entire project. But right now, it's just a rumor. What do you know about construction?" Bernstein asked.

"Enough to know that they probably overcharged you a few million dollars, which is small potatoes on a project that size."

"True," Bernstein said, laughing again. "Nickel and dime. Which is why I'm not losing any sleep over this. But you never can tell."

"What about the cost overruns? That's usually where the hanky-panky happens."

"I had three of the Big Eight accounting firms working on this—they were down there on-site. They approved all the pay-outs," the billionaire oil man explained. "We had ours, Morrison Knudsen, the American construction firm, had theirs. Citibank, the lead bank on the deal, had the third."

"Harold, it isn't easy to con a Big Eight firm."

"I agree. And we had three for good measure. I don't think we went over budget because of theft, but I'll sleep easier if you sniff around. Talk to this guy in Panama, the engineer. See if you think it's worth the trouble," Bernstein finished.

"As soon as I'm done with what I'm working on, I'll go."

Harold's problem didn't seem too pressing, which was good. I was right in the middle of a search to find the sixteen-year-old son of a New York businessman. The kid had been gone for weeks, and the police had given up looking for him. In desperation, the father contacted me. The guy couldn't afford to pay me—he even offered to sell his car for my expenses. But I was so moved by his anguish that I took the case for free.

It turned out the kid had a drug problem. We put surveillance around the youngster's friends and found him after a couple of days at a local Westchester County amusement park. His suppliers—operating out of the shooting arcade—had him all strung out in the back room.

I picked the kid up and drove him back to his relieved father.

With that task complete, it was time to tackle Harold Bernstein's problems south of the border.

I flew to Panama and met with Bernstein's engineer, Andreas Offerman. It was obvious that the nervous builder didn't want anyone to see us together. His domed, balding head was highlighted by worry wrinkles above his eyes. When we met, he kept looking over his stooped shoulders to see if anyone was watching us. I led him to a hotel room I had rented so we could talk in private.

Also obvious was that the tall, gentle Offerman was that rarest of humans: an honest, decent person who was being tormented by his conscience.

"Look, I'm kind of like a mentor—a father figure—to many young engineers down here. A lot of young people from other countries come here to work with me," Offerman explained. "Maybe that's why I'm sticking my neck out. I've tried to teach them how to work honestly. And I just can't stomach what happened. I won't be able to look my friends in the eye if I let this go."

"Maybe we can put a stop to that?" I suggested.

"Maybe. Probably not." The pessimistic engineer paused. "In Central America, you have to expect business to be done this way. Everyone has their palms out. But this project, this pipeline, was like nothing I've ever experienced before. Everyone had both hands in the till. We can't allow robbery to occur on this scale again. If this kind of behavior becomes the norm, the construction industry in Panama will crumble."

Offerman's motives were critical because his story was a whopper. If it was true, Harold Bernstein wasn't going to sleep for a solid month. The engineer was convinced that instead of shaving a few million here and there, the pipeline project had been rife with wholesale looting to the tune of $50 million. If Offerman was telling the truth, most of the vast "cost overruns" could, in fact, be attributed to theft.

I informed Bernstein of this when I briefed him a week later at Northville's corporate headquarters on Long Island. He listened and paid me a $100,000 retainer to investigate further.

"Dig deeper. Tell me where the money went, how they hid it, and who's got it now," Bernstein said.

Digging was the appropriate word. The first thing I did was get copies of every record that pertained to the project. That included thousands of microfilm pages covering billing statements, material orders, change orders, work orders, purchase orders, progress billing, inventory control forms, cost overrun sheets, and so forth. It was all plugged into a computer database so it could be cross-referenced.

When the numbers started getting crazy, I flew Offerman to New York to help me translate the documents. After the first few times, the translations became redundant.

"This one's bogus. That's a fake. That work was never done. This work was completed two months earlier. That replacement wasn't needed. They never bought any of those materials. This is a mirage . . ." It was endless.

After two months of grinding computer work, the first payoff came. For some reason, more than thirty of the independent Panamanian subcontractors used the same P.O. box for their billing address. And all thirty had worked directly with Morrison Knudsen, the American money tree handing out the disbursements like sugar-coated gumdrops.

Either someone in Morrison Knudsen's accounting department was asleep at the switch, which was highly unlikely, or this P.O. box was the critical "green hole" I was looking for, the swirling orifice through which the money was being sucked.

One of the Panamanian subcontractors using the address was a giant firm that handled building projects all over Central and South America. The fact that this huge conglomerate was sharing a billing address with loading operators, painters, and other one-horse companies seemed insane.

Unless, of course, they owned or controlled those small and midsized companies and wanted to make it look as if they weren't monopolizing the contracts.

My instincts told me that was the case. This big firm no doubt had its sticky fingers in everything. That made them the key to finding out just how extensive the bloodletting had been, and who at Morrison Knudsen was working with them.

Proving this, obvious as it appeared, wasn't going to be easy. Paper can only tell you so much. Whatever the engineer said was bogus, someone else could say was real. On a project that large, there are literally millions of places to hide.

Instead of trying to trace old records, I needed to experience the skimming process in action. And I wanted to be part of it, to be in on the action. To accomplish this, I devised a plan right out of *Mission: Impossible.*

"Harold, I want you to build another pipeline."

"What?" he exclaimed, perhaps thinking I'd caught a malarial fever on my last trip to Panama.

"In order to catch the thieves, we have to give them another opportunity to steal. And this time I'll be right in the middle of it."

"But to build another pipeline? . . ." he said.

"Not build it," I corrected with a smile. "Just say you are going to build it. I'll take it from there." Bernstein stared at me for a second, and then he slowly began to grin.

"Why, you devil," he said.

"Exactly," I answered.

Despite the strenuous objections of his jittery lawyers, Bernstein did as I asked. He made a showy announcement that the first pipeline was so successful, he was going to build another! At my urging, he personally notified the president of Panama.

Technically speaking, the project was absurd. That didn't stop the word from spreading like wildfire in the steamy Central American nation. It was front-page news in all the papers and was the lead story on evening television broadcasts. (Even the *Wall Street Journal* bit.) General Paredes, the real power in Panama, embraced the idea, as did his officers, including intelligence head Colonel Manuel Noriega, then in an early stage of his power-mad career.

The army's reaction wasn't surprising. The Panamanian military, taking a cue from the Mafia, had extorted millions from the first project by providing "protection." They quickly offered their services for the second.

As I suspected, no one questioned the need for another pipeline. Everyone was too busy anticipating "Thieves Paradise—Part II."

With the hook sufficiently baited, I went to work rounding up my cohorts from the "Mexican Team." We located and purchased a ripe shell company in Mexico to establish our credentials. The firm, with the suitably vague moniker National and International Representatives (NIR), had previously been used as a corporate shell by the former president of Mexico during construction of the Mexico City subway. That made it perfect for our plan. It was large enough, at least on paper, to handle a massive project like the pipeline. Even better, anyone who checked would be told that it was associated with Mexico's ruling party. Not bad, considering that the purchase price—$10,000—amounted to that of a small car.

After the papers were signed, I transformed myself into "Don Antonio," billionaire owner, president and CEO of this international construction company.

Don Antonio joined the rush of eager companies from around the world bidding on Pipeline II. Holding back my stately presence, I had my associates wine and dine various political leaders, and in turn be wined and dined themselves by the local construction companies—including the one I'd targeted. This process intensified when Northville—on my cue—began spreading the word that my firm was the leading candidate to oversee the project.

Jumping to the top of the list had many advantages, but also had the disadvantage of making me a bigger target. A number of local builders and government officials decided to check me out with the Mexican Embassy. What they checked, however, was not me, but "Don Antonio" and NIR.

Because my associates and I had taken the time to create a credible cover, both came up clean.

Once everybody was hooked, it was time for Don Antonio to appear—but not in Panama. In true royal fashion, the president of the big Panamanian contracting company, a man named Jose Duran, was summoned to Mexico to appear before me.

Spreading around some pesos, I had Duran and his top executives whisked through the Mexico City airport VIP style—without the hassle of having to go through Customs. A squad of heavily armed bodyguards then ushered the builders through the city and checked them into the Presidential Suite of the Hotel Aristos, one of Mexico City's finest hotels. Among the suite's lavish decorations was a little feature my Mexican team added—complete audio and video surveillance.

I arranged to meet the men over drinks at the Mexican capital's swankiest private nightclub, the Focolare, located a few blocks from the hotel in Mexico City's Zona Rosa.

When I made my entrance, the singer, a well-known Latin-American recording star, stopped her set, came down off the stage, and gave me a big, showy kiss.

"Don Antonio! It's wonderful to see you," she cooed, earning the $2,000 my associates had previously slipped her. "I dedicate the rest of my performance to you!"

"Thank you, my dear," I said.

Finally, after all the hoopla, my burly bodyguards led me to Duran's table.

The Panamanian, a dark man of Italian descent, was traveling with an obsequious entourage that included his attorney and his brother. He also brought along an infamous American contractor who was now living in exile in Panama after years of dirty dealing throughout the States. The tall, gracious, slow-talking American had teamed with Duran to keep his shady cement operation going in Latin America. Individually or collectively, these weren't people I had to mince words with.

"My associates tell me that you're the people to do business with in Panama," I opened after the introductions. "But I must tell you, right off, pulling no punches, I don't know how you do business over there, but here, in Mexico, I get my fifteen percent. Off the top. How are you going to take care of me if I decide to use your company?"

"We'll have no problems taking care of Don Antonio," Duran said, winking to his associates. "It's easy to squeeze extra money out of the Americans."

Swallowing the hook even faster than I anticipated, Duran began to brag about just how that could be done. I had to stop him so he could say it on tape upstairs.

"Not now," I cautioned, motioning toward the singer. "We do my friend disrespect." When she finished her set, I motioned for everyone to regroup in the Presidential Suite.

"Okay, as you were saying? I need assurance that this can be done cleanly."

"It can, because we already have," Duran laughed. As I expected, he began to explain how they plundered Northville the first time around. It was nothing fancy. Just typical double billing, triple billing, mystery billing, and repairing problems that didn't exist. I listened patiently, waiting for him to ID the players at the heart of the scam.

"Did anyone ever check?" I asked.

"We had a top manager of Morrison Knudsen on our payroll!" Duran boasted. "Paid him two hundred and fifty thousand dollars for his 'special assistance.' Same with two auditors."

"That's good," I laughed. "You guys are better than I imagined. Maybe I could learn a thing or two from you."

I met with Duran at least ten times over the next six months, solidifying our business relationship while learning more about the theft. To stay in character, I arranged for the phone company to have any incoming calls to Mexico City routed to my office in New Jersey, without the caller's knowledge. Every time Duran dialed Don Antonio's number in Mexico, he'd reach Octavio Pena at my compound in Fort Lee.

As the pipeline start date neared, I flew Duran and his men to Long Island to meet Bernstein and finalize the building contracts. That set the hook deeper. And several times Duran and his minions, along with some Morrison Knudsen representatives and a bean counter from one of the Big Eight Accounting firms, flew to Mexico to meet with me. Don Antonio got them to explain, in detail, how they were going to pay my 15 percent off the top without getting caught. So much for Big Eight accountants.

It looked like easy sailing from there. So easy that I began to have premonitions of disaster. The glitch came over the phone.

"Don Antonio. It's Jose. I need to meet you tonight!"

"Tonight? I don't know if that's possible."

Hell no, it wasn't. Don Antonio was entering data in a computer in Fort Lee, New Jersey! Duran wanted to meet me in Mexico City.

"Oh, come on, my friend. It won't take long. We're going to be there. I need to see you."

"Why?" I said as nonchalantly as possible.

"It's a surprise. Just meet us at the top of the Mexico City Hilton nightclub tonight at eleven. It's very important, Don Antonio."

I could tell from Duran's voice that it was critical that I attend. With great misgivings, I agreed.

There were a lot of red flags about this. When a mark calls for a mysterious late-night surprise meeting with an undercover agent, it's generally not a good sign. On top of that, I had to fly to Mexico with little time to spare. I made a rash of last-minute arrangements to reestablish my identity, then caught the next flight to Mexico.

I arrived in Mexico City with an hour to spare and immediately hooked up with some bodyguards. Ironically, this time the bruisers weren't just for show. If Duran was luring me into a trap, I'd need them!

At the nightclub, I was confronted with the first of a series of mistakes born out of not having enough time to plan ahead, mistakes that could have cost me my life. The first came right at the popular club's entrance. With no time to call ahead, I was forced to queue up in line. If Duran or his men spotted the famous Don Antonio standing in line like a regular schmo, waiting to fork over the hefty cover charge, it would have been curtains. Guys like Don A don't pay covers, and certainly don't do lines.

Even worse, when I reached the doorman, I didn't have any pesos! All I had were American greenbacks. Thankfully, American money is accepted almost everywhere, including at the door of a snooty Mexican nightclub. I quickly paid the $50 fee for myself and my bodyguards and breezed in.

Reclaiming my royal aura, I searched the dark environs for Jose. The moment I saw him, my tension eased. He was sitting at a table surrounded by beautiful women. The important meeting was nothing more than an "important" stag party for Duran and his buddies.

No sooner had I greeted Duran and taken my place among the beauties when disaster, in the form of the cashier, struck again.

"Senor, please take your money back," she said apologetically, handing me the greenbacks. "I didn't know you were with Senor Duran." It couldn't have been more obvious if the woman had held up a sign. I felt the sweat drip down my back as the cashier thrust the money back at me. I quickly grabbed the American dollars and stashed them out of sight, then searched the eyes of Duran and his boys. Did any of them understand the implications of what had just happened?

Naaah. They were too drunk and too infatuated with the women.

I had escaped again, yet something told me the nerve-wracking night wasn't over. I kicked myself for agreeing to a meeting in which I wasn't in total control.

"Don Antonio, I want you to meet an associate of mine," Duran effused. "This is Colonel Guittierez. He's the head of the Panamanian air force. I think you might have some common friends."

"Is that so?" I commented, tensing up. How could that be? Don Antonio had no friends in common with anyone, since he didn't exist!

An old nightmare flashed through my head. Once, while on a case for a Fortune 500 company in the Dominican Republic, I'd pretended to be a bigwig Central American businessman. The only problem was that the cover I'd constructed actually belonged to a real person! My cover was blown one night by an associate of the people I was targeting. I dumped the operation and literally hopped on the first plane out of the airport without ever checking out of my hotel.

What hell awaited me now?

I shook the Air Force colonel's hand, instantly relieved that he was Panamanian, not Mexican. It turned out that he'd trained in Mexico and had once been friends with many influential Mexican politicos.

"Don Antonio knows the president, don't you?" Duran said as he ogled another woman at the table.

"Then you must know Ramon," Guittierez smiled.

"Ramon?"

"The president's pilot. I trained with him."

"Really," I answered, praying a chandelier would drop on his head.

The colonel moved his chair closer. I looked over at my body-guards and checked their position. At any second, my cover, the whole Northville investigation, and possibly my life could end. The colonel smiled at me and asked a highly specific question about the presidential pilot's family. I smiled at him, pretended that I didn't hear him, and thought frantically of a way to get away from the table. He leaned closer and asked again. Oh shit, I thought. This is it.

"Oh, Don Antonio, why didn't you tell me you were coming tonight!" I turned to my left. It was the nightclub singer from the Focolare. By a magical coincidence she was performing at the Hilton that night. She was also improvising for another $2,000 tip, which I would have happily tripled. The sexy songbird leaned down, made a big show of hugging me, then sang her next song from our table. It was the perfect distraction. By the time she finished the nosy colonel had forgotten his stupid question. And I wasn't about to let him remember. I made some quick excuses about having to see someone across the room, then bolted out of the place.

"Damn," I groused to myself in the elevator. "I flew all the way from New York just to have a few drinks with these bozos. And because of it, everything nearly fell apart."

Of course, Duran didn't know how far I'd come. He thought I just drove a few miles across town. His request that I join him and his women was just business as usual.

After that close call, I jetted back to New Jersey. With renewed speed, I knotted the loose ends of the yearlong investigation.

The final picture wasn't pretty. Certain executives at Morrison Knudsen had not only engineered a staggering amount of false billing, they kept the fraud going by staging a phony labor strike. The alleged work stoppage enabled them to pocket another $15 million in bogus cost overlays. The money was one thing. What really sickened me was the fact that during the orchestrated strike, two workers were killed by the military. I never discovered whether anyone else at Morrison Knudsen was aware of what the rogue executives were up to.

It was time to end the charade.

"Jose, I need you and your associates to fly to New York as soon as possible," I said.

"Hey, Don Antonio. What happened to you the other night?"

"The usual," I ducked. "A woman made me an offer I couldn't refuse."

"You dog," he said.

"Anyway, can you make it here?" I asked him.

"When?"

"I'm arriving tonight. I'll meet you at the airport tomorrow."

"Okay. What's wrong?" Duran asked.

"We've hit some last-minute snags we need to iron out before we break ground. The lawyers are gumming things up again. Nothing to worry about," I assured him.

I picked up Duran and his top assistant the next afternoon at Kennedy Airport. This time, instead of carting them to the Carlyle Hotel in Manhattan as I usually did, I brought the two Panamanians to my office in Fort Lee, New Jersey. Despite the extreme change in routine, they suspected nothing.

"Where's Señor Bernstein?" Jose Duran finally asked. I ignored him and ordered one of my associates to close the door.

"Sit down, Jose, I've got some bad news," I opened. Duran and his aide joined me around the conference table. The construction magnate's eyes were suddenly sharp little points. I noticed them checking the two exits.

"My name is not Don Antonio. It's Octavio Pena." Their expressions remained blank. "I'm a security consultant for Northville Industries."

That's all I needed to say. Duran's face froze into a mask. Luis, his personal assistant, actually blanched, his hands clutching at the table. I stared down at the two businessmen. Duran's mask cracked, he licked his lips, and then his eyes flicked toward the door again. The shock quickly turned into the realization that I had the goods on them. The realization was quickly replaced by raw fear. Luis began to visibly shake, and Duran could barely speak. They were certain I was about to kill them.

"No, you've got it wrong," I reassured them. "This is America, not Panama or Mexico. I mean you no harm. None of you." I waited for that to register, then continued. "I'm not going to hurt you. I know how business is done down there, okay? And I know it was the Americans, the auditors behind all of this. I've talked to Harold Bernstein, and he'll forget about your involvement if you agree to testify against everyone. That's the deal."

Duran slowly nodded his head. It didn't take him long to figure out he'd been outmaneuvered and should cut his losses.

That night, I invited Duran to meet Grace and have dinner at my condo overlooking the Hudson River and the New York skyline. This was to assure him Latin American-style that he was not in danger. By the evening's end, a relieved Duran agreed to provide as much documentation as he could, including the testimony of one of the accountants on the project, to prove Northville's case against the executives at Morrison Knudsen.

Two weeks later, Harold Bernstein met with a senior executive of Morrison Knudsen in a room at the Waldorf Towers Hotel. On Day Three of their intensive negotiations, Bernstein told me that the contractor decided to refund $30 million back to Northville.

That was it. No arrests, no indictments—nothing. It started out being about money and ended up being about money. Crimes were committed. People were betrayed. And when the shouting was over, the score was settled in a hotel room with a handshake between two gentlemen.

MR. T AND THE EXTORTIONIST

IN ITS HEYDAY, The Lynch Company handled thousands of cases a year from its fifteen or so branch offices. Mostly they were small-scale investigations involving minor corporate theft, missing persons, trial assistance, and so on. Lynch's investigators, mostly retired FBI agents, handled them well. But the big cases came to me.

Lynch called from Los Angeles one afternoon with just the kind of case that required my input. "I'm in a hotel with a client who wants someone to deliver $100,000 in return for some stolen documents. You want to handle this?"

"I'll talk to him, but you know how I feel about paying ransoms. Is he open to other suggestions?"

"I don't know. You deal with it."

I caught the next plane to L.A. and met the man that evening.

Lynch had told me little about the client's background or what the case entailed. All I knew was that he was a rich entrepreneur in the shopping center and electronics businesses. From those bare facts, I figured someone must have snatched some high tech-trade secrets.

I was caught off guard by the man's appearance. Instead of the suited, gray-haired businessman I was expecting, in walked a handsome young dude in his thirties decked out in jeans, cowboy boots, and a colorful sport shirt. His hair was long and stylishly cut, his mustache dark and thick, and a string of gold chains sparkled from around his neck. He looked like he should be the drop man, not me.

"Hi, I'm Jack," he beamed. "So you're the guy who's going to make the drop?"

"Not so fast," I cautioned. "I want to talk to you about that. I don't think you should just hand somebody one hundred thousand dollars."

"It's a hundred and fifty thousand now. He upped the ante this morning."

"See? That's exactly what I mean. You pay once, you pay forever. Guys like this must be stopped in their tracks."

"I hear you, but I need those, uh, records back. I need them back bad, man."

"What exactly are these records?"

The young businessman danced around the question.

"Listen," I interrupted. "You want me to help? You have to tell the truth. What's this all about? Before I can recommend a course of action, I need to know the facts."

The guy started dancing again. I repeated my statement, more forcefully. The guy had to come clean or I was on the next flight home.

"Okay, you win," he sighed. "Someone took my books."

"Your accounting books?"

He nodded.

"So?"

"They took the real ones," he said, a bit sheepishly.

"Ah, I see. You keep two sets."

"Exactly."

"Why didn't you just say so?"

The man shrugged.

"So someone snatched the real books, and they're holding them to your temple like a giant cannon. Beautiful. I can see why you're willing to buckle under so easy."

"I need them back. If those government assholes get hold of them, they could be misinterpeted. I've got a complex tax situation."

"That you do," I said with a chuckle. "Don't worry, we'll get them back. But you can't pay this person. If you pay, you'll be in more trouble. You'll become their retirement plan, paying yearly dividends. We've got to get the books, then run the person out of town."

"I don't know. If anything goes wrong . . ."

"Trust me," I said.

The extortionist was calling Jack at his office, at his home, and at his sister's home. By the second day, the ransom had soared another 300 percent, topping out at a whopping half-million. I told Jack that we would practice my time-honored strategy of stalling the enemy. Jack told them he couldn't get the cash while I used the extra time to plan an effective counterattack.

This was definitely an inside job. The books had been stashed in Jack's safe at his office. Although he had 200 employees, very few had access to his safe. That narrowed down the suspects. Unfortunately, it might have been too narrow for Jack's liking. In situations like this, it's often someone very close who's turning the screws.

"Don't tell anybody, not a soul, who I am or what I'm here for, okay? Don't breathe a word of this to anybody," I cautioned.

"Okay," he promised.

The next evening, Jack took me to dinner at a local restaurant. He brought along his steady, a striking woman from Argentina. When Jack excused himself to go to the bathroom, she asked me, in Spanish: "So tell me about the plan to get Jack's books back!"

"It's none of your business," I said calmly, ticked that Jack had already blown my cover. Afterward, I cornered the electronics whiz. "Why did you tell your girlfriend who I was?"

"Ah, she's okay."

"No she's not! She could be a suspect! At this point everyone's a suspect. And what do you really know about her? She's from South America, for goodness sake!"

"She's okay," he insisted. "She wouldn't do that to me. I can trust her."

"Someone took something from your safe, Jack. Think. Use your head. You can't trust anyone right now. Not your sister, partner, girlfriend, anyone. Even if she isn't the culprit, who is she going to tell? She blabs to her best friend, her best friend tells her mother, and pretty soon it's on the front page of the *L.A. Times*! If you keep talking, you could put my life in danger. Understand?"

"Completely," he said.

Jack couldn't keep a secret, but he was better when it came to working the phones. He managed to stall the deep-voiced extortionist for a month. Meanwhile, a mole inside Ma Bell relayed the records of all the calls made by those in Jack's tight circle of friends, relatives, and upper-level employees.

The extortionist, who identified himself as Mr. Brown, wasn't making it easy on his end. However unprofessional he acted in other areas, he kept his calls under a minute so they couldn't be traced. But he didn't know enough not to make them from his home phone. That was his undoing.

Combing through the phone records, I found a call someone made to Jack at his office that matched the exact time Jack was talking to the shakedown artist. We had our man.

As is so often the case, the creep squeezing Jack was the same man Jack was paying to protect him—the owner of the security company contracted to secure his businesses. I'd paid particular attention to this guy because he was one of my main suspects from the beginning.

"See, it wasn't my girlfriend," Jack said with a smile when I told him what was what.

"Not this time," I shot back.

"She really does love me."

I let it slide.

"So, what do we do next? I don't want any cops," Jack said, getting back to business.

"This guy's an ex-cop, so the police are out of the question. What we need to do is give him a scare. We'll make him voluntarily give back the books and then we'll run his fat ass out of town."

"How?"

"Just wait," I teased.

I spent the next week doing a complete background check on the cop turned shakedown artist. Mr. Brown was a big, bulky Italian, a mean, blackjack-to-Rodney-King's-skull type of guy. After putting in his twenty with the LAPD, he retired to a resortlike planned community with security, a swimming pool, and tennis courts.

Through various sources, I learned something else about our Mr. Brown, something very interesting. Since his retirement from the force, he had started fancying himself as a pseudo-mobster. He strutted around town in fancy suits, drove a sleek sportscar, talked tough, and encouraged speculation that he was connected to the big mob families in New York. Perfect. I had my winning gambit. If he wanted to play Mafioso, we'd indulge him.

The next evening, I rented a long black limousine, picked up Jack's beautiful sister for window dressing, hired some off-duty motorcycle cops as security, rented a tow truck, and rolled up to the secured entrance of Mr. Brown's planned community.

I had told one of the biker cops exactly what to say at the gate. "The boss needs to pick up one of his cars."

The security guard—one of Mr. Brown's own men—looked at the beefy cop, the limo, and the tow truck, then waved us through without question. If you act like you own a place, nobody messes with you.

We drove to Mr. Brown's house. The off-duty cops quietly hot-wired his garage door, and then pinched his cherished Nissan 300 ZX right out from under his nose as he slept. (Jack had actually loaned Mr. Brown the money to buy the sports car and held the title to it.) After hooking it to the tow truck, we breezed back out the security gates. The ZX was towed all the way to the next block, where I'd rented an apartment that gave us a clear view of Mr. Brown's pad.

At 2:00 A.M., I had an associate from Brooklyn call Mr. Brown from New York and patch the call through to me so that I could listen. We watched as a light snapped on in his house.

"Mr. Brown. Mr. T wants ta meet wit youse," my associate ordered in his best gangster voice.

"Who? What?" the groggy ex-cop said.

"Mr. T needs ta meet wit youse."

"I'm not Mr. Brown. You got the wrong number."

"We don't have the wrong number. We know exactly who youse are, Mr. Brown. Mr. T wants to meet with you, pronto. The meet's at the beach at six A.M. We'll send a car to pick you up."

"I'm not going to no fucking beach! Are you crazy?"

Slam. The phone went dead.

The next thing we saw was the garage door open. Our extortionist was headed for the hills—only he was in for a surprise. A frantic Mr. Brown soon appeared and ran around in circles in his driveway, wondering what had happened to his prized wheels. Gaining his senses, he sprinted a few hundred yards to the security gate.

"What the fuck happened to my car?" he raged.

"What car?"

"The red 300 ZX!"

"The boss came and took it."

"The boss? What fucking boss?"

"He just said the boss," the guard shrugged.

Exasperated, Mr. Brown ran back to his house. His phone was ringing as he entered. It was my associate again. I could barely keep from laughing as I listened.

"Where the fuck's my car?" Brown frothed.

"Mr. T wanted to get your attention. If you want it back, you better do as he says."

"I'm not going to no fucking beach at six A.M.!" Brown said again.

"Mr. T no longer wants to meet you there. He's very unhappy about how you're behavin'. You stay put. We'll contact you later. Mr. T is unhappy." Click.

At 6:00 A.M., we motored through the gates and parked the limo in front of Mr. Brown's house. The two off-duty cops, posing as Mafia muscle, knocked on his door.

"Mr. T is here to meet with you. Now."

Mr. Brown tried to shut the door, but the cops bullied their way inside.

"He'll meet you out back by the pool," one of the bruisers informed him.

With two hulks inside his house, Mr. Brown suddenly lost his desire to put up a fight. He nodded and led the men out the back door.

Prior to going to his house, I had the cops place two lawn chairs on the grass by the pool so that they faced each other. Mr. Brown was plunked down into the westernmost chair—the one facing directly into the rising sun.

The driver then cruised the big limo ever so slowly around the block. He eased it to a stop at the opening near the pool. Once parked, I waited ten minutes before making my grand entrance. I wanted the sun to start hitting his eyes.

I emerged from the ominous vehicle, clad in a pinstriped suit, pink shirt, and dark sunglasses. As I approached, all Mr. Brown could see was my dark image silhouetted by the blazing sun. I sat down and looked hard at the ex-cop turned extortionist. He was squinting to see me. His hands were trembling.

Suddenly I spread my arms apart in front of me in the classic "what the fuck are you doing?" posture.

Mr. Brown nearly jumped from his seat.

"You have taken something that belongs to me," I said.

"I didn't take anything . . ."

"You know what I'm talking about. The books, you shithead."

"I'm sorry, Mr. T," he groveled. "I didn't know they were yours."

"What's the matter with you? Why are you fucking my partner around? Taking his records. You made me come here all the way from New York to straighten out this mess."

"I didn't know. I swear!"

"Here's the deal. I want you to give me all the books you stole, and all the copies. Don't even think of holding anything back, or next time I come I won't be so nice."

"Yes, sir," he gulped, his hands still shaking.

"After that, I want you out of town. I don't want you ever even thinking about bothering us again."

"Yes, sir."

"And let me tell you something. You better pray for Jack's health. Because if his jet crashes, I'm coming after you. If he gets drunk and smashes his Porsche, I'm coming after you. If he sits on a park bench and gets a splinter in his ass, I'm coming after you. You got that?"

"Yes, sir."

"Okay. When can I get the books?"

"This afternoon."

"Bring them to Jack."

"Yes, sir."

I signaled to my men, then turned and disappeared inside the limo.

That afternoon, Mr. Brown sheepishly appeared at Jack's office with all the stolen books. As instructed, Jack accepted them without saying a word.

Within a month, Mr. Brown sold his security business and moved to another town. A week before he pulled up stakes, Jack bumped into him at a local bank. The retired extortionist took one look at Jack, froze for a second, then dashed out of the place.

And that was the last anyone ever heard of him.

As for Jack, he showed his gratitude to me by presenting me with a copy of *The Art of War* by the famous Chinese military strategist Sun-tzu, which I treasured and still read. Inside the thin leather covers, I finally found someone else who thought the same way I did.

I like to think that somewhere up in the heavens, Sun-tzu was smiling at the way I neutralized Mr. Brown. We let the enemy defeat himself using only his own overheated imagination.

NIGHTMARE IN MONTEGO BAY

W E HAVE A CLIENT with a big problem in the Caribbean. Mr. Lynch said to run it by you before we pass." The caller was a retired FBI agent heading Lynch's office in San Francisco. It was another big case they wanted me to handle.

"What's the problem?"

"The man's daughter was kidnapped by Rastafarians. They've shanghaied her to Jamaica and want a million dollars for her."

"Rastafarians?"

"Yeah. The father's in a panic. Doesn't know what to do. You think you can rescue her?"

"Absolutely!" I said without hesitation. There's no situation with higher stakes than a kidnapping. I qualified my enthusiasm before I made a 100 percent commitment. "I have to get the details, but sure, let's go for it. Tell the father to fly to New York immediately. I'll brief him and if it looks good, I'll go."

"You sure?" the ex-G-man cautioned. "Those Rastafarian rat bastards are nasty sonsofbitches. And you'll be playing in their ballpark."

"I'll handle them. Just get the client here."

Although the case seemed like the kind of challenge that piqued my interest, I wasn't taking the agent's warning lightly.

Technically, the long-haired, dreadlocks-wearing, Caribbean Rastafarians are a peaceful group who speak a happy, lilting version of
the English language. Their beliefs center around the late Ethiopian
Emperor Haile Selassie. Rastas view Selassie as a divine savior, and
see Ethiopia as Eden. They also believe that the descendants of
black slaves snatched from their homeland and scattered around
the world will one day be repatriated to Africa.

The name Rastafarian comes from Selassie's original name,
Ras Tafari. And they use marijuana as sort of a religious rite. A lot
of marijuana.

If they were just about religion, few outside of Jamaica would
know them. What sets Rastafarians apart is the tremendous impact
their members (or those who follow their look and style) have
made on the world's music community. While the truth about the
Rastafarian religion may not be widely known, everyone's heard
their music. Whether it's the immensely popular reggae, or off-
shoots like ska and world beat, there's hardly a corner of the globe
where a Rastafarian-influenced band isn't playing riffs by Jimmy
Cliff or the late Bob Marley—Jamaica's two international music
superstars.

The dark sides of the Rasta force are the splinter groups and
gangs that traffic in the drug trade. While waiting to return to
Africa, these less patient members stay high, fiercely defend their
territories, often lean more toward black magic and voodoo than
the teachings of Selassie, and have been known to torture and kill
without a semblance of human compassion.

Because of their dramatic look, close-knit community, and
unusual language and behavior, these bad Rastas are exceedingly
hard to infiltrate. And if you do get in, you better not get caught. All
of which makes them a tough bunch to tangle with, especially on
their home turf.

While I waited for the client to arrive, I made some phone
calls around the New York law enforcement community to get a
picture of the Rasta subculture. What I learned didn't make me
too comfortable.

"We don't go into Rasta-dominated neighborhoods, Octavio, it's
that simple. If we have to arrest one, we bring triple the number of
officers," a high-ranking NYPD official named John Maguire told me.

"Why?"

"Drugs, usually. They're so hopped up, they'll do anything.
Including shoot a cop. If you're dealing with criminal Rastas, you'd

better be damn careful." Maguire was referring to Rastas in New York. I didn't tell him I was thinking of taking them on in Jamaica.

The last thing I did before the father arrived was to get a complete briefing from Lynch's San Francisco office. What they said made me curious about the whole affair. Apparently the young college student was married to a Rasta. It wasn't clear if the marriage had happened right before she was kidnapped, or sometime during the previous college semester. When the Lynch people went into her condo in Los Angeles they found it in a shambles—from packing and hard use, not from being ransacked.

Armed with the husband's name, I ran a check on him and found a phone number in Montego Bay, as well as some interesting phone call patterns to California and Brooklyn, New York.

The following day, the father, a wealthy Jewish industrialist, arrived at my office with his oldest daughter and son-in-law in tow. Tall, tanned, with refined, aristocratic features, the father was the kind of man who took bold risks and was used to giving orders.

In normal circumstances, that is. With his daughter in the clutches of a bizarre religious sect, his strength of character was being strained to the limits.

The oldest daughter was in her late twenties and looked as if she had once been attractive but got married, put on weight, and lost interest. The son-in-law was a studious type who wore glasses and was a half-decade younger than his wife. He was still attending the same college as his kidnapped sister-in-law.

The father handed me a picture of his youngest daughter, Jody. Unlike her sister, Jody was a beautiful, vivacious blonde of the Nicole Brown Simpson genre. The father explained that he had recently given Jody a million dollars from a trust account for her eighteenth birthday. Her first purchase was a blue Datsun 2PO, which was also missing.

"When did she disappear?" I asked. There was an embarrassed silence. Their eyes searched the ceiling or dropped to the floor.

"Look, she was in college. You know how it is," the father said sheepishly. "She didn't call us as frequently as I'd like."

I could tell we weren't dealing with the closest of families here, but that didn't matter. What mattered was getting Jody back.

I sensed that Jody's sister was particularly uncomfortable with the subject of her sister's spotty family communications. It was apparent that there were things about Jody that she felt I should know, but didn't want to say in the presence of her dad.

I made some excuses and got the sister alone for a few minutes.

"Tell me about Jody," I asked, giving her the opening she was seeking.

"Jody's wild. Really wild," she said, sighing. "We're not very close. I'm religious. She's into drugs."

"What kind?"

"You name it. Pot, cocaine, pills. Daddy was crazy to give her the money. She's just going to blow it up her nose. And it made her . . ." The sister choked on the words. Wild as Jody was, she was still her sister.

"It made her a target," I completed her sentence. "A rich, confused young girl with a drug problem. Like shooting ducks in a barrel."

The sister nodded.

"She was into reggae music and that whole Rasta scene. She dated Rastas. That's how they got her."

"How often did she check in with the family? You all seemed hesitant there."

"She'd be lost for weeks. That's why we don't know how long she's been gone. My husband would see her around the college sometimes, but other than that, it wasn't unusual to not hear from her. If her . . . if the kidnapper hadn't called, we wouldn't have known she was gone."

"You mean her husband, right?" I said.

The sister shook her head and sighed.

"That's what he says. It was a surprise to us."

"You'd better start at the beginning."

"A few days ago, I received a call from Jamaica. A man—one of those Rastas—said he was Jody's husband, that they had recently eloped to Montego Bay. Then, after the marriage, he said Jody was kidnapped." She paused, trying to remember the exact words. "He said he'd paid them all he could but they wanted more. He said we had to help him."

"I'll bet. How much help does he need?"

"He said he was negotiating with the kidnappers. They've demanded a million dollars."

"An even million? And he plans to handle the payoff. He wants you to send him the money?"

She nodded. Now it was my turn to shake my head.

I had a nagging suspicion that we were witnessing an interesting new wrinkle in a very old game. Jody might have now been

Mrs. Rasta, but I had a feeling she was coerced into it. The husband was probably the point man for the kidnappers.

"He's been calling you, not your father?"

"No. Just me."

"Good. Let's keep it that way. When is he going to call again?"

"I'm supposed to call him."

Every plan has its weakness and Mr. Rasta just revealed his. He might be chuckling over his marriage ploy, but on the other hand, we had a kidnapper we could call anytime we wanted. And that would make what we had to do much easier.

"These guys must be sure of themselves. Are you positive they even have her?"

"She's not at her apartment. And the car's gone. And eight hundred and fifty thousand dollars has been transferred from her account to a bank in Jamaica, a joint account she had with her . . . with that bastard," she spat out.

They had her all right. They probably thought they'd hit the mother lode.

"Okay, let's bring your father back into this."

We went back into the room where Jody's father sat, staring out over the New York skyline. I laid it out for him.

"Okay, here's how it goes. You're not going to pay these guys a dime. If you pay them once, you'll be paying forever."

"I just want her safe," the father said.

"We'll bring her back. But I need your full cooperation."

This was going to be one of my most difficult undercover operations. I had to become as conversant as I could in the Rasta world. I had to find an angle, a weakness, a slight opening that I could exploit to free Jody. For background, I picked the brains of several people in law enforcement and intelligence who knew about Jamaican Rastafarians.

The next day, I met with psychologists who were experts at reconstructing the psyches of kidnapping victims. After that, I spent several hours with operatives skilled in armed rescues.

The next day, I began assembling my anti-Rasta team. That wasn't an easy task. Many of my most trusted associates begged off.

"You can't go against the Rastas," one knowledgeable source told me. "They own the place down there, and they're mean, drug-crazed, voodoo-practicing psychos. You can't trust anybody in Jamaica. Count me out of this one."

I heard that refrain repeatedly before I finally assembled a squad that initially consisted of a pair of young, tough, fearless Puerto Ricans who were as cool as an island breeze. One, Eddie Ramirez, was a particularly slick character. He was a street-smart, handsome jive talker who instantly got along with everybody, including, I hoped, Rastafarians. His partner, Hector Gonzales, was more low-key but equally hip.

"You two go down to Montego Bay, rent a condo near the house where the girl is being held, and learn everything you can about the area," I instructed. "The roads, alleys, I want to know where every pothole is. If you can, get a vantage point on the house and do some light surveillance."

"Got ya, boss."

"I want hourly briefing calls, if possible. Okay? You're my eyes and ears down there."

While Eddie and Hector were jetting south, I phoned the U.S. consul in Jamaica. Generally, these calls are a major hassle. The last thing the official U.S. government representative wants is trouble. A SWAT team of mercenaries sweeping in on a native's home to rescue a kidnapping victim can amount to lots of trouble—particularly if people get shot, or something goes wrong. The consuls invariably try to talk me out of it, going so far as demanding that I stay away. I always ignore them. The only reason I call at all is that I want them to be aware of the operation so they'll stay out of our way. In some instances, if the consul or ambassador is decent, they might even be able to help.

In this case, the consul, a woman, was more understanding than most. She couldn't give us her official blessing, but she stopped short of ordering me to steer clear.

"You should know that we don't have decent relations with the police in Montego Bay," she said. "The Rastas are particularly powerful there."

"So we're on our own," I answered.

"That's right. Good luck." Her tone indicated she expected to read my obituary in the *Kingston Times*.

After settling in at Montego Bay, Eddie called with his first report.

"We can see down on the house from the mountain above," he said. "It's a big, beautiful place overlooking the bay and the airport. It's surrounded by some other houses."

"Now we know where the girl's eight hundred and fifty thousand dollars went."

"Yeah, that would probably do it."

"What kind of traffic?"

"People are coming in and out all the time."

"What kind of people?"

"Rastas. Rastas all over the place, and a number of the local police."

"Wonderful."

"Hey, I thought you'd like that part," Eddie joked. This was going to be more difficult than I thought if the constables were partying with the criminals.

"Can you ID the husband?"

"Not yet. He's just one of the Rastas."

"What about the girl?"

"Haven't see her yet. But the car's here."

"The Datsun?"

"They drive it around."

"Okay. Watch that. Chances are the guy who drives it, or drives it the most, is the husband. Here's what I want you to do. You guys become one with the neighborhood. Hang around. Cruise the streets. Make yourselves obvious. Let people get used to seeing you. Then start spreading the news that you're from New York and are looking to score some drugs. Don't go to our targets first, just spend some money, go out with some women, drink a little bit. A little bit, Eddie, and make some friends."

"Anything else, boss?" Eddie said. He could tell I was a bit anxious because I wasn't on the scene.

"Make an ID on everybody around that house. Make maps of the roads to the airport and marinas, footpaths, access to the house. Who lives next door. You know what to do."

"Okay. And then what?"

"Then I'll let you know." I hung up, wishing that I could be there. But the time wasn't right. I still had to figure out a way to break down the Rastas' defenses.

Back in New York, it was the same old story with the husband/kidnapper—dangle the money, negotiate to death, and stall, stall, stall. The process was made easier by the kidnapper's own ruse. Since he was supposedly a good guy who was now part of the family, he couldn't play tough and make threats. And he didn't have to worry about short calls or phone traces, because he'd already revealed who he was and where he lived. These factors enabled us to play him like a big, fat tarpon roiling in the bay below his new mansion.

It helped that Jody's sister dutifully played the part I gave her. She pretended to be friendly with the Rasta, telling him that he was their only hope to rescue Jody. At one point I advised her to suggest to Mr. Rasta that she should fly down to Montego Bay with a "friend" (me) to negotiate with the kidnappers, but he slammed the door on that idea, saying he was the husband and he'd handle it.

"I just need da money, and Jody be free," he said.

The sister blamed the payoff delays on her father, who was traveling in Europe and was difficult to reach.

"We'll get you the money as soon as we can," she promised. "We want Jody back as much as you do. We just need to talk to her or hear her voice. To know that she's still alive."

A few hours later, the husband was back on the phone with a tape.

"Please have my father pay so I can get out of here," a woman slurred.

The sister identified the voice as Jody's.

"Please, just pay the money!" Jody said again.

"That was quick," I whistled. "It's easy when she's right there beside him."

The tape, and the strange way Jody talked, forced me to consider an element I'd yet to mention to anyone. Was Jody herself part of the kidnapping? Maybe she planned it? If that was true, then she wouldn't take kindly to our rescue. She could put the whole team in danger at the most critical point.

I had to get someone inside that house to tell me exactly what the situation was. (By this time we had already obtained the building plans to Mr. Rasta's mansion from an attorney in Kingston, Jamaica. We knew how many rooms there were, the layout, and doorways, etc., which would prove crucial if we had to storm the place.)

To increase the odds, and bring in a little muscle, I sent a second team to the tropical island. It was headed by Frank Musumici, a half-Italian, half-Puerto Rican tae kwon do expert who had previously worked for Lynch before establishing his own martial arts academy. Frank brought one of his prize students with him, an athletic blonde destined to become his wife. I gave Frank the same instructions as I had to Eddie. "Move into the area. Learn the roads. Befriend the neighbors. Chart the local police and determine when they make their rounds. We need to ID all the cops who are with the Rastas. Become a known presence in the area so that when I arrive with the rescue squad, no one will suspect anything."

With my two teams in place, it was time to develop my own cover before I flew down to Montego Bay. Because we had access to the Rastas' phone records, we knew that they regularly called a fellow group of dreadlock-sporting druggies in New York. I arranged an introduction to the Big Apple Rastas, and with my associate Don Calogero pretended to be a porn producer who wanted to shoot stag films and throw wild parties in Jamaica.

The leader of the New York Rastas practically drooled to introduce us to his friends in Montego Bay because he thought he would get a piece of the action in my newfound profession—especially since we were looking for a nice house by the water to film our masterpieces.

With my cover in place, we stalled the husband for another week while Frank got himself situated. By then, three weeks after the initial call, with all the intelligence I'd gathered, I was ready to formulate my final plan.

From the building blueprints, we knew that the house was fed by two large water tanks perched on the roof. Slip an industrial-strength "mickey" into the tanks, and I'd be able to waltz in and grab the girl while everyone was dreaming of their Ethiopian Eden and its divine savior, Haile Selassie.

To accomplish that, I again needed to get someone inside. The critical task fell to Eddie.

Eddie's technique, a standard practice in the intelligence business, was effective and quick. He staged a minor accident with one of the Rastas who frequently visited the house. Whipping out a wad of cash, he immediately cooled the man's temper by grossly overpaying for the damage. As the pair became friendly, Eddie inquired about making a score. The Rasta gladly accommodated him. Within days, Eddie was not only tooling around with his new pal, he had established a pipeline for Jamaica-grown marijuana to the eager buyers on the streets of New York. Eddie was not only in, he was part of the gang.

Naturally, he wrangled an invite to the house.

"She's there all right," he told me afterward.

"Is she being held, or is she with them?"

"Hard to say. She's all strung out. A total mess. They keep her drugged twenty-four hours. My guess is she's a victim."

With Eddie on the inside, it was nearing D-Day. I sent a third team down to increase our numbers during the actual raid, then turned to one of my associates, psychologist Karen Kronman—the woman who helped me crack Claude Smith on the Frito-Lay case. I had Karen debrief Jody's sister to learn all she could about Jody's life and childhood. This would come in handy if Jody fought the rescue, or freaked out during it.

Karen and I were the last team to arrive. I'd barely touched down at the airport when I made a critical mistake that nearly blew apart the operation. Passing through Customs, I declared our equipment, and the $10,000 in cash I was carrying in case we needed to pay someone off.

Eddie picked us up outside the airport just before midnight. As we were talking, I noticed a young boy bent down behind Eddie's car, inspecting the tires. Distracted by Eddie's conversation, I put the incident out of my mind.

During the drive to the hotel, Eddie kept looking in the rearview mirror.

"Damn it. I think we have a tail, boss," he said.

"Okay, stay calm."

The next thing I knew, the car was bouncing wildly on the road.

"We also have a flat," Eddie announced. "A tail and a flat. Not a pleasant situation."

"They're after the money I declared at Customs," I deduced. "Damn, I knew I shouldn't have done that. Okay, what's up ahead?"

"There's a lighted bus stop a couple of miles down the road."

I looked out the window. All I could see was black jungle, glinting in the moonlight. There were no other cars in sight. Fortunately, Eddie knew where we were.

"Pull over when you get there," I said, grabbing a gun and a pair of binoculars. "When we stop, we go on the offensive."

I peered through the binoculars and focused on the car trailing us. Although we were only going about ten miles an hour on our bad leg, the tail had not passed us or even gained ground. They were definitely waiting for us to stop.

Through the magnified lenses, I could see that there were two men in the car. From what I could tell, they weren't Rastas.

"They just want the money," I repeated. "Okay, Eddie, when we stop, I'll handle the driver, you take the other guy."

After bumping along for two miles, we arrived at the bus stop. Eddie pulled over. We waited for the tail to park behind us, then Eddie and I leaped from the car with our weapons at our side and ran toward the hijackers.

"We don't need any help. Thank you," I yelled as I approached the driver's door.

The men were caught off guard by our aggressive action. I, in turn, was caught off guard by a gleaming set of white teeth coming from the back seat. I'd counted on two men, not three. The extra hijacker scared the shit out of me. Fortunately, we scared the shit out of them worse. They cranked up their vehicle and drove away.

"That gets the blood going," I cracked as Eddie wiped his brow.

Back at the car, Karen was thoroughly relieved that the incident had ended without bloodshed. I touched her shoulder to comfort her, then quickly helped Eddie change the tire. I didn't want any Johnny-come-lately robbers to try and take advantage of our situation.

We made it to the hotel without further incident. The next morning, I regrouped the whole team at the beachfront apartment we had rented. I briefed everyone on our strategy. By then, Eddie had introduced Frank and his girlfriend to the Rastas as easy marks in the marijuana-buying market. Soon they were also accepted inside.

The plan was simple. The Rastas, as usual, were having a big party in two days. Sometime during the festivities, Eddie was to slip out of the house, climb up the water tanks, and pour in sleep-inducing drugs. The Rastas would be so drugged anyway that they'd hardly notice when people began passing out. I just hoped they occasionally drank water.

Once everybody was unconscious, we'd march in, grab the girl, drive to the airport, and fly her home in a ready and waiting Learjet.

Everything went as scheduled. The only wrinkle was Eddie's utter revulsion at what went on during the party. The Rastas, including Jody's husband, had nothing but contempt for their victim. It wasn't enough to keep her drugged. They sexually humiliated and debased her in every way possible. Rasta after Rasta would disappear into her room to rape her, including bums they dragged off the street. It was apparent that Jody had become the gang's sex slave. The girl was drugged out of her mind, but still, I knew, the scars from this experience would last a lifetime. And if we didn't get her out of there, that lifetime wouldn't be very long.

Eddie broke away from the perversion, which included ritual-
istic animal sacrifices in the back yard and other grotesque rituals.
He poured the drugs into the tanks. "Take this, you sick bastards!"

The next morning, we marched in, big as life, and entered the
Rasta nest. I was wearing a crisp white suit, a psychological ploy
designed to show any Rastas still conscious that I was in charge.

The house was totally trashed. There were beer cans, liquor
bottles, food, dope, and garbage strewn everywhere. Rastafarians
were scattered about, passed out on the sofas, beds, and floors.

As we searched the house, a dreadlocked man stumbled out of
a room, spotted us, saw Eddie, gave a slight wave, got something to
drink, and wandered back into his room. A second man repeated
the procedure a few minutes later. Recognizing Eddie and Frank,
the drugged, hungover Rastas never raised an eyebrow. They probably thought that their sleepy cohorts had simply scored some
killer weed the night before.

We found Jody all alone in a back bedroom.

"Shalom, Jody," I said. "We've come to take you home to your
father."

Jody backed away toward the wall like a frightened child.

"It's okay, Dee," Karen said, calling her by a childhood nickname. "Your father and sister are waiting for you. Please come
with us." The nickname did the trick. She began to cry.

Jody took Karen's hand. We lifted her up and helped her walk
through the house and out to the driveway.

The trip to the airport was uneventful. I carried Jody to the
Learjet and buckled her into a seat. Within minutes, we were air-
borne. Her long nightmare was over.

In New York, I contacted Immigration and explained that we were
bringing in a kidnapping victim who had no passport or identification of any kind. I'd previously advised the State Department, so
that process went smoothly.

After her joyful reunion with her family, Jody was taken to
Europe and was checked into a drug detoxification and psychological counseling center. When she returned, she presented me with
two camels carved from wood grown on Mount Olive in Israel. I
cherish these gifts.

Jody's father didn't want to take any further action against the
men who kidnapped, raped, and horribly abused his daughter. He
allowed them to keep the house, car, and whatever money they

had left from her trust account. He was just happy to have his daughter back.

About a year later, I was disturbed to learn that Jody was back in Los Angeles living the wild life. Not only that, but she had fallen right back in with a new group of Rastafarians.

At her father's behest, I flew in with some muscle, grabbed the Rasta leader, and told him in so many words not to mess with her again.

Apparently he got the message. Jody, through no help of her own, has managed to remain free. Knock on Mount Olive wood.

FOREVER IN BLUE JEANS

THE AUDIT FROM HELL

Sixteen years ago, during the Watergate affair, we learned the professionalism of the IRS was compromised by an imperial Presidency. . . . Today we find the IRS mired in its own form of Watergate, which like its predecessor, involves greed, seduction, cover-up, the victimization of innocent citizens by intimidation and retaliation, obstruction of justice and criminal activity . . . If we fail to effect [changes], it will be extremely difficult for this government to re-establish its faith with the average taxpayer citizen.
— U.S. REPRESENTATIVE AL BUSTAMENTE, TEXAS,
CONGRESSIONAL IRS HEARINGS, 1989

IT WAS BLACK TUESDAY, January 28, 1986, the day the space shuttle *Challenger* exploded in the Florida sky. The Earth's vibes must have been universally bad that morning, because it was also a disastrous day at Jordache Enterprises in Manhattan. The $500 million international blue jeans company was about to embark upon its own four-year nightmare.

At 9:20 A.M., as the doomed shuttle sat on the launchpad awaiting countdown, a fleet of vans pulled into the entrance of the underground loading bay at Jordache's aging, red brick, ten-story office building on Seventh Avenue. The van doors opened with a loud metallic clatter. More than fifty heavily armed Internal Revenue Service and U.S. Customs agents poured out into the cold air.

The elite Treasury department storm troopers were gearing up to sweep through the building like an invading army, manhandle Jordache's 240 employees, and rip the company apart.

At 9:30, Jordache's in-house counsel, Robert Spiegelman, walked out of his office to run a quick errand. As he passed the elevator doors, they hissed open.

"This is the IRS! U.S. Customs! This is a raid!" an agent bellowed as the mob swarmed into the office complex. "You are all to stand up, get away from your desks, and place your hands at your sides. Move! Now!"

Guns drawn, barrels up, the federal agents waved their badges above their heads like winners at the local church bingo parlor. Barking commands, they shoved people aside, causing waves of chaos and fear to ripple through the office workers.

Uncle Sam's gangbangers were storming the place like it was a crack house full of armed lunatics instead of a blue-chip Manhattan business populated by meek secretaries, accountants, and suited office workers.

The lead IRS agent, Steven Levy, ordered all the Jordache employees to queue up and submit to being frisked like common criminals. Properly humiliated, the emotionally spanked wage earners were then sent home. The only Jordache staffers allowed to remain were a few scattered lawyers and executives.

For the next forty-eight hours, IRS and Customs agents chewed through Jordache, grabbing records by the cartload. They rummaged through files, peered in trash cans, emptied desks, snatched a child's report card from his mother's drawer, removed personal belongings and photographs, and grabbed private letters. Like a trail of worker ants feasting on a freshly killed carcass, they carried the spoils down the elevators and stairs and piled them into their vans.

Right from the beginning, something stank about the raid. The only people the IRS usually invades with such heavy-handed tactics are drug dealers, mobsters, and corporations long under investigation. The IRS's elite goon squad, the Criminal Investigations Division (CID), is only allowed out of its cage after more evolved agents have certified "probable cause" by painstakingly corroborating all evidence of criminal activity.

In contrast, Jordache was never notified of any previous irregularities regarding the IRS or Customs. The blue jeans company's taxes were prepared by Coopers and Lybrand, a respected Big Eight accounting firm with a reputation for straight shooting.

"What are we under investigation for?" Spiegelman asked Levy.

"Criminal tax fraud," Levy snapped.

"Why didn't you just subpoena us?"

It was a good question. Levy apparently had no answer. He simply walked away.

There seemed to be no rhyme or reason for the oppressive raid. The government just swallowed everything in sight, enough to shut down Jordache for weeks at the cost of millions of dollars.

Spiegelman paced with increasing frustration as the agents combed through the place. There was nothing he could legally do to counter the criminal search warrant a federal judge had signed.

However, it was a different story when the storm troopers tried to barge into his locked office.

"Get away from there!" he screamed. "You guys can't touch legal documents. That's attorney-client privilege!"

"Move the fuck out of the way," spit an IRS man. "We can take whatever we want."

Spiegelman refused to give. He was shoved aside and watched helplessly as they unscrewed his door off its hinges, rifled through his papers, took personal notes and secret litigation strategies on current court cases, and then drilled open his safe.

It appeared highly improper, but they were the IRS. There was nothing anybody could do.

The following day, Jordache was vilified in the media. Rumors spread that they were an Israeli organized crime front guilty of everything from tax evasion and smuggling to drug dealing. The jeans company was not only under the guns of the IRS and Customs, but was caught in the crosshairs of vaunted U.S. Attorney Rudolph Giuliani, the feared Mafia hunter who operated out of the Southern District of New York.

Not surprisingly, business plummeted.

The once dominant blue jeans manufacturer now teetered on the brink of collapse. And they had no idea—not the faintest clue—as to why. After six months of this hell, they called me.

I was about to embark on the biggest case of my career—one that forever changed the way I felt about justice in America. It was also a case in which I was forced to use all my accumulated skills to save my own skin.

In the executive boardroom of one of New York's swankier law firms, Avi Nakash—one of three Israeli brothers who owned and operated Jordache Enterprises—outlined his problems to me. Nakash, a refined man with olive-toned skin, was dressed informally—in contrast to the bevy of $500-per-hour attorneys accompanying him—sporting a tennis shirt and a pair of the high-priced jeans that had made him wealthy. The casual clothes didn't detract from the air of money and power that exuded from him. I sensed that he could be ruthless if he needed to be.

Right now he was extremely worried.

Of all the horrors he had been through with Customs, the IRS, and the U.S. Attorney, what seemed to eat at him the most was a massive lawsuit in California that he was now starting to lose.

The three Nakash brothers were in a vicious legal battle with, ironically, another band of immigrant Jewish siblings, the four Marciano brothers of Hollywood by way of French Algeria and Marseilles. Thirty-six months earlier, the seven brothers had hashed out a deal where Jordache bought 51 percent of the Marcianos' little company, Guess Jeans, along with a smaller division called Gasoline. Jordache paid $5 million to close the deal, and threw in a personal credit guarantee to aid Guess's expansion.

Although the serious and conservative-minded Nakashes were the majority owners, the dashing, gregarious, party-happy Marcianos continued to run the company.

Thanks to a nifty advertising campaign, fashionable designs, and Jordache's know-how, the public began clamoring for Guess's stonewashed jeans. The California firm rocketed from an $8 million operation to an industry titan, raking in more than $200 million in annual sales in less than three years.

The Marcianos, no doubt feeling that they acted too soon and sold out too cheaply, desperately wanted to rid themselves of their straightlaced New York partners. To do so, they filed a thunderous civil suit charging that the Nakashes had enticed them with the investment cash so they could steal their designs for Jordache.

"If I wanted to steal their designs, it wouldn't have cost me five million dollars. I'd just go to Bloomingdale's and buy a pair of Guess jeans off the rack for fifty bucks," Avi lamented. His lawyers nodded in agreement behind him.

Prior to the IRS raid, things had been going well for Jordache in the California court. Afterward, with all the bad press, Jordache started getting hammered.

"So what can I do?" I asked.

"Our attorneys and investigators have not made much progress. We need you to find out if the Marcianos are extorting their sewing contractors, if they've stolen from us, taken kickbacks, things like that. Plus, what's going on with the lawsuit."

Avi also wanted me to do some checking on the Marcianos' history overseas. There were allegations that one or more of the brothers escaped France to avoid paying millions in back taxes.

After perusing the legal records and bringing myself up to date, it appeared to me that, vicious and costly as it was, the legal battle in Los Angeles was little more than a typical sour-grapes ploy by someone who wanted to weasel out of a financial arrangement—all goaded on by an army of attorneys only too happy to pour oil on the flames of the dispute. The current suit was actually the third the Marcianos had filed trying to accomplish the same goal of eradicating the Nakashes. In one of the prior suits, the Nakashes had generously compromised by giving the Marcianos back a critical ownership point, making the two sets of brothers equal, fifty-fifty partners.

The whole thing struck me as routine legal mudslinging—until I glanced at a packet of legal papers on a peripheral case. After they hit the big time, the Marcianos filed a similar court action designed to break a licensing agreement with a small garment company owned by a man named Jeff Bohbot. Bohbot had been granted the sole distributorship of Guess in the USA back when the jeans company was tiny. Now that the Marcianos were raking in the dough, they wanted to control its distribution. No surprise there. If the Marcianos went after Jordache, they'd surely go after some small fry. I was almost ready to cast the file aside when I spotted something that made my blood run cold. Shortly after getting slapped with the civil suit, Bohbot's company was placed under investigation by the IRS.

No, it can't be, I thought. *The garment district is full of crooks. It must be a coincidence.*

After some careful sniffing around, I brushed aside my fears and officially signed aboard, but not before setting down some tough ground rules to Avi and his attorney, Spiegelman. Since I assumed the Marcianos had bugged the offices, we met in safe places or offices that I knew were clean. "You have to keep me secret. No exceptions. Nobody knows I exist except you two. Not even your brothers. And the same goes for any informants I develop. I have to protect their identities at all costs.

"Also, Jordache's offices should be swept for electronic bugs on a regular basis. And no phone calls to me from there. If one of you needs to reach me, use a pay phone and call collect.

"I can probably answer your questions on whether the Marcianos have taken kickbacks, extorted their contractors, and stolen from Guess in a couple of months," I continued. "But there are some things I won't touch. Your problems with the IRS are yours. And I can't really help you with Giuliani. As far as the grand jury investigation goes, that's your problem."

After that, we set my fee, a $50,000-a-month retainer and expenses, plus a healthy bonus for success, in this case $500,000. Nakash further sweetened the deal. He offered to pitch in an extra $150,000 if I could finish the case in three months. Piece of cake, I thought.

Since most of the footwork would be in Los Angeles, I assembled the core of my Mexican team. Antonio, Jesus, and Manuel were happy to be back in the game, as were some other Mexican associates with more specific abilities that might be needed on a case like this—things like security and self-defense. I also added a young attorney with unusual skills named Sally Godfrey. Sally had previously worked in counterintelligence for the FBI, spoke several languages, and was a martial arts expert. Better yet, at five-seven, with long blonde hair and big green eyes, she was a literal and figurative knockout. Sally could get any man to talk to her. If he got out of line, Sally could kick his ass.

To my surprise, Avi Nakash had done a little clandestine butt-kicking himself. After the lawsuit was filed, he had detectives collect the trash at both Guess and the headquarters for a chain of retail stores the Marcianos owned called MGA. The sixty boxes of paper the PIs had grabbed proved to be a gold mine. There were financial statements, incorporation documents, bank accounts, cash transaction records, and investment accounts at Drexel Burnham and Merrill Lynch. I entered it all, including the names of everyone listed, into a rapidly growing computer database.

One of the first things the valuable trash told me was that the vast amount of Guess clothing stocking the shelves of the Marcianos' MGA stores didn't match what the Guess records said they had been supplied. In other words, the Marcianos were apparently siphoning money from themselves, i.e., stiffing Jordache, and probably the IRS. Clever, but no earth-shaking revelation. The Marcianos, of course, denied everything.

The trash also revealed the extent of the Marcianos' egos. They had retained a prominent Hollywood public relations firm headed by the son of actor James Mason and given the flacks a truly bizarre assignment. They wanted Mason to arrange it so they wouldn't have to rub shoulders with the hordes of unwashed peasants down at Immigration when they received their U.S. citizenship. Instead, they wanted to be sworn in during an elaborate ceremony at the White House! And why not? Mason referred to the litigious jeans barons as "France's gift to the United States"!

While Mason spun a wonderful new image for the greedy brothers M, Sally Godfrey and I were uncovering an entirely different picture. We quickly unearthed a legion of angry Guess employees and ex-employees who were more than happy to rat out their Scrooge-like bosses. The stories were all the same. The Marcianos forced kickback payments from their sewing subcontractors, mostly small Mexican and Korean firms. They then apparently used the skimmed money to buy real estate and invest in the stock market.

The sources—including ex-Guess production managers Cary Nadler and Marsha Knotts—said, among other things, that the Marcianos demanded $1 per item from the beleaguered sewing shops, which were producing 60,000 garments a week. Not a bad under-the-table take.

They also reported that upwards of 50,000 pairs of Guess jeans and jackets had marched out the door unchecked and reappeared on the display hangers at MGA. On top of everything else, the employees charged that the socially charming Marcianos were the kings of mean, verbally abusing their staffs on a regular basis.

An overseas check produced more of the same. The French Minister of Taxation confirmed that the four brothers bolted France owing close to 60 million francs in unpaid taxes and penalties from their previous business endeavors. The Marcianos, it seemed, didn't exactly rank up there with the Statue of Liberty when it came to benevolent gifts from France.

It was time to contact the IRS and tell them the good news about Guess. In a case like this, the tax collectors usually take over from there. I thought that after a few IRS interviews with the unhappy employees and subcontractors, it would be "all she wrote" for the French quartet. If life were only that easy.

I phoned an IRS CID manager in L.A., identified myself, and started spilling the beans. However, before I'd spilled enough to feed a small squirrel, the tax man interrupted. "Let me give you a tip. Off the record, okay?"

"Sure."

"If you bring a case out here against the Marcianos, it's you who will be investigated."

My grip tightened on the phone. "Me? What do you mean?"

"This is way off the record, okay? You ought to know that the Marcianos just hired a former IRS Criminal Investigations branch chief. Guy by the name of Howard Emirhanian, one of the bigger dogs out here. They hired him to be their Chief of Security, only Howard has no idea what security means."

The IRS man lowered his twangy, Midwestern voice. I had to strain to hear. "They're about to hire the Criminal Investigations Chief of the entire L.A. region, Ron Saranow, the top dog out here. Saranow and Emirhanian are close. You want to investigate the Marcianos? Then the IRS will go after you. That's all I'll say." He said a lot.

It was very peculiar. Why would an IRS agent, on a cold call from a stranger, break the agency's famed code of silence? In one short conversation, he had revealed a great deal of disturbing information. It sounded like a cry for help. I stared down at the telephone. Could the situation be that bad in Los Angeles?

I switched on my computer and punched in Saranow and Emirhanian. Pay dirt. Scattered among the Guess trash were literally thousands of phone messages that the Marcianos had discarded. Some listed names, times, and even the substance of the call. Dozens had come from Howard Emirhanian and Ronald Saranow, the two top dogs in the Los Angeles IRS Criminal Investigations Division.

Emirhanian was already on Guess's payroll. Saranow had a standing offer to join him.

I breathed a deep sigh of relief. Thank goodness for the Good Samaritan on the telephone. Had I waltzed into that IRS office with all my dirt on the Marcianos, I might not have made it back out. If I was going to get anywhere, I'd have to bring my evidence to another IRS district, one where I could vouch for the players' integrity.

Fortunately, I just happened to know a very good IRS agent, George De Los Santos from Dallas. George and I had worked together on the Frito-Lay kickback case, and I knew he was above reproach.

"Send me the material," he said in his Texas drawl when I phoned. "I'm sure there's nothing wrong out there, but we'll do this according to procedure."

I prepared the materials and Fed-Exed them to Dallas, confident De Los Santos would change his tune once he saw the papers.

Meanwhile, my Mexican team continued to put the squeeze on the Marcianos. Sally Godfrey, the karate attorney, had transformed herself into Kelly Grace, freelance writer. Kelly G called *Playboy* magazine, pitched an article on the Marcianos, and got an editor to agree to see it on spec, meaning no promises. That was good enough to establish her cover.

Kelly G then started calling people around the Marcianos, and eventually the big four themselves. Paul Marciano, the most brilliant and aggressive brother, called her back. A charming man, he tried to sweet-talk her, even when she began to poke him with some penetrating questions about kickbacks, French taxes, hiring IRS honchos, and other sticky matters. Paul ducked them all, going so far as to deny that he hired Emirhanian.

Shortly after that conversation ended, another began—one that was far less pleasant. On Kelly G's horn was one Marshall Grossman, the Marcianos' pit-bull attorney. Grossman wasn't any deskbound corporate weenie, he was a killer, take-no-prisoners trial lawyer, the top of the breed.

Grossman started stabbing Kelly back, accusing her of slander and misguided muckraking. She defended herself by tossing out more evidence that we had on his clients, things like currency violations in Italy and a peculiar contribution to a synagogue in Marseilles. Caught off-guard by the pinpoint data, Grossman temporarily withdrew his counterattack.

While Sally/Kelly was verbally wrestling with the Marcianos and their high-priced brawling barrister, I was reaching out to a contact I had inside the L.A. IRS. The source nervously confirmed

what I'd already been told: that Emirhanian was working for the
Marcianos and that Saranow had been offered a job. He also told
me that the Marcianos were IRS informants, and ran their information through a CID manager named Al Lipkin, a pal of
Emirhanian and Saranow.

"Lipkin targets the people they give us," the contact explained.

"The Marcianos are IRS informants?" I echoed, surprised by the
news. "Is it common knowledge that Emirhanian works for Guess?"

"Everybody knows. They haven't tried to hide it. And Saranow
brags around the office about his job offer and a red Porsche he's
been promised." After a long pause, the agent spoke in an eerie
whisper. "Be careful. This office is a nest of vipers."

The whispered warnings were getting to be serious, and quite
unnerving! Still, it's not in my nature to back off. Instead, I did the
opposite. I directed Sally, i.e. Kelly Grace, to call Mr. Lipkin.

Despite the hard questions she asked about his boss, Lipkin
was a cheerful type, especially when he found out who she was
allegedly working for. "*Playboy*! You going to model for them, too?
You sound like you're good looking enough to pose."

"They wanted me to," Kelly responded, feeding his fantasy.
"But they don't pay."

That got him going. He said he would be in Chicago soon
(*Playboy*'s headquarters), and wanted to take her out for a beer.

Kelly steered him around that, then burrowed in with the
$64,000 question. "I heard the Marcianos just hired someone out of
CID in Los Angeles. Did he retire, or what? I'd like to call him, if
you could give me his name."

"I don't know anything about that," Lipkin dodged. "You know,
L.A.'s a big office."

"My source said it was a big honcho, like a supervisor . . ."

Yeah, like your supervisor, Lipkin! I thought when I heard the
tape.

"No. No," he repeated, then went back into his get-a-date-in-
Chicago mode.

The next day, Sally/Kelly placed a call to Howard Emirhanian
at Guess headquarters in L.A. About an hour later, he phoned her
service, left a message, and represented himself as being from the
Los Angeles IRS CID office. That was interesting. Call a security
guy at Guess, get a return call from the IRS.

An hour or so later, my phone line lit. It was a deep-cover
source my Mexican team had developed inside the Marciano

camp. "The Marcianos have gone berserk! Some journalist called them. Grossman, too. The brothers are scared shitless. Paul's even talking about chartering a plane to Canada to get their secret papers out of the country. And they're shredding documents faster than hell. I mean, they're really rattled. Georges even mentioned a settlement with the Nakashes."

"Good. Just stay low and keep me posted."

At the end of August, George De Los Santos asked if we could meet with Avi Nakash at the IRS headquarters in Washington, D.C. He'd read my materials on the L.A. office and wanted to discuss it further. The fact that he wanted to do it in Washington told me the matter was being taken seriously. We arranged a meeting the following week. "Avi, we need to talk," I said, calling my client. "Meet me at the usual place."

I had an associate shadow Avi and watch for a tail as the tycoon left Jordache headquarters and began to walk across 37th Street toward 9th Avenue near the Port Authority bus terminal. I wanted to talk to him in a noisy place away from his office in case the place was bugged. We met on the sidewalk.

"Evidently, the whole L.A. senior IRS CID staff is going to work for the Marcianos," I told him. "Can you remember anything else about the IRS and the Marcianos?"

Avi pulled me into an alcove. He told me that an Israeli businessman, Hardolf Wolf, had acted as the go-between during the original deal that brought Jordache and Guess together. Afterward, when things started getting nasty with the lawsuits, Wolf returned to his role as go-between. "'Avi, you'd better settle on the Marcianos' terms, $12 million for the Nakashes' 50 percent,'" Avi quoted Wolf as saying. "'Settle, or they'll drop an atom bomb on you guys.'"

"When did this guy Wolf say this to you?" I asked.

"December, 1985."

"The IRS raid was when?"

"A month later. January."

"Did Wolf mention the IRS specifically in the context of the atom bomb?"

"Yes!"

IRS raids are virtually always emergency reactions by the tax agency when they discover that someone under investigation is shredding documents or destroying other evidence. How did the Marcianos know about the possibility of a raid a month in advance? As I drove back to my office in Fort Lee, New Jersey, I realized I had been sucked into the one area I wanted to avoid like the plague—Jordache's problems with the IRS. But there was no way to escape it. The IRS, the Marcianos, and the lawsuit appeared to be tightly intertwined.

Bad for Avi. Worse for me!

It was Mexico all over again. It's a regular practice in my native land for the rich and powerful to use the Fiscal Police (Mexico's IRS) to attack their enemies. But in America? Could a rat pack of French Algerian immigrants, some with criminal records, buy the most powerful government branch in the United States and use them as their own trained Dobermans? It boggled the mind. It was also extremely frightening.

At my request, Avi arranged for Wolf to fly in from Israel the next morning. I needed him to repeat his "atom bomb" statements on the record. We gathered at the St. Tropez restaurant on 36th Street for lunch on September 3.

The well-dressed Israeli was of medium height and had brown wavy hair. He appeared to be in his forties, and was sporting a red tie. Despite his jet-lagged exhaustion, he seemed like a shrewd businessman.

The conversation quickly focused on a settlement. "Look," he said, "unless I create an earthquake in Georges' [Marciano's] mind, we will not move him an inch."

Wolf now wanted to do the same thing to the Marcianos that he had done to the Nakashes ten months earlier, force them into a settlement. He was playing both ends against the middle. "I go to Georges and tell him, 'Georges, beware! If you don't settle by Thursday, it will be bad,'" Wolf said. He added that until then, the Marcianos felt that the Nakashes had nothing on them. Georges, Wolf added, told him as much: "'If they had someone to use against me, they would have used it a long time ago,'" he quoted Georges as saying. "'They would not sit idle after I made what I made with the IRS . . .'"

There it was! Another indication that Georges Marciano and clan were directing IRS raids against their business enemies. And in doing so, they managed to get the U.S. Attorney's office, the famed district run by New York mayor-to-be Rudolph Giuliani, to do their heavy-handed bidding.

I kept talking, trying to get Wolf to spell it out in clear language.

"Georges told me to tell him [Avi] that unless he did this and that, he would throw the IRS on him. This means extortion? No! No!" he repeated. "It's not extortion."

He remained convinced that earthquakes and atom bombs were the only way to play the game. The allegorical Israeli continued to press us for a "bullet" to "hold to Georges' head." We had nothing to give him. To push our hand, he repeated that the Marcianos had played the game first by using the IRS, and it was only natural to retaliate.

"They were committing extortion!" I insisted, trying to get the unflappable Israeli to understand the import of his suggestion.

"Well, they got away with it," he finally admitted.

"They've been paying the people from the IRS," I explained.

"They didn't get paid directly, but got paid by someone, okay?" Wolf confirmed. "And they [the IRS] did what they were supposed to do . . . The IRS was supposed to find some papers . . ."

So that was it. It never was about taxes. It was about intimidation, and bringing the Nakashes to their knees. It was about the Marcianos getting their hands on papers, no doubt the Jordache attorney's privileged attorney/client communications, trial preparation notes, and anything else Guess's legal team could use in the trial. The one thing that the Marcianos really wanted was the same thing the IRS had no business grabbing.

Avi, his attorney Spiegelman, and I arrived at the IRS Washington, D.C. headquarters at 1111 Constitution Avenue the next afternoon. The tax agency has a way of striking a chill in one's heart, that's for sure. One could sense the power of the place standing outside, dwarfed by the blunt, off-white building.

We were ushered into a plush, wood-paneled conference room on the fourth floor where George De Los Santos and his Dallas manager, Duke Van Carlton, waited.

De Los Santos greeted me with a reserved smile and firm handshake. I noticed that his stocky frame supported a bit more weight than the last time we'd met, during the Frito-Lay case six years earlier. He still wore a well-groomed beard, which complemented his broad, handsome Mexican face.

When I finished briefing the men, Van Carlton agreed to open a formal investigation of the Marcianos. They would start by interviewing the sources inside Guess that Sally and I had developed.

Just as I was once again starting to feel good about the case, another fly fell into the ointment. On September 8th, the Nakash attorney Spiegelman called me collect from a pay phone, as I'd instructed. He had just received a letter from Grossman, the Marcianos' attorney, claiming that there had been death threats made against his clients. Spiegelman wanted to know if any of my associates had threatened the brothers.

"I'm not that stupid, and neither is she," I answered in a huff, referring to Sally, the only person who had spoken with one of the brothers personally.

I chuckled when I received a faxed copy of the letter to Spiegelman. It was nothing more than clever lawyer bunk solely designed to steer attention away from his clients and toward the Nakashes. Grossman termed Sally's calls intimidating and added that afterward, the Marcianos had received death threats. That was a new one: death threats from a journalist. It's generally the other way around.

My interest was piqued near the end. Grossman, brilliant as he was, made a mistake. He mentioned that Sally/Kelly "claims she was formerly with the FBI . . ." The only person she had told that to was that ol' smoothie Al Lipkin, he of the playmate centerfolds dancing in his head. Someone in the L.A. CID office had directly or indirectly relayed Sally's call to Lipkin to the Marcianos. Who was working for whom here?

When I relayed the information to Sally, she had some news of her own. "I received some interesting messages on Kelly Grace's answering service," she said, rolling the tape.

"Stop the investigation or you'll end up in the hospital," growled the first caller. "We're gonna break your legs," grunted the second.

Who was threatening whom?

Following Watergate, Congress learned that a powerful President could use the IRS to harass his political opponents, as President Nixon did. To counter that, they passed the "Disclosure Laws"—section 6103 of the tax code—which states that the tax agency cannot give out information concerning taxpayers to anyone, including the Justice Department, without the taxpayer's consent or a court order. Even the FBI was handcuffed by the law.

It sounded good on the surface—protect the public, rival politicians, and protest groups from political harassment. In reality, the Disclosure Laws gave even more power to the already hugely powerful IRS. It placed them above the law. Thanks to Disclosure, no one could investigate the IRS except for Congress, and even with Congress, the IRS could stall and hide.

Instead of an independent review body to keep them honest, the IRS was left to police itself with its own Inspection Division. As with every closed-door internal security group, their official function bore little resemblance to what they actually did. Officially, they were to weed out corruption. Unofficially, they covered it up so that no one would ever know.

The Jordache/Guess squabble proves how the Disclosure Laws had become a maddening Catch-22. If the IRS was feeding information to the Marcianos, they were breaking the law. But the same Disclosure Laws they were breaking protected them from prosecution.

That meant, as the Los Angeles IRS office no doubt realized, they could operate with impunity.

Somehow, I had to get around this ironclad IRS shield.

I began shifting my emphasis from Guess to the IRS itself. A new set of moles needed to be cultivated inside the tax agency, especially the cancerous L.A. branch. I knew that would be difficult because the retaliation against anyone caught talking would be harsh. But I also knew that within every agency or business, there are honest, moral employees like the man who initially warned me about trying to take on the Marcianos. These people, though naturally frightened and nervous, are usually upset enough about what's going on inside their organization that they're almost desperate to talk to the right person.

By the end of September, I had befriended the first of what would eventually be more than a dozen disgruntled IRS agents and managers eager to give me an inside view of Uncle Sam's tax collectors. It wasn't a pretty picture. And it was only the tip of the proverbial iceberg.

With all that I was learning, I had to be insane to go on with my campaign to bring the Marcianos to justice and get them, and the corrupt IRS agents and U.S. attorneys, off my client's back.

George De Los Santos, an idealist who believed IRS corruption only went so far and could be easily eradicated, began to carry the ball. He set up a meeting with his Los Angeles counterparts to present my evidence against the Marcianos and their IRS puppets. The meeting was set for the Pacific Shore Hotel, a beachfront lodge in Santa Monica.

When I phoned George at the hotel before the meeting, something strange happened. After a long pause, the operator asked me who was calling.

Hotel operators usually don't ask who's calling, like somebody's personal secretary. They don't know callers and guests from Adam. The L.A. IRS guys were apparently spying on the Dallas group.

I brushed her off, then huddled with De Los Santos and Van Carlton that evening. The Mexican, in his easy Texas manner, wasn't alarmed when I told him about the operator. He said he figured as much and had changed rooms at the last minute to avoid bugs.

I asked who from the L.A. office had attended the meeting. He replied that CID Branch Chief Phil Xanthos was there, along with an agent named John Anderson.

Uh-oh. John Anderson had been the point man on the investigation of Jeff Bohbot, the Guess licensee whom the Marcianos had fed to the tax agency like a white mouse to a python. That triggered a thought. "Did you ask if the Los Angeles IRS granted the Marcianos immunity?"

I shuddered in anticipation of the answer to this important question. If the Marcianos had immunity, the ball game was over. They were out of reach.

De Los Santos's boss, Van Carlton, said he asked that same question and was assured that the brothers were flying naked; they were just informants.

"Who else was there?" I wanted to know.

"Well . . . Al Lipkin."

"Lipkin!" I exploded. It was bad enough Anderson was there, but not Lipkin.

"Lipkin may be the guy leaking information to the Marcianos," I ranted. "I was told that Lipkin is one of Saranow's boys!"

De Los Santos squirmed, then said the connection didn't matter because Saranow had disqualified himself from anything having to do with the Marcianos. That was because of his job offer from Guess, which Xanthos had confirmed. Xanthos added that it wouldn't be a problem because they would simply "cut Saranow out of the loop." Yeah, right. And there's a bridge in Brooklyn I'd like to sell.

The two Dallas agents waved off my concern, insisting that the L.A. gang was excited about the information and were preparing to raid Guess. The IRS had confirmed that the Marciano brothers were shredding documents, and that, unlike the situation with Jordache, they now had a legitimate reason to call out the CID dogs.

It all sounded good, but I had my doubts.

Two days later, an informant told me that Saranow confronted Xanthos four times, demanding to know the details of the Pacific Shore meeting. Remarkably, Xanthos held firm.

Saranow's demands confused me because Lipkin and Anderson were obviously his boys. He could have gotten the information he wanted from them. His bullying, if true, had to be nothing more than intimidation.

I flew back to New York confident that everything was going to be taken care of. Xanthos appeared to be the kind of guy who wouldn't back down, not even to his own boss. And besides, Dallas was involved. Saranow's reach couldn't extend that far. I began to mentally ease out of the case. Once the IRS officially acted, my part would be over, or so I thought.

Man, was I naive.

WATCHING THE WATCHERS

KARATE ATTORNEY Sally Godfrey unwittingly unleashed a chain of events that was about to rain on my expected IRS-raids-Guess parade.

Godfrey said someone had been trying to squeeze the answering service we had used four weeks earlier to establish her cover as a *Playboy* magazine writer. Tracing the harassment trail backwards, I discovered that the Marcianos were using a powerful private investigative firm in New York named Kroll Associates, which we confirmed from the Marciano trash.

According to the answering service, a Kroll sleuth had teamed with an AT&T official to hound the answering service in an attempt to discover the real name and address of "Kelly Grace." When the initial attempts failed, a New York City police captain from Brooklyn paid the midtown Manhattan answering service a visit.

The implications of the attempted breach ran deeper. Kroll was supposed to be a glossy company known for helping out with corporate takeover fights. Apparently they could also get down and dirty with the best of them. Getting a telephone executive and a police captain to do their bidding didn't sound like the pristine

Kroll I'd read about in the *Wall Street Journal*. And if they'd sink that low to uncover Kelly Grace, how far would they go to smoke me out?

The more I learned about Kroll, the uneasier I became. For a handsome fee, Kroll's operatives had developed the original "evidence" against Jordache, the questionable tax fraud information later given to the IRS and the U.S. Attorney. And presenting their bullshit case wasn't difficult. Several of Kroll's top staffers were ex-Giuliani lieutenants from the Southern District, including an influential managing director named Bart Schwartz. Bad Bart had been Giuliani's chief of the criminal division.

Everywhere I turned, the water kept getting muddier. And I was in for a big dunking.

"Hey, Octavio, something's up," De Los Santos said over the phone from Texas. "I just got a call from Inspection here in Dallas. The guy wanted to know the name and address of my informant for the Los Angeles CID case against the Marcianos. He said he got a directive from Los Angeles Inspection to find out who you are."

"Why?"

"I don't know. He didn't say. Maybe Inspection wants to interview you. Should I give him your name?"

Confident that the Marcianos and their IRS puppets were about to take a fall, I nearly said yes. "No, not yet, but it sounds great. Give me twenty-four hours. Let me think about it, and then we'll decide."

It took considerably less than twenty-four hours for the smell to hit me. Why would IRS Inspection in L.A. call a Dallas Inspection agent and have him make the pitch to De Los Santos? Why the runaround? Why not ask De Los Santos directly?

I contacted my L.A. IRS mole. The source said that the Dallas CID visit had rattled the L.A. office, and the internal battle between Xanthos and Saranow was getting nastier.

I phoned De Los Santos at his home. "Something's wrong here. Don't give this guy my name."

"Okay. It's your call."

The next day, the Dallas Inspection agent, Jorge Urquijo, pestered De Los Santos again. And again. And again. He kept riding the guy. When De Los Santos refused to cough it up, Urquijo threatened to investigate him with a detailed audit.

Despite the pressure, De Los Santos felt that Urquijo could be trusted.

"Set up a phone call between the three of us. I'll identify myself as 'Mr. George.' Let's ask him some questions," I suggested, going on the offensive.

Five minutes later, we were all on the phone, George De Los Santos, Mr. George, and Jorge, which is George in Spanish.

Urquijo was more forceful, confident, and energetic than the laid-back De Los Santos. I instinctively read him as being honest. I also liked him.

"Why are you leaning on De Los Santos so hard? He's just doing his job," I said.

"You think I'm harassing De Los Santos? This woman [in L.A.] threatened to discipline me if I didn't find out who his informant was. She's calling me every day. Very insistent. She wants me to seize all of De Los Santos's records."

"Is that normal, Mr. Urquijo?" I asked.

That gave him pause.

"Well, to tell you the truth, actually, no. She certainly rubbed me the wrong way."

I gave Urquijo a quick rundown of the case in L.A., what happened to Jordache, and explained why they couldn't reveal my identity. I finished by asking Urquijo to check it out himself. If he could honestly tell me that Saranow and the Marcianos were clean, then I'd give him my name.

Urquijo agreed, then gave me some information. The IRS senior inspector bearing down on him was named Debbie Jones. In her telex to Urquijo, she gave "internal housekeeping" and the need for a "collateral investigation" as the reasons she had to know the true identity of the mysterious Mr. George. She also mentioned Saranow and the fact that he'd recused himself from the Guess investigation, and confirmed, once again, that Howard Emirhanian was working for Guess.

Those last references seemed out of place in the telex. She was protesting too much, as the saying goes. It appeared as if she was anticipating my response.

Jones's telex gave me the chills. I didn't know proper IRS protocol, but the whole thing sounded like bullshit to me.

Urquijo suddenly stopped talking in midsentence. "Man, this shit stinks. This whole setup stinks," he mumbled. The Dallas agent explained that Jones's telex didn't contain a case number. That didn't mean anything to me, but it made Urquijo's skin crawl. The IRS is a stickler for numbering everything, including internal memos. Every sheet of paperwork must be accounted for.

"What you are telling me," I said, "is that this telex, and all of Jones's phone calls, don't officially exist?"

"That's right. Without a case number, no one knows about this memo except me and her."

The fog was lifting. L.A. had done the end run around De Los Santos because they knew he wouldn't rat. He might, however, give my name to a trusted associate from his own office. And once it was relayed to L.A., it was sure to go right to Ron Saranow and the Marcianos.

That's why the request wasn't numbered. It wasn't IRS business. It was Marciano business!

Debbie Jones, gender aside, had to be one of Saranow's boys. I contacted one of my new IRS moles in L.A. to determine how close Jones and Saranow really were. The answer chilled my blood again. "Debbie Jones and Saranow have gone out together. Everyone knows they're socially close."

Boom! There went the supposedly impenetrable wall between IRS Inspection and the Audit and Investigative units.

"Is that allowed?" I wondered.

"No fucking way. The Inspection people aren't supposed to hang around with other agents. Inspection is supposed to be the watchdog here. But everyone—and I mean everyone out here in Los Angeles—knows that whatever they tell Debbie Jones, or even the other Inspection agents, goes right to Ron Saranow.

"Ron Saranow has total control over this office, because he controls Inspection. He can get away with literally anything. He knows everything that goes on here. . . . Octavio, Ron Saranow is without a doubt the most powerful IRS Criminal Investigation Chief in the nation. From what I hear, even the Commissioner is afraid of him. He's owed favors by everyone. He's got his claws sunk into people everywhere. Be careful. The man's very dangerous."

Another dire warning, this one the creepiest yet. Boy, was I getting tired of those! Tired, but not worried. Any day now, Saranow was about to have his eagle wings clipped by the Dallas gang and his own internal investigators. Once the Marcianos were raided, the IRS Big Cheese was certain to go down with Guess's ship. His reign of terror in Los Angeles would be over. I had nothing to fear, I told myself.

In mid-October, George De Los Santos called me in a rage. I'd never heard him so animated. "They dropped the fucking case! Los Angeles dropped the criminal case against the Marcianos!"

"What? I thought you had the raid sanctioned!"

"I swear to you, I haven't seen anything like this since the Frito-Lay investigation. They just killed it."

My inside source had been right all along. Ron Saranow was indeed a powerful man. And he was still out there, more powerful than ever, no doubt extremely angry.

The target of his anger? Me.

De Los Santos recovered from the L.A. shock when Los Angeles transferred the information to the Laguna Niguel office just south of Saranow's kingdom—supposedly to cut Saranow further out of the loop. But it was still too close. Within weeks, Laguna Niguel also killed the investigation. De Los Santos said the reason he was given was that the amount of Guess kickbacks weren't enough to warrant it.

I phoned the Laguna Niguel CID agent, a woman named Linda Dunlap. She admitted that the Marcianos failed to declare under-the-table revenues, just not enough to bother with. From the evidence I provided, the IRS could "only" document $1 million in kickbacks.

"Isn't that enough?" I screamed.

One million! The IRS tossed baseball legend Pete Rose in the slammer for failing to declare $50,000! And Rose didn't push people around. He earned the money by signing autographs and attending memorabilia shows.

Dunlap's lame excuse was total bullshit. The Marcianos had gotten their IRS lackeys to protect them again.

On November 13th, I gathered up all the evidence and brought it to a man named Jim Berliner, an Assistant U.S. Attorney for the Central District of California. My Organized Crime Strike Force contacts told me that Berliner was a good egg.

Berliner was an intense man in his mid-thirties with dark brown hair and a thin, athletic build. He seemed like a no-nonsense individual, so I didn't mince words. I asked him if he knew Saranow and/or the Marcianos, and if he had any problem with taking on the IRS. He responded that he only knew Saranow by reputation, didn't know the Marciano brothers, and wasn't afraid of the IRS.

The problem was, he quickly added, that because of the Disclosure Laws, he'd have to use IRS agents to spearhead any investigation. Without their help and cooperation, there was nothing he could do.

I suspected as much, but hated having to hear it.

Nonetheless, Berliner promised to get back to me after studying the materials.

Before leaving the coast, I spent some time cultivating new IRS sources. One agreed to meet me inside Pan American's First Class Lounge at Los Angeles Airport.

"You've got balls investigating these bastards, let me tell you," he opened.

After an hour of small talk, the source got down to business.

"If Saranow finds out I'm talking to you, he'll destroy me. That's what he's done here to whistle-blowers . . . and that's what they do in Washington."

"Are you telling me that Washington doesn't care about corruption?" That caught my attention because De Los Santos said that a high level internal security investigator from the capital wanted to meet with me.

"The agency is so decentralized that no one's in control," the source continued. "Several of the regional chiefs, guys like Saranow, have more de facto power than the Commissioner."

I'd heard that before. It was hard to believe, but all these sources couldn't be wrong. This one in particular appeared to be letting go of years of pent-up anger and frustration.

"They're like Mafia kingpins owed favors by people in every walk of life," he went on. "Chiefs like Saranow have the power to do anything. Raid you. Investigate you. Fuck you up. And you can't fight them. If I tried to blow the whistle on Saranow, he'd come after me. Transfer me to Alaska. Audit me. Harass me. It's really frightening. And I'm a man! You wouldn't believe the amount of sexual harassment in the service. I know two female agents in California who filed internal IRS sexual harassment claims, but nothing was done. Except they were harassed more."

"We're going to nail them all," I assured him.

"In only a couple of months, you've done more than Inspection ever has. I'm impressed. And Saranow's scared, I think. There's so much corruption inside the IRS it's unbelievable. And you never hear about it. Why? You always hear rumors about other government agencies, but never the IRS. I'll tell you why. They're so fucking powerful with these Disclosure Laws, and they go after anyone who tries to stop them."

Before he left, the man said that the next time I was in L.A., he'd introduce me to a couple of cohorts who knew even more.

A second IRS source related another eye-popping story. She said that behind the iron curtain that surrounded the L.A. tax agency offices, a number of supervisors were having sex on their desks late at night, going on drunken binges, and smoking pot. That was some mental image: tax men romping around their cubicles, then, after hours, rolling joints with W–2 forms. Who says accountants are boring?

De Los Santos phoned on November 20 with a familiar problem. The Washington internal security bigwig he'd previously mentioned, Keith Kuhn, was hounding him to reveal my name. It was Jorge Urquijo/Debbie Jones all over again, this time at a higher level.

"Okay, George, let me handle this."

By then, U.S. Attorney Jim Berliner had decided to investigate my allegations. He said that he'd call Kuhn for me, outline the corruption in the L.A. CID office, and get a read on the IRS man. If Berliner felt he was sincere, then I would phone next.

Back in New York, Avi Nakash phoned with some good news. He'd been contacted by a rabbi in L.A. who wanted to broker a settlement between the Nakashes and the Marcianos. The Marcianos, obviously feeling the heat, were said to be ready to compromise. The meeting was set for November 26 in Los Angeles.

Avi sounded happy and relieved. Win or lose, the lawsuit was costing him $10 million a year in legal fees. That, more than anything, was driving him nuts.

I couldn't help but wonder what spurred this latest extension of the olive branch. Were there more leaks? Did the Marcianos know about Berliner and Kuhn?

Two days before the big Nakash/Marciano lovefest, Jim Berliner called and said that he had met with Keith Kuhn in person and felt that the high-level IRS exterminator was on the level. Kuhn told Berliner that he had been suspicious about corruption inside the L.A. office for years.

Was Kuhn the man I was waiting for, or was it another well-laid trap to discover my identity? Berliner had come highly recommended, so I had to trust his instincts.

I scheduled my sitdown with Kuhn for November 26, the same day as the Nakash/Marciano gathering. My meeting came through. Avi's didn't. The day before the negotiation session in Los Angeles, the Marcianos backed out.

What happened? What made them change their minds? One minute the Marcianos are desperate to settle, the next they're standing firm again. What happened in the last few days?

Me. I happened. The thought made my stomach turn. Did the Marcianos have some renewed steel pumped into their collective backbones because they were about to identify the source of their problems? Had Kuhn relayed the news about our scheduled meeting?

There was a second possibility. Had the Marcianos suddenly been granted immunity by the U.S. Attorney's Office in the Southern District of New York?

I contacted a trusted confidant who could answer the immunity question. He confirmed my worst fears. There was a strong indication that the Beverly Hills brothers had been granted immunity.

If that were true, then there was no need to waffle over my decision to meet Keith Kuhn. Good or bad, he was the only option I had left to help clear my client.

So there I was, walking back through those massive, thoroughly intimidating doors of the IRS headquarters in Washington, D.C. *What the hell was I doing? Was it worth it?* I should have been a million miles away from this nightmarish structure. But if I ran away, who else was going to stop this cancer? I remembered a jumbled version of a famous saying: "Some seek greatness, others are chosen, and a few have destiny thrust upon them."

I was directed to the third floor, where destiny was going to be thrust upon me with full force. Kuhn's office was as impressive as the building. The dark oiled wood and expensive furniture fit the power of his position. As the Acting Assistant Commissioner for Inspection, Kuhn was one of the top ten IRS heavies in the country.

With one phone call, a guy like Kuhn could ruin a person forever.

Kuhn himself didn't fit my preconceived notion of the tax agency's top cop. He was a distinguished-looking man in his mid-fifties with receding gray hair and the air of a college professor. All that was missing was a pipe.

A much younger man with a decidedly crisp, clean-cut FBI look stood deferentially a few steps to Kuhn's right. He was introduced as Steve Jones, probably Kuhn's hatchet man.

I explained how I got involved in the case. Kuhn responded by confirming my suspicions that he was brought in by Jorge Urquijo.

Then he got down to business. He was aware of my allegations against Ron Saranow and the Marcianos, and knew about the pressure put on Urquijo by Debbie Jones. He repeated to me what he'd told Berliner, that he had suspected high-level IRS wrongdoing in L.A. for some time, but hadn't been able to prove it.

"Mr. Kuhn, I believe the situation just got worse," I said. "Yesterday I discovered that the Marcianos may have been granted immunity by the Southern District of New York."

Kuhn's eye's widened. This was clearly news to him. He motioned for Jones to check it out, then asked me to present my case. I gave him the extended version, the gist of which was that the Marcianos were using the IRS and the U.S. Attorney's office to pound their business enemies into submission. To drive the point home, I played him the infamous Hardolf Wolf "atom bomb/earthquake" tape.

When I was finished, Kuhn's reaction was more than I could have dreamed. He offered to put me on the IRS payroll to help him go after the L.A. office!

I was flattered, but it never crossed my mind to accept. I told him that Jordache was paying me enough, and I couldn't work for two different masters, anyway. Besides, considering what I'd found out about the tax agency, I couldn't think of a worse outfit to work for.

Kuhn promised full disclosure on his end, which was critical, and said both the IRS Commissioner and Assistant Commissioner were aware of my activities. Also aware was a man named Mike Bik, Inspection Chief for the Western United States.

My chest tightened. That was one person too many! The Commissioner and his assistant, I could understand, but this Bik character? If he was operating out west, then he fell clearly within Saranow's long reach. I kept my fears to myself. After all, I was set to jettison out of the quagmire any day now.

Not so fast. Kuhn's first directive was for me to fly back to the Laguna Niguel office, meet with District Director Mike Quinn, and present my findings again to see if they would reopen the tax fraud case against the Marcianos.

Wait a minute, I thought. Back to those guys? Back to Saranow's ballpark? I was about to protest when Kuhn floored me by saying he felt that Giuliani's office had been "duped" into investigating Jordache. My job was to pull my client, Jordache, out of the muck. With Kuhn expressing those feelings, how could I protest? I had to play along.

When I relayed Kuhn's statement to Nakash, he was ecstatic, so ecstatic he offered me a million-dollar bonus if I could prove that the grand jury investigation of Jordache was tainted, and get Giuliani's gang to drop it.

I accepted the challenge. It was all woven together anyway.

So much for jettisoning from the quagmire.

The meeting with Mike Quinn and his CID Chief, Bob Pledger, went relatively well. They listened to my by-now-well-rehearsed presentation and decided to reopen the investigation. Although Kuhn confirmed that the Marcianos had indeed been granted immunity by the Southern District of New York, he said the papers appeared to have been backdated and probably wouldn't stand up. That gave Laguna Niguel the go-ahead to take action.

Things started to sour once more from the moment the specific assignments were handed out. Pledger assigned the case to Linda "one million isn't enough" Dunlap! When I protested, he said she would be coordinating with U.S. Attorney Jim Berliner.

Either the fix was in again, or Dunlap just needed a kick in the ass from her superiors to get moving. I was praying it was the latter reason.

The more I checked into it, the more I realized that my prayers were falling on deaf ears. The Laguna Niguel office had originally been split off from L.A., meaning most of the people there had once worked for Saranow. Dunlap and her husband, a private investigator, were close to Howard Emirhanian, the former IRS honcho now on the Guess payroll. Bob Pledger himself used to work for Saranow, and Pledger's wife was a CID agent in L.A. still working for Saranow.

It gets worse. A former Laguna assistant CID chief named Alan Wells was a close friend of both Saranow and Emirhanian. Wells left the agency under a cloud of suspicion and formed a PI firm, Worth & Wells. Worth? He was a former Laguna IRS chief and another close friend of Saranow.

To top it off, after the Laguna Niguel meeting, I was approached by a "friendly" patron at the bar of a restaurant where I stopped to have dinner. He took a deep interest in my life, asking a lot of specific questions. After about five minutes, I abruptly left and made sure I wasn't followed. When I checked around later that night, I discovered that his business card was phony.

On December 16, there was another major breakthrough in the case. I was directed to a man named Steve Shaul, an Israeli who owned a small jeans stonewashing and dyeing outfit in L.A. What made Shaul valuable was that he had previously worked for both Jordache and Guess.

Shaul shooed me outside to the parking lot of his factory, then whispered a very interesting story involving my ol' pal Hardolf "Atom Bomb" Wolf, middleman extraordinaire. "Wolf said to me that the only way they could drive the Nakashes out of Guess was to prove that they were no good, that they were criminals. . . . So Wolf asked me to say bad things about them in court."

"Wolf asked you to lie about the Nakashes?" I marveled.

"No, not exactly. He said that I probably knew a lot of bad things about them, and that I should just tell the truth in court. I told him, 'I know nothing bad.'"

"What about the IRS?"

Shaul glanced around before answering. I recognized his look of fear, as if he were surrounded by an omnipotent enemy.

Shaul said Maurice Marciano phoned him in March and said he was coming by. Instead, two IRS agents appeared. The first was John Anderson, the L.A. agent who attended the big Dallas/L.A. IRS meeting the prior September. The other was Steven Levy, the New York CID stormtrooper who led the charge during the Jordache raid.

"They were like Wolf," Shaul said. "Levy kept asking me what I knew about the Nakashes. 'You were the bag man for the Nakashes, why don't you admit it?' he accused. 'You're trying to protect criminals, after they threw you out of Jordache like a dog . . .'" Shaul's voice vibrated with anger. "Levy threatened me and called me a liar. And then he said this, I'll never forget it, he said, 'I can destroy you.' He said that to me several times.

"He wanted me to invent lies about the Nakashes and Jordache. Levy then said that if I cooperated with the IRS and testified against Jordache for the grand jury in New York, he could guarantee I'd get more business from Guess."

Unbelievable! The IRS was apparently bullying an immigrant into giving false grand jury testimony. In return, they'd reward him by pimping blue jeans for a bunch of shady French Algerians. For a minute there, I had to shake off the sudden thought that I was in some banana republic south of the border.

"Did I agree to testify? No. I could not lie . . ."

"What happened after you refused?"

Shaul shrugged. A pained look passed over his face.

"I lost all my business with Guess. They were my major account."

"When? "

"The next day."

Beautiful. These guys were not only playing hardball, they were bringing out the billy clubs and blackjacks.

Shaul's revelations convinced Jim Berliner to convene a grand jury in California to investigate the Marcianos. That enabled me to turn my full attention to the IRS.

It was now January 1987. A full year had passed since the IRS raided Jordache. My three-month investigation was extending into eternity, and there was no end in sight.

During another visit to L.A. I ran into George De Los Santos by chance at the Embassy Suites Hotel. He was in California on another case, and we arranged to meet that evening for drinks. Another Dallas agent joined us at the hotel's piano bar.

As we talked, three gorgeous women approached our table and made some excuse to join us. One was Hawaiian, the other Spanish, the third Anglo. What was wrong with that picture? Three guys, three attractive girls? I'd been in this business too long to believe in coincidences.

Any doubts that it might have been our charm and good looks that drew in the ladies were dispelled when the Hawaiian started peppering me with questions. And instead of buttering up my buddies, her pals hung on my every word.

I decided to turn the table, returning fire with my own questions. The Hawaiian told me her name and said she worked at Hughes Aircraft near the airport. They were out celebrating her birthday. At the Embassy Suites? Unless they were trolling for airline pilots, that story didn't wash.

I quickly excused myself for the evening and left the bar. Hiding in an alcove, I watched as the troublesome trio quickly deserted my IRS buddies and disappeared into a cab. It was obvious they weren't out to party. I wanted to have them tailed, but there wasn't time.

When I returned to the bar, De Los Santos gave me a big grin.

"They sure liked you, Octavio."

"Yeah, but they were following you, not me."

"Me?"

De Los Santos thought about it for a moment, then slowly nodded his head. His L.A. counterparts were still terrified that he was on their case. And they remained desperate to identify "Mr. George."

The next morning, I paid a visit to the Hughes Aircraft plant. Neither the birthday girl nor her friends worked there.

The next day, a Brooklyn IRS agent called my Fort Lee office claiming to have just spoken to my old boss, Mr. Lynch. I phoned the agent back, and he pretended he had the wrong Mr. Lynch and promptly hung up. I alerted Keith Kuhn in Washington and he promised to investigate.

By then, I was commuting to Los Angeles on a weekly basis. Another IRS agent—a friend of one of my better sources—was ready to talk. I arranged another meet at LAX's Pan American First Class Lounge. The new mole told me that in September 1985—five months before the raid on Jordache—Saranow, the Marcianos, and attorney Marshall Grossman jetted to New York to huddle with the Kroll detectives. They then visited the New York IRS, and the U.S. Attorney's office. The purpose was to discuss the IRS case against Jordache.

After those meetings, my sources said, Saranow began bragging about his six-figure job offer from Guess and his new Porsche.

"How do you know so much about the meeting?" I asked.

"I've known Saranow for a long time. Plus, he's so fucking arrogant, he thinks he's above the law. He just brags about shit. The man can't keep his mouth shut. And his trip was officially recorded."

Near the end of the conversation, my new source began fidgeting and glancing at his friend who had made the introduction. "Saranow called the Chief of the Laguna CID back in December, and he pressured Bob Pledger to bury the case against the Marcianos," the source finally admitted. ". . . We told Kuhn in D.C."

"Kuhn knows about it?"

"Yeah, evidently Pledger also called Kuhn, because he was terrified that you and Internal Security had the entire Laguna CID office bugged."

That made me laugh for a moment. The mirth vanished when I realized that Kuhn wasn't giving me the promised full disclosure.

"Watch out for Internal Security and Inspection," the source warned. "You're going to find out what all of us agents have known for years. They're a bunch of whores."

I called Jim Berliner to see if he knew about the report that Saranow tried to influence the Laguna investigation. He said he didn't. Apparently Kuhn had shoved us both out of the loop. Not a good sign.

To Kuhn's credit, he 'fessed up about it. To his discredit, he whined that he still didn't have enough evidence to do anything about what was happening in L.A. I promised to provide the evidence.

I also mentioned the incident at the Embassy Suites with the three ladies. Kuhn responded by offering to have his men protect me. Protect me, or place me under surveillance to find out my sources? I declined.

Over the next few days, Kuhn continued to insist that I needed IRS shadows for my clandestine meeting with IRS sources. He sounded worried and made me wonder if he knew something I didn't. I agreed to allow him to send me a detail, on one condition. "When I meet an IRS source, your people disappear."

Kuhn agreed. He immediately arranged for me to meet my guardian angels on February 24 at the L.A. airport. The team would be headed by his assistant, Steve Jones. I immediately arranged to have my Mexican team tail my new IRS team. Spy vs. spy. Only my spies were a lot better.

When Jones arrived at the airport, he marched up to the Pan Am First Class Lounge receptionist and asked for "Mr. Pena." I couldn't believe it. These morons were on the job for two seconds and they had already blown my cover! I pulled him aside.

"You said my name to the receptionist!" I scolded. "Either I'm known, or I'm unknown, make up your mind!"

The young IRS henchman tried to brush it off.

"Be consistent, Steve, or we could be dead!"

If I'd known what was coming next, I wouldn't have bothered wasting my breath. Jones introduced me to my team of guard dogs: Debbie Corwin, an attractive, brown-haired woman in her thirties; Russ Davis, fiftyish, a senior inspection agent for the western region; and a third woman, whose identity was about to make my blood pressure pop off the chart.

"Mr. George, this is Debbie Jones. She's the manager for Los Angeles Inspection. Debbie [Corwin] and Russ report directly to her."

Debbie Jones! Saranow's "close, personal" female friend? The woman I was told he went out with! I pulled Steve Jones aside again and went ballistic.

"This is the woman who harassed the Dallas agent for my identity!"

He did a furious soft shoe.

"We checked her out. She's clean, okay?"

Not okay!

I later learned that checking her out consisted of a single question. They asked her if she had a personal relationship with Saranow. She denied it. That was enough to get her assigned as my lead pit bull.

Once again, I had to put aside all my doubts and suspicions, cool down, and go along with the program. It was my only option. Maybe Jones was the proverbial woman scorned, and wanted to get back at Saranow. Or maybe she had an integrity and loyalty to the job that went beyond personal relationships, especially with Washington looking over her shoulder. And maybe the moon is made of Philadelphia Cream Cheese.

Steve Jones proceeded to outline a surveillance scheme involving satellite dishes, walkie-talkies, and constant sightings. It was a cumbersome plan right out of some B-grade spy movie. Anyone with half a brain would spot Jones's lumbering crew in ten minutes. (And my Mexican team certainly did.)

I had a better idea. I'd been told that the U.S. Attorney was about to drop a subpoena on the Marcianos. All we had to do was get a court order to put electronic surveillance on Saranow and everyone around him, and wait and see what happened when the Marcianos took the hit.

The IRS team agreed. Steve Jones said he'd ask Berliner to petition a judge for a court order to tape the Los Angeles IRS CID phone lines, as well as Saranow's home phone.

The following afternoon, everything came unglued. I couldn't reach any of my new IRS friends. Then Steve Jones and Russ Davis sheepishly paid me a visit that evening. The pair explained that the plan had changed. Steve Jones was bowing out. Davis, a laid-back type, was given the task of heading the investigation.

When I asked what happened, Jones started stonewalling and hiding behind the IRS Disclosure Laws. Furious, I ushered Jones to a local Pizza Hut, leaving Davis behind. "Don't fuck with me!" I raged. "I want to know why my plan was killed!"

Jones bobbed and weaved, revealing squat.

"I've been running investigations for over twenty years, and I know when one has been compromised," I accused. "You and

Kuhn know it. You know there's a cover-up, so don't bullshit me. I know how cover-ups are engineered. You get some low-key manageable type to investigate so it looks kosher, and you get an official report for the record that says nothing happened . . .

"You brought her [Debbie Jones] in on this, and you compromised our investigation. . . . Go back and tell your bosses in DC that if I find out that the IRS has covered up for Ron Saranow out here, then I'm going to bring my evidence to the United States Congress!"

After cooling down, we made up. I was obligated to my clients to do everything I could to fight the IRS and U.S. Attorney's pending attacks against them, so if there was a minuscule chance these guys could be shamed into playing on the level, I had to take it.

A knowledgeable IRS source contacted me the following day with the lowdown on Russ Davis, star investigator.

"Davis has never investigated a corruption case before. All he's ever done is routine background checks on prospective agents. He's never 'made his bones.'" He was also, my source emphasized, a year away from retirement. That meant he wasn't about to step on anybody's toes.

This move revealed something far more sinister than ever. The cancer inside the IRS seemed to go above and beyond Ron Saranow.

THE WATCHERS COUNTERATTACK

IN MARCH, a pair of New York IRS Inspection agents paid me a visit on the pretense of investigating why someone from their office had previously called John Lynch. Within minutes, they revealed their true purpose—to flush out my IRS source in L.A. "We want to be notified if you have any personal knowledge of any instances where IRS agents have been corrupt," one said.

How about here and now, you assholes?

I blew the goons out of there.

On St. Patrick's Day, I received a frantic call from Avi Nakash. He was in California to attend a Guess board meeting and was being stalked by a pair of thugs! "He's coming toward me! He's not five feet from me!" Nakash whispered fiercely over the phone.

"Tell me very calmly what's going on. No one's going to kill you in the lobby of the Beverly Hills Hilton. You're okay."

Avi said the brutes had been following him all morning—from the hotel restaurant, to the bathroom, and into the lobby. So far, all they'd done was glare.

I took the threat seriously. I sent my Mexican team to the hotel, with some extra bodyguards. I then called Jim Berliner and asked for his help. The U.S. Attorney begged off, saying he couldn't provide protection. The IRS in Laguna Niguel sang the same tune. Their denials were upsetting. Avi was a potential government grand jury witness in both their cases against the Marcianos, yet they refused to protect him.

For the next two days, the thugs shadowed Avi, and my guys watched the thugs. When Avi went to the California State Courthouse to check in on the Jordache/Guess trial, the gorillas followed him right inside the courtroom! Avi's attorney protested to the judge, who asked the Marcianos if the men were indeed their employees.

"Yes," Paul Marciano admitted.

The judge tossed them out.

Things slowed down considerably after that. As predicted, Russ Davis's investigation wasn't going anywhere. Nobody inside the IRS would talk to him. That included the dozen-plus sources I'd cultivated. I can't say I blame them. They knew better than anyone that the game was fixed. "Whatever we tell him will end up on Ron Saranow's desk. And then we're screwed," an IRS source explained.

I was also having trouble with some of Avi's army of attorneys. Sad to say, the $10-million-a-year legal team wasn't interested in anything that might short-circuit the pending IRS and U.S. Attorney investigations of Jordache. I had the impression that a good portion of the carnivorous lawyers were actually eager for arrests and indictments. Then they could drag out their lucrative fees for years to come. If the IRS were blocked and the indictment defused before it came down, the party would be over.

It confirmed one of my major credos—your own attorney is usually your worst enemy. As Roger Burman warned me years before, the more trouble a person gets into, the richer his or her attorney becomes. And the more that attorney loses, the more profitable it is. If a case is thrown out on a motion, the attorney's billing ends. But if they can lose motion after motion, lose the trial, or better, get a mistrial and lose the second trial, and then lose appeal after appeal, they get stinking rich! Therefore, it wasn't surprising that Avi's attorneys undermined my efforts, denigrated my evidence, and basically tried to ignore me. Whenever I came up with something that was too big to ignore, their response was the same. "Great. We can use that at the trial," one of them actually had the nerve to say.

Avi didn't want a trial! He wanted the bogus IRS investigations ended before the situation reached that point.

Trouble was, Avi didn't have the understanding or intestinal forti-tude to overrule his parasitic attorneys. And second, he had too many of them! That was one area where I had to admire the Marcianos. They were smart enough to hire one kickass Doberman, Grossman, and stick with him the whole way. That made their efforts more coor-dinated and effective. (But not cheaper, as I would later discover.)

After three months, it became apparent that another attorney, Jim Berliner, wasn't accomplishing very much either. His grand jury probe had stalled. The IRS was dragging its feet in providing him with evidence (or confirming my evidence), and that com-pletely hamstrung the Assistant U.S. Attorney.

Morale among my IRS sources plummeted. Trying to fight the IRS was like battling that liquid metal robot from *Terminator 2*. Burn him, blow him apart, blast holes in him with a shotgun, chop him up, didn't matter. He just melded himself back together and kept right on coming.

Still, there had to be a way for the white hats to win this gun-fight. I couldn't allow my informants, or myself, to give up. I stayed at it, bolstering the old sources and cultivating fresh new ones at every opportunity.

"You have to realize that these guys, particularly the CID guys, spend their lives investigating people who make millions and mil-lions of dollars," a mole close to Ron Saranow rationalized. "And here they are G–12s or 13s making eighty grand at most. It's human nature that a few would want to pad their retirement eggs. Ron Saranow's not unique in that he would take a job with the Marcianos and influence investigations to protect his future job. Shit like that happens all the time. The problem is, they can't get caught under the present system.

"Listen, Saranow is wired into the very highest levels. His mentor used to be an Assistant CID Commissioner in Washington, Richard Wassenaar. His friends in Washington give Saranow enor-mous clout."

"Enough clout to start this IRS probe of Jordache in New York?" I asked.

"Saranow organized the whole damn raid. The evidence against Jordache was bullshit. . . . But when a man like Saranow says to investigate, you investigate, even if you're Rudolph Giuliani. CID chiefs are that powerful. Remember, only the IRS can control tax-related evidence. It would be very easy for Ron Saranow to bamboozle a U.S. Attorney."

The source then gave me a solid tip. "Ask them [Giuliani or his assistants] if they've ever seen the information that the Marcianos originally provided the IRS before their raid on Jordache. Probe them on it, because it was bullshit." I filed that away.

"Are there other instances of IRS corruption that you know about outside of the Marciano affair?" I asked.

"Saranow apparently has invested in the real estate properties of a company under investigation by the IRS."

"You've got to be kidding me!"

"Nope."

When I checked this story out, I discovered that Saranow, Emirhanian, Saranow's mentor, Richard Wassenaar, who was then Assistant Commissioner of the IRS in charge of Criminal Investigations, and others had formed a real estate partnership called El Monte Industrial Properties, Ltd.

After they got some rather sizable loans from the IRS credit union, El Monte bought a prime piece of property for about $1 mil from a guy named George Green, the president of Elco Manufacturing. Nothing wrong with some Feds investing in the private sector to make a few bucks—this is America.

Nothing wrong at all. Except Green was under investigation by the L.A. CID!

Worse still, I discovered that Green apparently loaned the partners $250,000—in the form of a mortgage—to close the deal! A taxpayer under investigation loans money to the very people investigating him to buy his own property? When the deal closed, so did the investigation.

The audacity of it all made my head spin. I mean, the *head* of the IRS Criminal Investigations Division—a guy charged with catching shenanigans like this—was involved.

But my new source wasn't finished with his tale of IRS woes. He added that one L.A. IRS agent actually prepared the tax returns for a local Mafioso. "The mobster bragged that he 'had an IRS agent in his pocket.' So after [Organized Crime Strike Force prosecutor Marvin] Rudnick discovered this, he decided to prosecute both the IRS agent and the mafioso. . . . Rudnick told Saranow that he would go after him [the dirty agent] with everything he could, felony, corruption and co-conspirator charges, you name it. . . . Saranow told Rudnick that he should just try for a misdemeanor charge!

"Rudnick made recommendations to the IRS Inspection Division to look into what might have been a case of deep Mafia inroads inside the IRS Los Angeles office. And it was killed. . . . Nothing was done. . . . When Rudnick complained to his supervisor about Saranow's actions, nothing was done either. . . . Rudnick was removed from the case. . . . And the Justice Department terminated him—get this—for insubordination."

If Saranow could squash a powerful, mob-hunting U.S. Attorney like Marvin Rudnick, what chance did I stand? (I was told something else about Saranow that gave me pause for thought: The powerful CID Chief was once given a $10,000 line of credit at the Stardust Hotel in Las Vegas—when he was making less than thirty grand a year. I also learned that in the early seventies, the Inspection Division had investigated Saranow for ties to organized crime in Chicago. Saranow had told a reporter that "no evidence had been found that substantiated" the charge, but in an eerie parallel to this case, I learned that Internal Security mysteriously dropped its investigation before anything definitive was found.)

Another new source told me that the IRS may have covered up a major scam involving a number of prominent law firms that were billing a large metropolitan city thirty hours a day per attorney for contracted public defenders.

"The IRS has a longstanding policy: Never prosecute prominent lawyers or politicians," the informant explained. "They'll audit you and me and the mom-and-pop businesses until we die, but the big fish swim free." My source added that the cases against Jordache and Jeff Bohbot were part of Saranow's overall "garment industry project."

"Let me guess," I interrupted. "All these cases were directed against the Marcianos' business enemies, right?"

"It certainly looks that way. They [the Marcianos] were the only sources for the project. . . . The CID managers on the case told the agents that they shouldn't number the [Bohbot] case until Bohbot filed his first quarter estimated taxes. Do you know what that means?"

"It means that the IRS started to investigate the guy before he ever did anything illegal!" I exploded.

"Which is against IRS rules. They were just looking for him to fuck up. . . . Same thing happened with Jordache. The agents working the case told Saranow that there wasn't probable cause for an investigation. . . . Saranow ordered the case kept open."

I knew from my research that the Marcianos had settled their differences with Bohbot that April. I asked the source if the agency was still on Bohbot's ass.

"The IRS officially dropped the Bohbot investigation a few weeks ago. In April." Naturally.

The vicious cycle continued its spin. Another source offered to introduce me to a dissatisfied ex-IRS Inspection agent who had recently quit the tax agency because of the widespread corruption. His name was Jorge Urquijo—the same Jorge Urquijo who had tried to pry my identity from George De Los Santos! Urquijo was now working for Customs.

This was one man I really wanted to chat with. After a brief introduction and small talk at Las Brisas, a beachfront restaurant in Laguna, California, Urquijo opened up.

"There's too much corruption," Urquijo sighed. "Inspection can't handle it, so the top brass just lets it go. Don't rock the boat. . . . If the taxpayers only knew how much corruption there is in the IRS. . . . Either I quit, or I joined the stuffed suits and buried my head in the sand. So I quit."

Urquijo went on to tell me what happened when one of my "guard dogs," Debbie Corwin, tried to blow the whistle on her bosses. "Debbie Corwin knew that Debbie Jones was close to Saranow. She told me, and I told Keith Kuhn."

"Kuhn knew?"

"Yeah, Kuhn knew. Debbie Corwin didn't want me to tell Kuhn that she was the source, but I had to, and she got screwed because of it."

Urquijo explained that Corwin, in traditional "David and Bathsheba" style, was then sent off on a dangerous mission as her punishment.

"She was supposed to infiltrate a gang of Jamaican drug dealers. They sent her to a fucking tanning salon, so that she could pass as black. Can you fucking believe it? She had no undercover training. She had no case officer watching over her. Inspection simply left her to hang out to dry. . . ."

Over the next few days, Urquijo opened up further. He said that Mike Ranelli, the Assistant Chief of Inspection for the Western Region, and his branch chief, Mike Bik, ganged up on Kuhn and got their Washington-based superior bounced off the Saranow case.

"How could they do that?"

"Regional chiefs, like Saranow, or like Ranelli, have enormous power. Kuhn pissed in another dog's territory, dogs who were close to Saranow. Saranow and Ranelli and Bik all know each other. They're part of the IRS old boy network. They protect their own.

"You told me that Kuhn's investigation was a top priority inside the Washington office?" Urquijo continued. "That the Commissioner himself was interested, right?"

I nodded.

"Who else knew about your activities?"

"John Rankin, the Assistant IRS Commissioner for Inspection."

"John Rankin and Ron Saranow have been friends forever! I heard he's protected Saranow for years," Urquijo said, shaking his head.

I rushed over to the U.S. Attorney's office in L.A. and laid this out to Jim Berliner. Didn't matter. I could have paraded a hundred eyewitnesses before him, and he couldn't lift a finger until the IRS's chosen investigator, Russ Davis, coordinated the effort. And nobody would talk to Russ Davis because he reported to Debbie Jones, another Saranow good ol' boy . . . Round and round I went.

Remembering what happened with the crooked bankruptcy judge, I decided it was time to bring in the press. I knew the media could be a powerful tool to cut through all the stonewalling and cover-ups. Against the wishes of his numerous attorneys, Avi Nakash arranged for me to meet an intense young reporter from *Forbes* magazine named Richard Behar who had expressed an interest in the inside story of the Guess-Jordache battle royale. I introduced Behar to a number of my sources, and the brash young reporter quickly realized that he'd hit on a "holy shit" story.

Behar's report on the IRS-Marciano connection appeared in an early November 1987 issue of *Forbes*—sixteen months after I took the case. Titled "Does Guess Have a Friend in the IRS?" the article outlined the "vicious blood feud" between the Nakashes and the Marcianos over the spoils of Guess Inc., now a $400 million company.

The story covered all the bases: the jobs at Guess for Emirhanian and Saranow; the Jordache raid; the killed Guess investigations; and the "plodding" and ineffective IRS internal investigation. At the end of the article, Behar wrote that the IRS in Washington had warned *Forbes* not to conduct any more inquiries into the matter. I guess that meant audit hell for Malcolm Forbes.

The *Forbes* article appeared to shame the IRS into action. What kind of action remained to be seen. The IRS Commissioner,

Lawrence Gibbs, issued a statement promising to "thoroughly review all aspects . . ."

In the weeks after the article ran, my phone was jammed with calls from IRS sources updating me on the fallout. Saranow was transferred to San Francisco, but not before going on a witch hunt for agents suspected of talking to *Forbes*. Georges Marciano was making noises about leaving Guess and going back to Europe. The rest of the brothers were said to be equally shaken.

On the other hand, the sources spoke darkly of administrative efforts to close ranks and institute a whole new set of cover-up maneuvers. The venal tax agency intensified its efforts to identify, harass, and fire suspected whistle-blowers. Among those fired was Debbie Corwin, the honest agent on my original guard detail. She was let go on the spot when she refused to cough up the source who confirmed Debbie Jones and Ron Saranow's personal relationship. (This firing was eventually overturned.)

Behar and *Forbes* printed a short follow-up two weeks after the original article ran. They reemphasized that the IRS wanted to cover up its cover-up of Saranow, and quoted Keith Kuhn as saying that the IRS raid against Jordache resulted from "a lot of duped people" in the U.S. Attorney's office.

The second jab from *Forbes* kicked up a new wave of witch hunts and reprisals inside the IRS. George De Los Santos was among those dragged in by Inspection goons to be grilled about the Guess/IRS scandal.

In response, angry IRS managers and agents from all over the country began writing and phoning *Forbes* with additional stories of massive corruption. One particularly scathing letter suggested that IRS Inspection check the travel and expense vouchers for the past two years covering Ron Saranow and a "female employee, a manager whose career has risen meteorically since she became socially close to Saranow . . ."

That was an all-too-familiar pattern in the L.A. IRS office. *Forbes* received so much information that Behar and his editor, Christopher Byron, were planning a third article. Among some of the allegations and rumors I had learned that they were checking:

- Three IRS managers in Chicago who were retaliated against in Chicago after they blew the whistle on a boss who had apparent mob connections.
- A high-level Inspection official based in Cincinnati who was

apparently cheating on his taxes. After he was caught, there was an alleged tradeoff: the Criminal Investigations Division would drop its case against him if Inspection dropped its case against Ron Saranow.

- Senior IRS managers with mob connections in Miami, Milwaukee, Los Angeles, and Atlanta.
- A southern district director taking kickbacks from a computer company in return for purchasing all hardware and software from that firm.
- An Inspection manager fired for uncovering the above kickback scheme.
- A cattleman in the Southeast blackmailed by an IRS Internal Security officer. When the poor schmuck paid the $500,000 ransom to make his IRS troubles go away, he was arrested for bribery. The case was thrown out because of entrapment.
- Myriad stories of honest agents being crushed for reporting the corruption of their superiors.
- A particularly disturbing report that Saranow called the IRS Commissioner and threatened to spill his guts about the real IRS unless they stopped investigating him.

With top IRS officials madly trying to plug holes in a rapidly breaking dam, it was no surprise that they'd want to plug the biggest hole of all: me. I was angered, but not surprised, when George De Los Santos relayed the tax agency's latest effort. A senior Inspection Division official from Washington blew into town and began to apply some real pressure, trying to get him to detail my so-called "illegal acts."

"I can take this heat from Washington for a while, but I'm telling you, watch out. They're gunning for you now. They want your ass in a sling!"

De Los Santos's latest interrogator was IRS Inspector John Gibson. His interest in me was strange because his official duties were strictly limited to investigating IRS employees.

I got Gibson on the horn. He stammered a bit, assuring me that I wasn't under investigation. No kidding! He had no power to investigate me in the first place! How could he admit it?

I assured him that if he was trying to be cute, he was abusing the public trust and I wasn't going to stand for it.

This stuff was really starting to piss me off. For a long time, I wanted nothing more than to shed myself of this nightmarish case.

But now things had changed. The personal attacks, relentless warnings, and constant threats did nothing but heighten my resolve. It was now do or die. I was in it to the bloody end.

In mid-November, a Jordache attorney introduced me to Gerald Kurtz, the former Commissioner of the IRS. Kurtz was said to be able to work out a meeting with current IRS Commissioner Lawrence Gibbs. I laid out my evidence to Kurtz, evidence now well known in the media. Kurtz, now on Jordache's payroll, took it to Gibbs, who sent word back that he'd like to meet with my sources. However, when I tried to arrange the meetings, Gibbs got cold feet. Kurtz called the second week of December and said that the Commissioner no longer wanted to meet my informants. He referred them to John Rankin.

John Rankin! Another Saranow crony! This was the Debbie Jones fiasco all over again, and it had come directly from the top!

At that point, Kurtz himself started acting strange. All he cared about was the upcoming *Forbes* follow-up article. He kept hounding me about what I knew about it, when it would be out, if I could get an advance copy, and so on. Once an old boy, always an old boy.

In the end, Kurtz and his pals had nothing to worry about. Malcolm Forbes killed the third IRS story. It was plucked from publication at the last minute—after it had been edited, titled, and ready to hit layout.

Forbes's decision was heartbreaking, but not surprising. A man of his wealth was sure to have played fast and loose with the IRS at one time or another. And Forbes had, in fact, been embroiled in squabbles over taxes for years. I was told that the pressure on him came directly from the IRS—an allegation so disturbing that the *Wall Street Journal* ran an article about it, which essentially confirmed the spiking of the article. (Forbes denied the charge that the IRS had called to kill the article.)

That was it, the end of the road. I'd climbed to the top of the IRS mountain, and was slapped down the entire way. There was now only one step left: the United States Congress.

As I neared the two-year anniversary of the IRS/Jordache raid, I was greeted by a new wave of fireworks. Someone tried to break into my office complex. The burglars made it through the first set of alarms, but were tripped by a secondary layer. The intruders didn't steal anything, and they didn't even grab the files on Guess and the IRS, which they had access to after getting inside the building. Apparently they were trying to plant a bug inside my inner office.

The attempted break-in intensified my efforts to expose the IRS before Congress. I hooked up with a sharp Jordache attorney, Arnold Kalman, who supported my plan.

Meanwhile, the IRS concluded its crack Russ Davis investigation and outlined the happy results in a letter to U.S. Attorney Rudolph Giuliani. Tapping some sources, I got my hands on it. The letter claimed that Davis had interviewed forty witnesses. This from the guy who kept saying nobody would talk to him? It went on to report that Assistant U.S. Attorney James Berliner had advised them that "there did not appear to be sufficient evidence of any federal violation which would warrant criminal prosecution. . . ." The letter ended with a complete exoneration of Saranow.

What a move! The IRS was solely responsible for giving Berliner sufficient evidence. Instead, they furiously covered everything up and sent Berliner a pile of shit. Then they turned around and used Berliner to say they were in the clear. Beautiful. And to top it off, Giuliani asked the judge to place the letter under seal so nobody could ever challenge it.

My anger boiled until I realized what I had. I was holding concrete, written evidence of the IRS's massive cover-up. When the shit hit the fan, the letter would come back to haunt them. All I had to do was get the shit to the fan, i.e., Congress.

That proved to be difficult. People tend to yawn at government corruption inside the Beltway. After a number of false starts, I finally found someone who listened. David Burnham, a former *New York Times* reporter famous for breaking Serpico's story of New York City police corruption (and subsequently the author of *A Law Unto Itself* and *Above the Law*), heard my story and introduced me to a congressional staffer named Peter Barash. The hero was Barash, Staff Director of the Commerce, Consumer and Monetary Affairs Subcommittee of the House of Representatives Government Operations Committee. The tongue-twisting group was chaired by Douglas Barnard, the Democratic Congressman from Georgia. Barash and Barnard were said to be among the handful of people on the planet who didn't fear the IRS.

After taking five hours to present my case against the IRS, Barash agreed to interview my sources. I flew out to L.A., bolstered everybody's confidence, assured them of their anonymity, arranged

protection, and scheduled the secret meetings. On May 19, Barash
sent two of his investigators, Leonard Bernard and Richard Stana,
to Los Angeles. For two days, Stana and Bernard spoke with a suc-
cession of IRS agents in both CID and Inspection.

As I shepherded each nervous source into the hotel room, I felt
that the tide had finally begun to turn. Rumors of the pending Congressional investigation caused more IRS horror stories to pour in.
A Texas agent called and said he had uncovered a secret slush
fund for George Bush's presidential campaign. When he reported it
to his CID manager, he was transferred to another district.

Bribes, kickbacks, additional IRS managers on Mafia payrolls,
destruction of records, disappearing evidence, extreme sexual
harassment, sex and drug parties inside IRS offices, the accusations were endless. The one constant was that IRS Inspection knew
about it all, and did nothing.

Meanwhile, Ron Saranow was keeping busy in San Francisco.
A senior IRS Inspection agent told me that Saranow had given up
on the Guess job offer and was now planning to go into business
as a private investigator with an IRS official named Anthony Langone, the head of CID for the whole nation. The source charged
that Langone had pilfered government material, videos, IRS
badges, training materials, and so on to open their business. These
guys never quit.

Barash called a few days later with the good news that his subcommittee had decided to convene a major investigation of the IRS
based on my evidence and contacts. It wasn't a full-fledged
hearing, but we were on the way.

The IRS responded to the news about the official investigation by
sending out a memo reminding everyone of the Disclosure Laws
and noting that the congressional subcommittee "does not have
statutory authority to receive tax information. . . ." The IRS was
going to stonewall to the bitter end.

That's not all. The IRS immediately began harassing employees
they suspected of talking to the congressional investigators, and
threatened everybody else to steer clear. Among those under the
newly reloaded gun were Jorge Urquijo, who didn't even work for
the IRS anymore, George De Los Santos, and poor Debbie Corwin,
who had already been fired once and reinstated.

On the upside, Barash and his congressional investigators were
well on their way to gathering thousands of pages of incriminating

documents, and speaking with over a hundred IRS whistle-blowers. As summer faded into fall, their investigation began to pick up speed.

And yet the insanity continued. Despite all the evidence in the press that the IRS raid on Jordache was a scam, the rumbling out of New York was that Giuliani and gang were still planning to indict the jeans company! "They're going to screw Jordache just to save face," a prosecutor friend told me.

The congressional investigation was good, but I was being paid to keep my client, Jordache, out of trouble. The news that the U.S. Attorney's office was about to drop the dime kicked me into action. I had to get to Aaron Marcu, the Associate U.S. Attorney handling the matter.

Jordache's attorneys were no help. The way I saw it, they were too eager to collect the huge fees that an indictment would earn them, so they didn't want me to rain on their money parade. I was left to round up my own source, Ray Levites, a former Assistant U.S. Attorney who was on good terms with Marcu and his chief investigator, Tom Doonan. Levites agreed to make the intro.

Before the meeting, I learned that Marcu was a protégé of Bart Schwartz, the Kroll Associates manager who was once Giuliani's righthand man. At Kroll, Schwartz was responsible for the lucrative Marciano account.

That meant I would have to all but knock Marcu's socks off to get him to back off the indictment. That wasn't going to be easy, especially when considering that Giuliani's office had already refused a congressional request to come forward with their evidence against Jordache. (Jordache, to its credit, gladly provided Congress with its tax records.)

The bearded Marcu affected the arrogant posture of most federal prosecutors. His investigator, Tom Doonan, looked like the typically tough New York Irish cop, used to having his way, and comfortable intimidating information out of his suspects. He glared at me from the moment I entered.

I told my story, outlining the case and the evidence while the men listened attentively. Then, remembering what an IRS source told me, I dropped the question.

"Have you seen the information that the Marcianos and Kroll originally provided the IRS before their raid on Jordache?"

Marcu calmly answered "yes," but Doonan showed their true

hand by freaking out. He jumped from his chair and demanded to know if I was taping the conversation.

"No," I answered.

The investigator then asked to frisk me. I compromised by opening my jacket to show that I wasn't. (Which actually showed nothing.)

My IRS source was right. The question touched a raw nerve. These guys might have known all along that the original evidence against Jordache was bogus. And it was all probably moot anyway. The "evidence," no doubt, had long been buried inside an incinerator.

Once again, I was staggered by the implications of the meeting. If someone had enough money to buy Kroll Associates' unique services, they could apparently influence the U.S. Attorney's office.

When I arrived back at my office, I spotted a windowless black van parked nearby. Looking through a pair of high-powered binoculars, I could see the tip of a periscope poking through the air vent on the top. Later that day, two more cars arrived, positioned to follow me wherever I went. I was now being watched around the clock. That was unacceptable. If they followed me, that meant they knew where my family lived, where my children played, where they went to school, and who their friends were. I was vulnerable.

Not long afterward, I found a "black box" tracking device hidden inside the engine frame of my wife's car. I knew that the Marcianos were desperate to identify "Kelly Grace"—they might have thought she was my wife Grace—but whoever put it there was too good. I couldn't trace it.

The pressure and intimidation increased. Someone called my children twice, pretending to be telephone repairmen needing to "fix your phone lines." I had to train my eleven-year-old son Richard and thirteen-year-old daughter Elisabeth in the ways of the cloak-and-dagger world.

While all that was going on, the Marcianos instituted a well-designed smear campaign against both me and my evidence. I learned from my sources that they were going to hit me on two fronts. Grossman was planning to accuse me of campaigning to have the Marcianos deported by Immigration. Secondly, they got a hired-gun expert who claimed that the Hardolf Wolf "atom bomb" tape had been doctored.

Both charges were ridiculous. That didn't stop them from pressing forward.

Grossman additionally subpoenaed me for a deposition. To feed his list of questions, I was told that the Marcianos posted my photo in all their offices and factories and offered up to $100,000 to anybody who could provide some decent dirt.

A few days before the scheduled deposition I had the tense encounter with the bogus cop detailed in this book's introduction. The mounting intimidation didn't end with the car chase. At 3:00 A.M. the morning of the deposition, my private phone rang, jarring me awake. "Hey fuckin' Pena, you'd better tell the truth tomorrow."

I slammed the receiver down before the throaty voice made it to the "or else" part.

The deposition was a letdown. The much-feared Grossman was a big, beefy man who actually tried to stare holes through me like a boxer during the referee's instructions. It was so childish it just made me laugh.

His questions were routine. The attorney obviously didn't want me to outline my evidence against his clients. He peppered me about the Immigration and doctored-tape angles, which I'd already been warned about, so the probes didn't catch me by surprise.

The only interesting part was I was able to study Paul Marciano, up close and personal. The chief Marciano strategist was a short, stocky, handsome man with curly black hair and dark features. I knew the Marciano brothers liked the Hollywood party scene and fancied themselves Tinseltown players. Paul fit the part. Even though we were bitter adversaries, I could see how he could charm the pants off of friend or foe.

During a break, Paul Marciano walked up to me and shook my hand.

"You know, you are very good," he praised. "You're the only person who has hurt us."

I asked him why he didn't just settle with my clients. Before he could answer, Grossman shut him up. He was probably afraid Paul would do just that and ruin his billing bonanza.

After the deposition, the Marcianos tried a new tactic. They hired a powerful Washington lobbyist, an ex-congressman named Jim Jones, and gave him the task of discrediting me and derailing the congressional investigation. Jones boasted some heavy credentials. He served as Chief of Staff for President Johnson, and once chaired the Congressional Budget Committee, one of Congress's most influential bodies. In fact, it was Jones who helped draft the original IRS disclosure rules after Watergate. (Ironically, he's now the U.S. ambassador to Mexico!)

I had to hand it to the Marcianos. They only hired the best carpetbaggers.

Jones began a letter and phone call campaign to Congress and the press that basically accused me of doctoring the Wolf tape and setting out to destroy the wonderful Marcianos, "France's gift to the United States." Jones's strategy was simple: Smear me, and the whole congressional investigation would topple.

On December 17, I was hit with a one-two punch. George De Los Santos started it off by calling with some bad news. "I've just been terminated from the IRS!"

The agency used the excuse of an old neck injury he had from an auto accident to bounce him out on a medical. It was sad, and infuriating. George had never been one of my secret sources. He hadn't spoken to *Forbes* or Congress. He was just an honest guy doing his job.

A few hours later, the second blow came. Someone broke into my wife's car outside a mall in Hackensack, New Jersey, and lowered her electric windows. They didn't take anything. The mobile phone? The stereo? Nothing. They just lowered all the windows.

It was a chillingly effective message. And yet another reminder of how very vulnerable I was.

REMEDIES AND RETRIBUTIONS

NOT ONE TO RUN from a good fight, I volunteered to testify before the California court trying the Jordache/Guess suit. I wanted to face Jim Jones's and Grossman's charges head-on in front of an impartial audience.

What's the Bible say, "Pride goeth before a fall"? That was me, marching boldly into the courtroom, thinking I could out-smart a seasoned trial attorney like Marshall Grossman. From the opening bell, Grossman's barrage of questions blistered me like the California sun. What the hell happened to the lamb who took my deposition? I was suddenly in a death match with a roaring lion who twisted the truth like a strongman bending a metal rod.

And I was forced to try and defend myself with both lips tied behind my brain. As attorneys and judges love to do, I was limited to answering most inquiries yes or no. By carefully crafting questions around restrictive yes and no answers, a courtroom magician like Grossman could make Mother Teresa admit to having been on the grassy knoll armed with a deer rifle the day John F. Kennedy was assassinated.

My side, i.e. Jordache's attorneys, was supposed to note all the suppressed explanations and let me have at it when it was our turn. Except in my case, Jordache's attorneys detested and resented my presence, so they just let me flap in the wind. (The night before my testimony, a few of them told me to "forget" as much as I could on the stand—something I refused to do.)

The gist of my two-day appearance was that Grossman was allowed to give the impression that I went to Jim Berliner to try to have the Marcianos kicked out of the country, that I doctored the Hardolf Wolf tape, then redoctored the transcript (which was ridiculous), that I impersonated a federal officer, and that I traveled to Europe to plant false information against the Marcianos to get them deported. (I was actually in Europe on an unrelated court-sanctioned case that is still under seal.)

That's our judicial system. You stroll into a courtroom thinking you're Billy Graham, then skulk out looking to all the world like Timothy McVeigh. From where I was sitting—under oath—Grossman was playing fast and loose with the facts. The judge let him get away with it.

After my skewered testimony, Judge "Just Answer Yes or No" Epstein declared that I wasn't a credible witness, a searing brand that made my blood boil.

I thought of Epstein's accusation as I recalled a scene from the courtroom. Sitting next to Paul Marciano was Epstein's buddy, ex-judge Richard Schauer, the man Epstein handpicked to be the "impartial" arbitrator on the Guess/Jordache board. Schauer was impartial, all right—about as impartial as a rubber stamp. In 113 tie-breaking votes, he sided with the Marcianos 107 times! Despite the fact that Epstein charged him with investigating the Marcianos' activities inside Guess and with their various garment subcontractors, Schauer began socializing with the four brothers, attending a wedding, a bris, Christmas parties, and a Marciano birthday party. Worse still, I had a document from the Marciano lawyers that stated that Judge Schauer was on our side. Indeed, I was given a document from the Marcianos' lawyers that described Judge Schauer as being "on our side." All while he was supposed to be neutral.

For his troubles, the Marcianos and Guess paid Schauer and his law firm a whopping $1.5 million over four years. I later found out that Schauer helped Epstein get reelected to the bench.

And I wasn't credible? The whole episode depressed me. I'd come to this country to avoid the kind of arbitrary justice made famous by Mexican judges. And now I was experiencing the same thing here.

As a result, Congress refused to use the Wolf tape, even after an expert at MIT ruled that it hadn't been tampered with. And worse, my scheduled star witness appearance before the upcoming congressional hearing was promptly canceled. They still intended to use my evidence and sources; it was just that thanks to Judge Epstein's damning smudge, I had to remain in the shadows.

Now I know why President Ronald Reagan, when they dragged him before a judge in an Iran-Contra trial, kept saying, "I don't recall." It's the only way to beat the "yes or no" crap.

With my credibility damaged and some of my evidence shot to hell, the IRS was quick to exploit my vulnerability. There were new reports of criminal investigations and frontal attacks headed my way. George De Los Santos, now a civilian, was squeezed some more. This time, they wanted him to confess that the whole investigation of the Marcianos was a figment of our demented imaginations. When he refused to lie, he was audited six times, and had his expense records scrutinized going back to Noah's Ark. "I wish I had something on you, Octavio," he sighed, only half-kidding.

Giuliani's office followed the IRS's lead. Instead of investigating IRS corruption, the aggressive federal prosecutors began hammering loyal agents like Jorge Urquijo, prodding them to reveal dirt on me.

It was all a furious effort designed to derail Congress.

Only it was too late for that. A hundred honest IRS agents couldn't be wrong. The case now hung on their experiences and testimony, not mine. I decided it was time for me to bow out, however ungracefully. Fat chance.

In February, one month before the start of the public IRS hearings, IRS Commissioner Lawrence Gibbs suddenly announced his resignation. He was scheduled to testify, then got caught in a nasty flap over his meetings with ex-commissioner Gerry Kurtz. Gibbs kept telling congressional investigators and probing reporters that he never discussed the Jordache case and my evidence of IRS corruption with Kurtz. I provided Congress and the press with tapes of Kurtz detailing the meeting, and the killer—Kurtz's Jordache billing records. The ex-commissioner had dutifully billed the jeans company for an hour-long meeting with Lawrence Gibbs. See ya later, Larry. Florida or Arizona's a nice place to retire.

The critical congressional hearing that Gibbs apparently feared ended up being delayed by Rep. Dan "Rosty" Rostenkowski, chairman of the powerful House Ways and Means Committee.

Rostenkowski refused to press for a vote to waive the Disclosure Laws for the subcommittee. Investigator Barash said Rostenkowski was worried that if the American public discovered how corrupt the IRS was, they might stop paying their taxes. (Rostenkowski would later be embroiled in his own well-publicized scandals regarding the House Post Office pleading guilty to two felony charges that he misused his office for personal gain.)

The stalled hearings gave the IRS, the U.S. Attorney's office for the Southern District of New York, and the Marcianos more time to fight back. In mid-May, Giuliani's underlings had the gall to send a recommendation to indict Jordache to the Justice Department in Washington for final approval. Incredible! After all the evidence and witnesses, and with the upcoming congressional hearing breathing down their necks, the federal prosecutors pushed forward into the abyss.

Avi Nakash took the latest bad news hard. He had the most expensive attorneys in the world, and still he was afraid that he was going to end up in prison. He was so exasperated with the judicial system and the costs of clearing his name that he considered copping a fictitious tax evasion plea just to be done with it. Only Avi said Marcu would not even consider a plea until Jordache got rid of me. Avi's attorneys were all for that.

The U.S. Attorney's office made that stipulation, in my opinion, because they knew I had them by the balls. To get Avi off the hook, I signed a release that stated I was officially off the case. I still worked for him, of course. The only way to fight bullshit is with bullshit.

Meanwhile, Jorge Urquijo was discovering that U.S. Customs was too close to the IRS for comfort. He was now being investigated by his own people at Customs for supposedly threatening ex-congressman-turned-hired-gun lobbyist Jim Jones. The insanity here was that Jones had called Urquijo and tried to turn him into a source against me. When Urquijo instead told him that I was on the level and that it was Jones's big-paying clients, the Marcianos, who weren't on the up and up, Jones wasn't pleased.

I know there wasn't any threat made, because I heard the entire conversation between Jones and Urquijo! To protect Urquijo from just such a double-cross, I listened in. The biggest betrayal was that Jones promised Urquijo anonymity, then turned around and sicced the Customs dogs on him.

"Jorge, don't worry about it," I told him. "I have the Jones call on tape. We can prove he's lying," I said. But it galled me, nonetheless. Despite the fact that President Bush personally commended him for dangerous undercover work, Urquijo was never promoted within Customs. (And still hasn't been to this date. He believes it is because he testified about IRS corruption.)

Jones, apparently under pressure from the Marcianos, then made the mistake of going after the subcommittee, its investigators, and its esteemed members. I loved that! After all the shit that was being dumped on me, it was somewhat comforting to see some of it poured elsewhere. Not that I wanted company in my misery, but such a misguided assault by Jones would help convince Congress what I was going through. The insulted congressmen didn't stand for it. The ranking Republican on the committee, Dennis Hastert, wrote Jones a scathing letter that summed up Jones's entire campaign: ". . . You do your clients no service, and frankly, yourself no honor by demeaning our ability to control the subcommittee, by attacking the integrity of the subcommittee staff, and by engaging in a campaign of misinformation and trivia, all to divert attention from your clients' lack of cooperation with the subcommittee and from what you fear our investigation might reveal about their role with the IRS in Los Angeles . . . Jim, we must reluctantly conclude that you are playing the oldest game in town: deflect attention from the real issues and attempt to discredit the staff in the eyes of the subcommittee chairman and its members. It is not going to work and we deplore the attempts."

My sentiments exactly!

While momentum was building in Washington, they just didn't get it in New York. Aaron Marcu granted attorney Sally Godfrey immunity and dragged her before a grand jury to grill her about me. When she failed to give him anything juicy, she told me that he resorted to insults, asking her why she was protecting her "sugar daddy." What a horribly sexist thing to say to a woman who was a respected attorney, a martial arts expert, and was currently a Judge Advocate in the U.S. Navy. It reeked of a politically incorrect plantation mentality— the typical strongarm tactic prosecutors get away with all the time behind the closed doors of grand juries all over this country.

With Giuliani's goons breathing down my neck, you can imagine my elation when congressional investigator Len Bernard called me with some rousing good news.

"The hearings are a definite go on July 25th."

"Octavio, give it up! If you push this thing with the IRS, you'll end up dead. In Mexico, you'd be dead already!"

The caller was my brother Gabriel, phoning from his Mexico City law office.

"Gabriel, the United States isn't Mexico."

"Hey, even down here we know about the IRS. I'm just saying be careful. Governments are governments the world over." I hoped that he was wrong.

The last time I'd been to Washington, I passed through the impenetrable gates of the imposing IRS headquarters, the largest bureaucratic temple in the world. This time, I was going to the nation's capital to see if I could shake some rotten apples from the mighty IRS tree. I'd waited an agonizingly long year for the hearings, all the while deflecting personal attacks like Samson bashing an endless horde of Philistines with the jawbone of an ass.

The excitement of the pending investigative "Super Bowl" infected me all the way down the Northeast corridor and into the Washington train station. As Arnold Kalman, Robert Spiegelman, and I approached the gleaming white buildings dominating the Washington skyline, I felt goose bumps sprout on my skin. Here I was, a naturalized American citizen, and I'd convinced the most powerful legislative body in the world to look into my case. It felt like a dream.

To me, the fluted dome of the Capitol building stood for everything I had come to the United States to experience. It symbolized a land where a determined citizen can indeed fight City Hall. And there's no City Hall anywhere tougher than the IRS.

Underneath the dome, Subcommittee Chairman Doug Barnard, the congressman from Georgia, walked in and immediately set the tone for the hearings. "Our investigations indicate that there are serious employee integrity problems among senior managers at the IRS: Inadequate internal investigations and punishment of senior-level misconduct; a pervasive fear at all levels of the IRS over retaliation for the reporting of such misconduct; and a driving concern that publicly exposing wrongdoing by senior managers will tarnish the agency's public image and make its tax enforcement responsibilities more difficult . . ."

Yes!

Barnard, bless his courageous heart, went on to hit me with something I wasn't expecting. He directly addressed the Jordache issue and informed everyone that the original evidence against the jeans firm, the evidence that lead to the raid, *"had been destroyed by the IRS criminal investigator who had been assigned to the Jordache tax fraud matter early in its development. . . . The IRS special agent . . . failed to notify the U.S. Attorney's office that he was destroying the documents . . ."* That explained why Tom Doonan leaped out of his seat when I asked about the evidence during my meeting with Marcu. It was gone, and had been gone, according to Congressman Barnard, since January 1986! That meant Giuliani's office had kept a case open for three years, and sent it down for an indictment, without even having the original evidence!

I couldn't believe my ears. The United States Congress had just confirmed that the IRS and U.S. Attorney's investigation of Jordache was based on evidence later described as "bullshit," which was then destroyed. I could just hear the guys down at the Justice Department shredding the Southern District's indictment recommendation.

When the congressional investigators took their turn at the microphone, the charges intensified. "What our investigation disclosed was a powerful Criminal Investigation Chief [Ron Saranow], who, together with a cadre of loyal subordinates, was beyond the control of his Regional Commissioner and the IRS in Washington," announced Richard Stana. No shit!

Included among Saranow's litany of sins was bringing the tax fraud case against Jordache for his buddies the Marcianos based upon "dubious evidence."

Congressional investigator Len Bernard lowered the boom even harder.

"We believe that evidence demonstrates that the Marcianos exercised unusual influence over Ronald Saranow by cultivating a strong personal and social relationship with him and by offering him a job with a six-figure salary. Saranow, in turn, influenced his subordinates and others in the IRS."

Bernard added that despite the sacred Disclosure Laws the IRS used to hide behind, the Marcianos had access to the tax returns of their business adversaries.

After that, the tax collectors themselves, including some of my sources, took to the mikes and machine-gunned Saranow and the

IRS, confirming virtually everything I'd uncovered, including the Saranow/Debbie Jones relationship.

IRS investigator Russ Davis took the stand and read a five-page statement into the record explaining how much trouble he had getting fellow agents to talk to him because of the "strong personal relationship" between his superior, Debbie Jones, and the target of his investigation, Ron Saranow. This, of course, directly contradicted the IRS cover-up letter sent to Rudolph Giuliani, which "exonerated" Saranow.

Another agent testified how Saranow and Mike Bik, a senior Inspection official on the West Coast, interfered with the working of the Organized Crime Strike Force in Los Angeles, particularly the work of gutsy prosecutor Marvin Rudnick, the guy fired for insubordination when he refused to buckle under to the IRS.

At the end of the hearings, the Subcommittee recommended that the Inspection Division of the IRS be transferred to the Treasury Department so that the rampant corruption could never happen again. Better yet, the top five IRS officials resigned.

If life were really like the movies, the end of the congressional hearings would have meant the final curtain on my longest case. The *Mr. Smith Goes to Washington* screenplay would call for one last long shot of me taking the train home, happy to know that democracy was safe once again. The credits would roll against the gleaming torch of the Statue of Liberty, and the audience would breathe a sigh of relief that the good guys had won.

The good guys did win, but it wasn't over by a long shot—at least not for me. When powerful government bureaucracies get caught with their pants down, they look for scapegoats. The Southern District, in particular, had been badly embarrassed by the revelation that their whole case against Jordache was based on BS. And I was their scapegoat.

Retribution began just over a week after Congress publicly spanked the IRS. On August 8th the Marcianos filed a massive, $90 million lawsuit in federal court accusing me of all manner of crimes, including that I'd gone to Nice, France, and planted false information with an eighty-eight-year-old U.S. Consul regarding the Marcianos' criminal records overseas. A second source supposedly confirmed it.

It was all bullshit, but like any lawsuit, it was going to be costly to fight. More important, the lawsuit dovetailed with Rudolph Giuliani's boys' trumped-up grand jury investigation of me in the Southern District. Obviously, all the accusations mentioned in the Marcianos' civil suit would be used by the U.S. Attorney's office in its vengeful attempt to criminally indict me. In fact, it seemed to me as if the Marcianos were preparing the evidence for Aaron Marcu and his bulldogs—just as they had done with the bogus Jordache case—using the conduit of Kroll Associates. Both Marcu and his chief investigator, Tom Doonan, were telling my own government sources that I was a bad guy.

They would all try to destroy me one last time—as revenge for what I had done to them with Congress. It was my turn now to experience the cold fear that Avi Nakash must have felt knowing that he might go to jail because of the power of corrupt money.

I decided to meet the greater danger of the Southern District challenge first by marching into Marcu's office and shooting down his latest round of accusations. The stakes were high. After he granted Sally Godfrey immunity and grilled her, I knew he wanted to indict me. Marcu and Doonan had flown to France to investigate the Marciano charges against me, a highly unusual move for the number two honcho in a U.S. Attorney's office. It simply showed how much he wanted to nail me. The thought that I could be arrested scared me far more than hit men dressed as cops chasing me around New Jersey. That threat I could disarm easily enough. But how do you protect yourself—and more importantly, your reputation—against the full weight of the U.S. Justice Department? I'd spent twenty-five years building a sterling reputation, and Aaron Marcu could destroy it all in a matter of minutes.

The stakes got higher when Marcu informed my attorney, Ray Levites, that I should bring my passport to the meeting. *My passport!* That meant they might indict me on the spot. (The Feds take your passport so you can't flee the country on bail.) Everybody told me I was crazy to face down a powerful prosecutor like this without immunity. Levites pleaded with me to take the Fifth, but I refused. And despite what the law says, everybody knows that only the guilty hide behind the Fifth.

I'll never forget the night before I was scheduled to enter the lion's den of the Southern District. I went for a walk with my twelve-year-old son. Richard was unusually silent until I asked him what was wrong. Then he began to get choked up. "Dad, are you going to jail?"

It seared my heart. What could I say? I'd been teaching my children to obey the law, that the American justice system was the best in the world, and yet here I was, being railroaded by the same system. I tried to explain to Richard that sometimes bad men get into positions of power, and then they abuse that power.

When I arrived at the U.S. Attorney's Office the next morning, Doonan demanded the passport. I slowly took out perhaps my most prized possession—it symbolized everything I had ever dreamed or fought for. My fears dissipated when the small blue book opened and revealed a picture of Our Lady of Guadalupe, the patron saint of Mexicans, which I keep there. When I saw her, I knew I would be safe. Sure enough, after making a copy of the passport, they returned it to me.

The meeting unfolded the way I expected. To Marcu's surprise, I asked the Feds to tape the dialogue. They readily accepted, expecting me to incriminate myself. But the more I answered Marcu's questions, the more I deflated their—or should I say the Marcianos' and Kroll's—case against me.

Toward the end, things suddenly got interesting. Marcu and Doonan appeared particularly concerned about whether I had spoken to the congressional Judiciary Committee about them. As a matter of fact, I had. Although I didn't think that committee would do anything, I dropped some not-so-subtle hints to Marcu and Doonan about my meetings. When Marcu's face fell, I decided to push the envelope all the way.

"Do you work for the Marcianos?" I asked the Associate U.S. Attorney for the most powerful district in America.

"I work for the United States Government," he snapped. Marcu left the office shortly thereafter. Although Doonan continued to yap at my heels, the meeting ended when Marcu exited.

Two months later, Aaron Marcu resigned from the Southern District and went into private practice. And with him went my indictment.

All that was left was the Marcianos' lawsuit, and that was also about to crumble. Two days after the showdown with Marcu, I was contacted by an old CIA source who directed me to a man named John Quirk. Quirk was working for Varicon International, an outfit in Virginia staffed with former CIA agents, including Herb Saunders, who had been The Company's Assistant Director of Operations. The ex-spooks had been subcontracted by Kroll Associates to investigate me.

After we frisked each other for bugs, Quirk handed me some-thing that blew my mind. It was a portion of a report he had prepared for Kroll. I read a particular sentence out loud so I could record it on the tape recorder hidden in my sock—Quirk missed it during the pat-down.

"In summary, there is nothing substantial to prove that Pena planted any information. The police records on the Marcianos exist."

A second report Quirk filed cleared me of having anything to do with the Marcianos' immigration problems.

The ramifications of the reports were staggering. The Marcianos' own investigator had exonerated me on all the things they were suing me for—and all the things the Southern District had been trying to indict me over.

This was wonderful. It was also possibly too good to be true. Was I being set up again? Why was this guy Quirk telling me this? He read my mind. He said that Kroll Associates weren't happy with his reports, and he'd quit in a huff. "They got caught in a lie about you. . . . They're getting desperate. I didn't want to work for them."

Hallelujah. I'd finally found an honest man—from the enemy's camp, no less. This PI was turning his back on a lot of cash and future business from Kroll to help me out. He couldn't stomach the disinformation the Marcianos were spreading. It was obvious that he was pissed off that the Marcianos had lied to him.

Over coffee in a noisy Connecticut diner, Quirk continued to pour out the good news. He said that the two witnesses against me in Europe were plants, and that aside from not being able to smear me, what really burned Kroll's collective asses was that Quirk kept confirming that two of the Marciano brothers' had overseas arrest and conviction records.

"Let me tell you . . . I checked these fucking police records backwards and forwards. I had guys in the French police checking. They [the Marcianos] are well known to several services . . . A lot of these records exist, counterfeiting . . . civil complaints, bounced checks, all this bullshit. . . . These charges against the Marcianos, arrests, complaints, came up and hit me in the face. . . . And I said, 'These fucking guys are greasy. I don't want to work with them. . . .'"*

---

*The Jordache attorneys obtained the criminal records of the Marcianos: Armand was convicted twice for illegal labor practices in France, and Paul pleaded guilty to charges of counterfeiting T-shirts with Peanuts characters. The other two brothers were apparently clean.

On my drive home, it dawned on me why Quirk, aside from a sense of decency, was being so helpful. The Marcianos had hired Kroll, and Kroll had hired Quirk's firm, Varicon International, to do the dirty work on me. That meant if the trail of lies were exposed, Quirk would be the guy with his neck out. He was the first fall guy. (And the Marcianos would be three layers away from it. Brilliant. Quirk also said that the Marcianos had planted evidence against me in Nice and Marseilles, then hired him to "discover" it for them. Double brilliant.)

And now, because Quirk was refusing to play along, he would be placed under tremendous pressure by Kroll, the U.S. Attorney's office, and Grossman, the Marcianos' attorney.

I spoke with Quirk several times a day during the next few weeks. It was playing out just as I'd predicted. His reports were bombshells that could ruin his employer's grandiose plans. He was being put under intense pressure to change them. But it was too late. He'd already shown them to me.

The meetings with Quirk showed me something else, too: The Southern District and Kroll were still in bed together.

Before one of my meetings with the ex-Kroll operative, where I planned to videotape him, I had my attorney, Ray Levites, call the Southern District to inform them that I intended to interview and tape one of their grand jury witnesses against me. The next day, Quirk told me that Kroll's attorney knew about the meeting!

"She said she knew that we met, and that you were taping me!" Quirk blurted out.

When I looked into it, I discovered that Kroll's attorney on this matter had just retired from the Southern District! The same bed? Hell, they were sharing the same pillow.

One of the additional tips Quirk gave me was that the Marcianos were working with someone to write a book about the case.

That someone turned out to be Chris Byron, the *Forbes* editor who handled the original story I presented them. Byron had been terminated by *Forbes*—it was later reported that the ax fell because Byron distorted a story—and hooked on with *New York* magazine. Now he had somehow hooked up with the Marcianos. That was troublesome. If he was in the enemy camp, he could cause problems. Byron and the *Forbes* writer, Richard Behar, were given access to many of my Guess and IRS sources. I made *Forbes* sign a waiver to protect the informants' identities, but if Byron was on his own, I wondered if he would hold to it.

The answer came quicker than I imagined. I began receiving calls from frantic Guess sources saying that Paul Marciano was calling them in and playing tapes of their conversations with me and Behar. One source, Sonia Herrera, said she saw a stack of at least twenty tapes on Marciano's desk.

When I told Behar, who was now writing about the IRS, among other business topics, for *Time* magazine, he freaked. He explained that for several months he and *Time* had been fighting a subpoena from the Marcianos over his tapes of my conversations with sources. Behar promised to check into it.

Two hours later, Sonia called me again, even more frantic. She had just been raked over the coals by Paul Marciano for telling me about the tapes! Either my phone line was bugged, or something fishy was going on.

I called Behar.

"The circle's closed," he said wearily.

"What do you mean?"

Behar explained that right after we spoke, he phoned Chris Byron.

"He must have called Paul Marciano," Behar said. The *Time* reporter added that he gave his former editor the tapes to help Byron write his book.

I had a stabbing thought. Did he also give the tapes of the IRS sources? Behar said no, but it was difficult for me to believe that. If he had forked over the Guess tapes, why not the IRS?

Behar and Byron met.

"We were almost in a fistfight today," Behar explained afterward. "I have never been betrayed like this by anyone before. . . . You know, a lot of people are going to burn if this is what happened . . . with the tapes. He had an agreement with me and you have got to understand that he [was] like a brother. We worked on this story like two brothers. We were going to do the book together. He decided to do the book on his own. I provided [the tapes] for his own background. He had access to everything anyway, as my editor. So I gave it to him for his own background and said, 'Under no circumstances can you quote from it.' It was the worst judgment I could have made. But how can you predict people will do that?" Behar sighed deeply, then dropped another bomb.

"He offered to give me back those tapes . . . if I brought the [IRS] tapes that Guess wants from me and we made an exchange."

"You're kidding!"

"I'm not kidding. I'm not fucking kidding! He claims it's because he's interested in the truth. He wants the truth to come out. He thinks you duped Congress, me, the press and set up every single source. So he wants the tapes to get the truth out."

"What a fucking asshole," I raged. "Doesn't he realize that Congress interviewed every single person, and they never heard any of my tapes? Do you have any idea what will happen to those agents on those tapes?"

Other reporters go to jail to protect their sources, I marveled to myself. Byron? He gives them up to the targets of his own investigative pieces.

That betrayal went far beyond his confidential sources. Byron betrayed himself. He turned his back on an ideal—a free and independent press. And that was far worse to me than anything the Marcianos ever did.

It was close to midnight when I finally hung up, wondering who else the Marcianos could influence. When was it going to end? They had charmed or bought every major institution I could think of, the Judiciary, the IRS, the Justice Department, an ex-congressman, and now the media. I never thought that the maxim money can buy you anything and anybody would apply so blatantly in the United States.

Meanwhile, Quirk continued to come to my rescue. He provided me with a memo written by a Kroll executive regarding Kroll's assignment to acquire evidence of my so-called criminal activity. "We are still lacking anything hard enough to satisfy a skeptical or even impartial outsider (such as a judge). In the near term, which is to say by the end of this week, we must concentrate all our efforts on nailing down something concrete . . . we need a statement on paper from a witness."

The memo was dated August 6th. The lawsuit against me was filed on the 8th. That meant they went ahead and filed even though they knew they had nothing!

This same memo included a cryptic warning about "What is NOT our concern." Specifically mentioned as a no-no was "what criminal record or reputation the M's may or may not have in France." Kroll was doing the three-monkey bit—see no evil, hear no evil, speak no evil—unless it was about me.

Fortunately, Quirk kept his eyes, ears, and fax open. "The charges against the M brothers do exist," he repeated in another letter to Kroll, referring to French lawbreaking. "They have successfully avoided paying duty and taxes. They have violated Customs laws and tax laws. . . . These charges are not erased from the police. They have committed fraud. They are listed as dangerous people who have carried firearms and explosives. . . . They have bad records. They are known to the anti-fraud division French police. . . . Bruce [Dollar of Kroll], I know this is hard for you to swallow, because you are close to Paul." Regarding the Southern District, Quirk added, "Doonan by now has reached the same conclusion, as he has had access to IRS investigation."

In one of his final faxes to Kroll before he made the decision to reach out to me, Quirk wrote: "In summary, there is nothing substantial to prove that Pena planted any information. . . . The Marcianos' problems with the IRS may be caused by an agent provocateur, but there is no information that Pena instigated it. There is certainly no information that he created it. I think it is obvious from remarks made by all my sources that the police charges were not planted by Pena or anyone else inside or outside the French government."

Adios Marciano lawsuit.

To nail things down doubly tight, I flew with my attorneys to Europe, tracked down the two alleged sources against me, and had the lawyers interview them. Both admitted that they had never even met me.

On November 16, nearly four months after the congressional hearing, the Southern District of New York officially dropped its tax fraud case against Jordache.

The fact that it lingered so long on a respirator after it had been rendered brain-dead by Congress was disturbing, but I wasn't going to quibble. I'd done my job. Jordache's nightmare was officially over.

Mine, unfortunately, still wasn't. The Marcianos' case was crumbling all around them, and yet they continued to throw punches from the grave.

On November 8, 1989, someone broke into my storage house adjacent to my office and took twelve boxes of Guess materials and a box full of computer disks containing information on the Guess/IRS investigation. The disks were coded and encrypted, so I wasn't worried about that. But the mere fact that this kind of thing was still going on was depressing.

A few weeks later, I found a bug in my office. It was an innovative device connected to a telephone number. Dial the number, and you could hear my secretary sipping her morning coffee.

That was followed by additional break-in attempts at both my office and home. And worse yet, despite all the evidence I provided that the Marcianos' lawsuit was frivolous at best, the judge in California refused to throw it out! He whittled it down, but wouldn't boot the damn thing.

I was left with no option but to prepare a countersuit against the Marcianos and their entire legal team, including all the investigators and lobbyists.

Next came the news from a reliable source that I was a week away from being raided, Jordache style, by the IRS. It seems that a hotshot CID manager in New York wanted a pound of my flesh for what I had done to his pristine agency during the congressional hearings.

He was coming after me not because of anything to do with Guess or Jordache, but because of the Argentinean drug lord in the Iorizzo/Franzese Mafia case apparently having a mole inside the U.S. Embassy on his payroll.

The whole thought of going another fifteen rounds with these goons, this time with my neck on the line, was crushing. Thankfully, the week came and went without a visit from the IRS stormtroopers. Apparently some friends of mine in the National Security Agency vouched for me and cooled the IRS hothead.

On a steamy, late spring day, I received an emergency call from Avi Nakash. He was in Los Angeles. And I was in Washington, D.C. ready to depose Jim Jones.

"Listen, the Marcianos want to settle with us!"

"Hey, that's great!"

"You have to settle, too."

"What?"

"Octavio, I would like you to settle."

"I'm not going to settle! I have them by the throat. I spent all last night going over my countersuit. My attorney thinks I'll get a million bucks without going to court!"

When Avi persisted, I told him I would think about it.

Avi called a few hours later. He explained that the Marcianos wouldn't settle with him unless I dropped my threatened countersuit. He pleaded with me, saying the jury was out in the second phase of the trial and that his entire business was in danger. What choice did I have? He was the client.

"All right, I'll settle. My attorneys won't like it, but I'll settle."

The Marcianos ended up dropping their $90 million suit

against me, and dishing out $66 million to buy Guess back from Jordache. The only real winners were—as usual—the attorneys. Between them, the two sets of Jewish immigrant brothers shelled out nearly $100 million in legal fees.

Before the ink on the settlement had dried, Marciano attorney Marshall Grossman filed a lien against it because he claimed the Marcianos refused to pay his $10 million bonus, which with interest and other charges had ballooned to a whopping $17 million. Fitting.

In the end, everyone walked away from the blood feud relatively happy. And despite the harsh words from Congress, no criminal charges were ever filed against anyone involved in the dispute, including the IRS folks.

After retiring from the IRS, Saranow went into business with his old buddies Howard Emirhanian and Bruce Alan Wells to form the investigative firm, Saranow, Wells & Emirhanian, in California. He originally wanted to form a financial investigative service with Anthony Langone, the former Assistant Commissioner for the IRS CID and Robert Roche, the former chief of the CID in New Jersey. But the three IRS retirees had to put their plans on ice when Roche was indicted by a federal grand jury in New Jersey for mail fraud and violating the Ethics in Government Act for providing Saranow with nonpublic information. Right after that Roche quickly pled guilty to another charge that he misused his former office to help a convicted narcotics smuggler. The first indictment was dropped as part of the plea bargain.

Debbie Jones left the IRS to become an investigator with the Small Business Administration.

Russ Davis retired from the IRS to become a private investigator in Los Angeles.

Bart Schwartz left Kroll Associates to form his own private investigative firm, Decision Strategies, Inc. He recently said in an interview, "There's no substitute for being a good investigator and a good interviewer, and understanding schemes and the like." Somehow, I don't think that's why Kroll hired him.

George De Los Santos recently passed the bar exam in Texas and is a practicing attorney.

Debbie Corwin is studying law in Los Angeles and expects to pass the bar exam shortly.

Jorge Urquijo now works as a senior investigator with the Envirnmental Protection Agency.

Sally Godfrey recently married and works as a Legal Aid attorney in Jacksonville, Florida.

Marshall Grossman successfully sued the Marcianos for his fee and received a whopping $23,000,000 for helping the brothers drive the Nakashes out of Guess. After the settlement he said, "The pain was horrific . . . the pain is still there. To that extent, the recovery of the funds is not a full victory." Yeah, right.

As for the antagonists? Both Guess and Jordache continue to prosper to this day. The Marcianos, however, can't seem to get rid of the cloud over their heads. They soon squabbled and began suing each other over the use of Georges Marciano's trade name after he sold his stake to the other three clan members. (All of which made their attorneys ecstatic.)

Just this year, a Los Angeles newspaper reported that the owners of Guess have managed to get the Los Angeles District Attorney's Office, headed by Gil Garcetti, to target small companies allegedly "counterfeiting" Guess designs—cases the D.A.'s own prosecutors don't think merit much attention. Worse still, the D.A.'s "evidence" is stored in Guess warehouses.

How'd they get all the attention? By donating close to two hundred grand to Gil Garcetti's election campaign in 1992, which helped the powerful prosecutor pay off his campaign debt. According to law enforcement officials, the money has given the brothers M unprecedented clout with the D.A.'s Office. It's always the same: Dangle the money, and government officials will snap it up. Leopards never change their spots.

Regarding his betrayal of coworker Richard Behar, Byron publicly admitted giving the Marcianos two tapes to help Behar avoid being named as a codefendant in the Marcianos' lawsuit against me. The thought of Byron "helping" Behar after betraying all of Behar's sources—the cardinal sin in journalism—made me laugh. Behar, who bore the brunt of Byron's betrayal, didn't find it so funny.

Why Byron really gave those tapes to the Marcianos—as well as providing other materials—is anyone's guess. (Byron's professional reputation was raked over the coals by the congressional investigators, who publicly accused him of gross distortions and impugned his objectivity.) Indeed, after Byron was fired from *Forbes*, he embarked on a veritable odyssey of employment: From *New York* magazine, *Worth* magazine, and the *Daily News*, to *Esquire*. Today he pens a column for the *New York Observer*, at least for the time being. In contrast to his former mentor, Richard Behar now writes for *Fortune*, and has garnered several major journalism awards, including the Loeb Award, the Conscience in Media Award, the Worth Bingham Prize, and the prestigious George Polk Award for Journalistic Excellence.

The blue jeans fiasco had been my longest case, and the one that disillusioned me the most about our justice system.

But in the end, Congress came through. And nothing makes me prouder than having had input into protecting what most of us take for granted: our rights as American citizens.

Epilogue

Not long after the Jordache case was over, I was taking a train from Washington, D.C. back to my home in New Jersey. A woman walked by wearing Guess jeans. The sight of the stylish denim made me smile. Little did she know.

I sat back and glanced at the businessmen and women all around me. They were prosperous-looking capitalists carrying leather briefcases and decked out in crisp designer suits. I wondered how many of these all-American boys and girls were big-time criminals cutting corners, stealing from their bosses, demanding kickbacks, and trying every way they could to cheat their way to wealth and power. You can't get rid of them, I thought. All you can do is strengthen the laws, and make doubly sure the keepers of the law don't dry-rot the way the IRS had—from the head down. That's one of the many lessons I've learned during my career investigating white-collar crime, and helping corporations and individuals with seemingly hopeless problems.

More important, I've learned that as a citizen of this great country, I was able to bank upon the power of the truth, a power that enabled me to convince Congress to protect us from the abusive actions of a tax agency run amok.

Someday soon, another influential IRS manager will be seduced by the allure of money. An unethical prosecutor will indict someone on false charges, perhaps as a favor to old chums working in the private sector. A judge will compromise his court by hanging a "yes or no" albatross around the neck of an honest witness and feed him or her to an unscrupulous attorney.

Somewhere, a vicious mobster will threaten to break an honest man's legs. A band of idealists will use violence and murder to push their political agenda. A famous company will be destroyed from the inside by theft, extortion, or counterfeiters. An innocent young woman will again fall prey to a drug-crazed cult. Sometime soon, probably tomorrow, a bribed government official will try to ruin someone's life.

What can you do about the crime and corruption that swirl around us with greater force every day? The answer is, *never give up.* In the final analysis, the ultimate responsibility for our democracy lies with each and every one of us. Sometimes our long-cherished rights must be fought for.